GUIDED

BY

VOICES

GUIDED BY VOICES

A BRIEF HISTORY

TWENTY-ONE YEARS OF HUNTING

ACCIDENTS IN THE FORESTS OF

ROCK AND ROLL

With an Introduction by Steven Soderbergh

JAMES GREER

Black Cat
a paperback original imprint of Grove/Atlantic, Inc.
New York

Printed in the United States of America
Published simultaneously in Canada

Library of Congress Cataloging-in-Publication Data

Greer, Jim, 1961–
    Guided by voices : a brief history : twenty-one years of hunting accidents
in the forests of rock and roll / James Greer ; with an introduction by
Steven Soderbergh.—1st ed.
        p. cm.
    Includes discography (p.   ).
    ISBN 0-8021-7013-7
    1. Guided by Voices (Musical group)   2. Rock musicians—United States—
Biography.   I. Title.

ML421.G853G74 2005
782.42166'092'2—dc22
[Bs]   2005048123

Black Cat
a paperback original imprint of Grove/Atlantic, Inc.
841 Broadway
New York, NY 10003

05   06   07   08   09   10   9   8   7   6   5   4   3   2

To S. A.

"No dilettante can recognize a master. They take his mastery for egotism."

—Goethe

CONTENTS

PREFACE

The purpose of this book, whose secretly real title is *Hunting Accidents*—a marketing impossibility, obviously, as it might draw too many unwitting Ted Nugent fans—is to tell the story, to those interested, of how Robert Ellsworth Pollard Jr., who encompasses and created every Voice in Guided by Voices, came to be considered by some as one of the truly great artists of our time. Logically, that consideration should extend to his band; but because the notion of "rock band" as Pollard has reconceptualized it—through a combination of necessity, personality, and restless creativity—has acquired a complex subset of meanings, it's a little more difficult to prove the extended proposition, because doing so would mean making mostly arbitrary decisions like "Which band?" meaning "Which version of the band?" because there have been several; nearly fifty players have served time in its ranks, some more helpfully than others, but all in the service of a single, and singular, vision.

That vision: sustained and propagated in its infinite fractions by Pollard, the forty-seven-year-old baby whose personal history parallels, intertwines with, in fact is/ought to be the story of GBV, which is short-hand for Guided by Voices, though Bob, as Robert Pollard is known to his friends and fans, and Bobby, as he is known to his close friends, does not and never has liked the abbreviation. Even though it was his idea.

You see? A contradiction in the second paragraph of the preface! Guided by Voices contains multitudes, much like the homosexual poet Walt Whitman, who, in *Leaves Of Grass,* wrote a poem called "I Sing the Body Electric," and thereby invented rock and roll, as well as the art of elliptical song titles that Pollard himself has long mastered.

The Guided by Voices story—the *Brief History,* as the book's title semi-ironically has it—is unique in the annals of rock, and not in the way other rock stories are unique, but in a truly expectations-defying, non-cliché-embracing, uncanny, and purposely unpurposeful way, so that while Pollard et many al. are held in high esteem by their peers, it's unlikely, even (possibly) impossible that anyone will ever successfully emulate the road to—what?—plain endurance, mythology, cirrhosis, glory that GBV took. Today, you can look but you will not find a single band clearly influenced by Guided by Voices in the way that, say, a great number of very bad bands were clearly influenced by, say, Nirvana. Because to imitate Pollard's songwriting would entail digesting, as he has, the entire contents of the Book of Rock, and rearranging every sentence via a meticulous, intuitive, logically-deranged process that results in another book, almost as long, and just as enlightening to read. Such a thing is not very likely to happen in your lifetime. Though swatches of influence might crop up here and there (The Strokes, for instance—whose gratefulness to Bob for listening to the cassette they threw onstage at a Guided by Voices show and directing soon thereafter that they be asked to open for GBV on an upcoming tour did not extend to a willingness to contribute to this book—bear some traces of Bob's musical DNA, but have only been able to replicate that genetic affinity on the one song they keep writing over and over), no one will ever dupe or duplicate the Whole.

Three months is probably not long enough to listen to, never mind research and write about, the body of Guided by Voices' work. We had a head start, we will admit, and a decade's worth of warnings, but who takes warnings seriously until someone dies? Who stops smoking until their good friend contracts lung cancer, and even then, who stops smoking? (We do not endorse smoking.) Our twenty months, give or take or add or subtract, playing bass for GBV in the waning years of the last century and our decade-old friendship (Bob was the best man at our imaginary wedding to our imaginary wife) was in the end more obstruction than helpmeet, because we began this book lacking the chimera of objectivity that rules, or is meant to rule, the writer's right hand. We are left-handed, and hopelessly subjective. Opinions expressed in *Hunting Accidents* not directly attributed to others are a by-product of our own unhealthy addiction to solving puzzles, and should not be trusted.

You are encouraged to trust, instead, those included in the long list of acknowledgments that will follow—like fans queued at the door of the Greatest Rock Show Ever—the coda with which this paragraph will inevitably end, without whose support, help, encouragement, information, inspiration, time, threats, physical abuse, and money *Hunting Accidents* would be a much poorer excuse for a book. We will not bother to identify the contributions specific to each person or group mentioned, because they know what they did and you do not care. Having said that, we are grateful beyond words that anyone, never mind everyone, was in so many instances willing to direct so much of their time and energy toward the completion of this project, and we fully recognize that the motivating factor was a common love of the band. Guided By Voices' tradition of generosity has been, in part, the secret of its success, and now it is the secret of whatever success *Hunting Accidents* enjoys. A multiplicity of thanks to (in no particular order): Robert Pollard, the reclusive Jimmy Pollard, Rich Turiel, Tad Floridis, Tobin Sprout, Nate Farley, Percy Kew, Matt Davis, Billy Dixon, Bruce Horner, Mike Lipps, Mark Gibbs (*qui es in caelis*), Buffalo, Dink, Peter Buck, Bertis Downs, Gerard Cosloy, Chris Lombardi, Patrick Amory, Nils Bernstein, Robert Griffin, David Newgarden, Joe Goldberg, Bun E. Carlos, Steven Soderbergh, Dennis Cooper, Bryan Pollard, Sarah Zade, Greg Demos, Jim Macpherson, Don Thrasher, Kevin Fennell, Mitch Mitchell (in absentia), Dave Doughman, Michael Azerrad, Eric Miller, Richard Meltzer, Byron Coley, Todd Robinson, Jason Pierce, Jeff Warren, Ric Ocasek, Anna Crean, Vic Blankenship, Mark Spitz, Doug Gillard, Chris Slusarenko, Kevin March, Steve Malkmus, Andy Valeri, Tony Conley, Wing Committee, Monument Club, Postal Blowfish, Girl Called Captain, Grove/Atlantic and its many helpful tentacles, Pete Jamison, Aaron Blitzstein, Sam Powers, Janet Billig, Jim Romeo, Matt Sweeney, John Wenzel, Celia Farber, Pete Townshend, Jonathan Bernstein, and the forbearance of Danny Greenberg at the William Morris Agency and of Allen Fischer at Principato Young Management. Humble apologies to anyone whose contribution we have failed to note. Even humbler apologies to those who contributed and have found their efforts gathering dust on the cutting room floor. In such instances, physics rather than aesthetics dictated the limits of inclusion. Special extra *mea maxima culpa* to those members of Postal Blowfish and Girl Called Captain who, when called upon, took the time to send us personal anecdotes, photos, and, in at least one case, articles of beer-stained clothing, only to find little direct evidence of their donatory labors herein. Please rest assured that you are present in every sentence of this book.

Needless to say, though every effort has been made to ensure the accuracy of the names, dates, and facts cited herein, any errors or (especially) omissions are the fault of the author and nobody else; except in certain deliberate cases, where directed by a secret agreement with the Knights of Northridge under pain of pain not to reveal or treat of subjects or personages that would violate the Treaty of Geo (Hard Rain Amendment).

James Greer
Los Angeles, California

IN LIEU OF AN ACTUAL INTRODUCTION

Thirty-one random thoughts on GBV in a very particular order:

1. I am a filmmaker because I am not a musician.
2. I think the narrator of "Always Crush Me" is an insect. At least I hope so.
3. I would rather be Robert Pollard than me, but I'm glad I'm not. Still, we should watch *Starship Troopers* together.
4. Watching GBV perform live is exactly like something.
5. My *Best of GBV* playlist contains 123 songs.
6. The chorus of "Liquid Indian" gives me goose bumps. "My Feet's Trustworthy Existence" makes me sad.
7. GBV isn't famous because people are stupid. It's good that GBV isn't famous, therefore it's good that people are stupid.
8. If I had done a video for GBV, I would have screwed it up.
9. "Blatant Doom Trip" is a good name for a song, but then so is "Larger Massachusetts." Sometimes they give different names to the same song, but it doesn't feel like cheating when they do.
10. If, in public, you behaved the way Robert Pollard behaves onstage, you would be thrown in jail.
11. The entire time I wore my GBV hat, nobody knew what it meant.
12. Some of the really short songs are great.
13. I wrote lyrics for "Alright," but I'm not going to show them to you.
14. I promised Cameron Crowe I would make him some GBV CDs, but I never did because I couldn't figure out which song to put first.
15. "Queens of Cans and Jars," if you forced me.
15. When there is absolutely nothing to be done, do nothing. Or not.
16. It doesn't matter if this book is any good, as long as it's inaccurate.
17. I'm actually surprised they stayed together this long.

18. If you don't want to play air guitar when you hear "Little Lines," then I guess you're just too fucking cool.

19. My favorite lyrics might be these:
My favorite son has found
My gun
My favorite son has found
My favorite son has found
My gun
And now the fun begins
And now the fun begins
And now the fun be—
Now the fun begins

20. I don't know the names of all the people who have been in the band.

21. Most women are the same, but in completely different ways. Most men are the same in the same ways.

22. GBV is like a great breakfast cereal with a surprise inside.

23. Even though GBV is the most prolific band ever, in photographs they look really lazy.

24. I can't remember.

25. GBV uses lots of different chords, but not in a show-offy way.

26. I would not like to see Robert Pollard in control of an air force or behind the controls of an airplane.

27. "Chicken Blows"? Holy shit.

28. I'm pretty sure there are some GBV songs I still haven't heard. There's just too many of them.

29. That album Ric Ocasek produced was terrific.

30. I think Robert Pollard is the greatest songwriter since

31. They're just making music I would make, if I could make music.

—Steven Soderbergh
New York City

FINALLY

"I don't know, if it was me I probably would have kept Guided by Voices and continued to do the other stuff on the side."

— Peter Buck, R.E.M.

Driving into Dayton, Ohio, on the night before Christmas Eve, 2004, all you could see was snow. The previous day had brought a twenty-inch fall to the area: historic, unprecedented, without recent parallel. Comparisons were already being drawn to the Great Flood of 1913, which had succeeded the invention of flight—by native Daytonians Orville and Wilbur Wright—by a mere decade, and was considered by some superstitious natives as karmic payback for that God-defying machine.

Three days later, word spread that an earthquake of historic proportions had taken place on the other side of the globe, followed by a tsunami that killed many more people than have been killed by quake-driven tsunamis in years past, at least since 1964, the birth date—coincidence?— of the British Invasion.

The confluence of near-apocalyptic events so close to one another must (you're thinking) have a unifying cause. How about this: the final Guided by Voices show, on New Year's Eve, in Chicago, at a club called the Metro, right across from Wrigley Field. The culmination of twenty-one years' hard labor served in the Prison of Rock. Sentence commuted by the warden, who, as happens in the best and the worst kinds of movies, is also the prisoner.

Our story begins, as all good stories must, at the end. On New Year's Day, 2005, in Chicago, at the Metro, where, at approximately four o'clock in the morning, after playing for three and a half hours before a thousand-plus lucky ticket-holders who'd paid upward of $750 on eBay for the privilege (though the asking price was a mere 75 clams), Bob Pollard stands surrounded by a wall of well-wishers and family and friends and the ghosts of band members both past and present. "Smothered in Hugs" is a fan-favorite song from the 1994 GBV album *Bee Thousand.* Its lyrical content has absolutely nothing to do with the scene backstage at the Metro, but you'd be forgiven for applying that title to this event. People are teary-eyed, people are smiling broadly, people are hugging profusely and indiscriminately, and we'd like to think this blizzard of hugs, this hug-storm, reflects in micro-view the macro-effect of Guided by Voices—its legacy, in the broadest sense. Because the word that best applies to the awe-inspiring breadth of the band's double-decade output is one of the best words you can say about anyone or anything: generous. Guided by Voices is the most generous band in the world.

Some would say *too* generous, and it's hard to argue the point with those who feel that a recorded output surpassing eight hundred songs and a standard-issue two-to-three-hour live show overmatches the average listener's attention span. But Guided by Voices fans are not average listeners, and Bob Pollard writes, records, and performs for himself first and for his fans second. The average listener comes in a distant third, with the music business and its attendant truisms—a band can only release one album a year, a band must tour said album for two years nonstop, a band certainly cannot change musicians like underwear and record on a Radio Shack microphone strategically placed between beer cans in a basement on a four-track cassette recorder—left sitting in a corner, feeling neglected.

Result: cult status and failure to sell millions of records. B-side of result: complete creative control and the primacy of the song over the medium. "At the end of the day, there are no bands, there are no labels, there's only 'Three Blind Mice' and 'Happy Birthday,'" Pollard opines late one drunken night (there are only late, drunken nights in the Guided by Voices universe) shortly before the final show. "I'd rather find a great song than a nice guy," he said another late, drunken night over ten years earlier. "John Lennon was not a nice guy. But he wrote great songs." Bob's opinions are usually appended with an insistent "Wouldn't you?" or "Don't you agree?" to which there is only one real answer, because the question is rhetorical and you—if he's even aware of your presence—are for the most part a rhetorical device, or at best an audience. Disagree, and he will accept your opinion with equanimity, but will hold it against you for the rest of your life, though you may never be aware of that fact. He will not respect you for speaking your mind. He will dismiss you as an idiot.

The National Guard arrived the day after Christmas to begin the process of snow removal from downtown Dayton that would occupy the better part of its next three days, by which time the band was scheduled to move on to Chicago and the last two shows. In the meantime, Bob somehow managed to fit in an expanded version of Monument Club (see the chapter entitled "Ghosts" for a complete explanation); a meeting of the Wing Committee (self-explanatory—you go to a bar and eat wings—in essence a pared-down version of Monument Club); a movie (*The Aviator:* mediocre); Margarita Night at a place that may or may not have had the word "Azteca" in its name; the Last Ever Guided by Voices rehearsal; a recording session for a forthcoming solo Bob EP; a recording session for the demos of an upcoming Bob project; a visit to Marion's Piazza, holy grail for pizza lovers and second home to Bob and his bestest pals (the taping of which meal may result in Monument Clubber Billy Dixon's first comedy album, *At Marion's of All Places*); dinner at the Pine Club, a restaurant both blessed and damned on separate GBV album sleeves; and an intensive scouring of Bob's personal collection of Guided by Voices–related memorabilia for the purpose of inclusion in this book.

The cast of characters that forms and informs the Guided by Voices multiverse, you see, is not limited to Bob Pollard and band members, whether past or present (though even the present are past, now), which is partly why we will spend so much time detailing that cast of characters, because without context you will not understand the wellspring of Pollard's singular genius. Not that such a thing is ever clearly understood, but one of the purposes of this book is to explain, and not merely relate, the story of Guided by Voices. To do that, in a very large measure, is to explain and not merely relate the story of Robert Ellsworth Pollard Jr., Northridge, Dayton, Ohio, United States of America, the World, the Universe. Et emphatically cetera.

*   *   *

If you are merely a casual fan of the band, or not even a fan but you have heard of them, you probably know a few rudimentary things about Guided by Voices: that Bob was a schoolteacher for fourteen years before his band was "discovered." That he was consequently considered, at age thirty-six, an unlikely prospect for rock stardom. That the band made most of its records on a cheap Tascam four-track in the basement, spending very little time and even less money, which method became known as "lo-fi," shorthand for "low fidelity," of which the band was considered if not the inventor then certainly one of its leading practitioners. That its live shows range from borderline disastrous to exhilarating raw rock power of a kind rarely seen in the unfortunately labeled genre "indie rock." And that Guided by Voices drinks a lot of beer. A ridiculous amount of beer. An inhuman amount of beer.

If you have never heard of the band at all, that's a pretty fair introductory summation. All of these things are true, to a point, but what is perhaps less well understood is the history behind those four or five truths—the reasons, if you will, that GBV has been unfairly reduced to a few misleading bullet points, and that, for instance, the band has not been "lo-fi" for well over ten years, half of its existence, during which period Bob's songwriting improved exponentially and the band learned how to translate its unique sound into the context of real recording studios, sometimes helped by producers with famous names, sometimes on its own, and that once GBV had outgrown the superficial bounds of its self-inflicted mythology, it became, to many discerning listeners, one of the greatest bands in the world. Bob Pollard has left behind, with the help of his bandmates, a legacy that will likely continue to grow in influence and renown long after today's fame puppets are forgotten. He has been called in the press—before the press got overwhelmed by his unending output and turned off by his fanatical self-belief, mistaken for arrogance—"this millennium's William Shakespeare," and compared by *The New York Times* to Mozart, Rossini, and Paul McCartney in the same sentence. It's likely that Bob's familiar with only the last person on that august list, and likelier still that he'd be angry not to be compared to his idol, John Lennon, rather than McCartney, whom he considers a "square."

The initial adulation that greeted GBV's ascendancy ignited the chip on Bob's shoulder that had been built up over the years of negativity he'd endured from his family and even some friends who simply couldn't understand a) why he was even bothering; and b) why he was bothering when he clearly didn't have any talent. In order to understand the extent of his suppressed (and sometimes expressed) fury, you need to understand the history not only of the years of obscurity but of Bob's entire youth.

There was a lot of debate in its initial stages about what would and would not go into "The Book," as Bob kept calling it. Late into one night at Marion's, he banged his beer glass on the table with some force. "Fuck it," he declared, and it's entirely beside the point to say that he was, at this point, not entirely sober. "It's going in the book. This is the bible, goddammit. I'm not gonna puss out. I'm going to tell what happened, and I'm sorry if anyone gets offended. But it's called *Hunting Accidents,* and the way I understand it, when there's a hunting accident someone gets hurt." (This is a paraphrase. He could not possibly have been that articulate at that stage.) The funny thing is we cannot for the life of us remember what particular story he was trying to decide to use or not, and just then the tape cut out, probably because someone spilled beer or pizza on it or a ghost wandered into the room and its ghostly viscera coated the magnetic particles of the tape, rendering them inaudible. Which would be appropriate, in a way, because—again, in a way, albeit from a marvelously oblique angle of perception—the story of Guided by Voices is a ghost story. Even funnier is the fact that Bob's drunken promise of complete fidelity was tempered in subsequent sessions by his desire not to hurt anyone's feelings. Which is not the same as a disclaimer that any significant lacunae in *Hunting Accidents* are at Bob's request, but, at the same time, yeah.

Later that week the band drove up for the Last Soundcheck Ever, before the penultimate show, the first of two at the Metro, which is a very nice club and had always treated the band well and as such served as a fitting site for the farewell shows. The band ran through a few of the songs it had decided to add to the set, then retired to the rock room, which is Guided by Voices' slang for the dressing room. The opening band that night, appropriately, was Tobin Sprout, longtime GBV member, who has recently begun touring again, playing a mix of songs off his solo albums and songs he wrote or cowrote while in the band. Toby's always been an affable, low-key guy, and his music reflects his personality, which is not an insult. His set that night was an appropriate aperitif for the second-to-last supper. Most of the rest of that night was a typical riotous, joyful blur. Afterward, Bob went straight from the stage to the van and back to the hotel, as has been his habit, increasingly, in the last couple of years. Much as he feeds off the energy from talking to fans and friends after shows, he's lately discovered that the harm to his voice and energy is a potential disservice to those who pay to hear him sing. Also, he's old.

Next day, the day of the last show, the band members mostly stayed in the hotel for the day, recovering from the previous night's exertions, but by showtime there was a celebratory air in the rock room that had little to do with New Year's Eve. Though only Pollard and his brother Jimmy remained from the small group of Northridge friends who started Guided by Voices twenty-one years earlier, wilting fronds of connection to his distant past were present and accounted for: Billy Dixon, his high school football team center; Daryl "Dink" Deaton, his high school baseball team catcher; Tony Conley, guitarist for Anacrusis, Bob's first band (albeit a heavy metal cover band); Bruce Horner, another longtime friend, famous for his malapropisms, which will be addressed later; and others too complicated to mention. All these guys are still close friends with Bob, and were before he started playing music, and still are now that he's a "world-famous" (in quotes because it's funny, not because it's not true) rock guy. Many of them have obscurely derived nicknames; and the preponderance of middle-aged, graying, grizzled men dressed in sweat suits—and at least in one case in shorts, despite the subzero temperature outside—in the rock room made this scene unlike probably any other dressing room preshow gathering ever. Some of Bob's friends looked a little uncomfortable, even out of place. They're still not used to seeing Bob treated with this degree of adulation outside the playing fields of Northridge when they were growing up and Bob was a three-sport standout. "There's two different people. There's Bobby, and then there's Robert Pollard. Sometimes I forget," says close friend Mike Lipps. He's standing to the side, holding a beer, watching Bob surrounded by longtime, hardcore fans to whom he always allows access to the rock room.

"I just can't understand," continues Mike, "how a guy who can make you laugh until it fucking hurts, who talks about nothing but sports and shit when we're home, just like us, can write songs so beautiful they make you cry."

For the most part Bob Pollard is a genuinely nice guy—the exception to his own rule—who also happens to write genuinely great songs, and though his refusal to self-edit (despite that he does so far more than many are aware) rankles even some of his most ardent admirers, the ratio of quality to crap over the course of the twenty-one years of his band's existence remains surprisingly high, and there are those—Bob among them—who value the crap more than the quality. You can understand why—why a guy who can layer a heartbreaking melody over an intricate chordal arrangement without seeming effort might find such a thing unchallenging after a while, and resort to wilder sonic pastures—without agreeing, but even if you disallow Pollard's cherished experimental side, he'd still have more truly great songs in his catalog than any ten of his more widely known contemporaries lumped together.

Many of those songs he played tonight, on New Year's Eve, at the final show of a tour Pollard dubbed "The Electrifying Conclusion," complete with T-shirts featuring a clearly silhouetted leaping Bob, captioned "Mission Accomplished." The set list contained some sixty-odd songs, augmented throughout by ex tempore surprises like "14 Cheerleader Coldfront," a chestnut he dredged up without hesitation when he turned to see Tobin Sprout, who had wandered onstage looking for champagne (we'll explain soon) and who cowrote the song.

Bob had meticulously dotted the list with songs designed for guest spots from every former band member who was willing to participate; the band's lineup has changed more frequently than that of most minor league baseball teams, so these guest appearances were frequent, and brought appreciative roars of nostalgia from the crowd. As has been his wont over the past few years, Bob engaged in frequent lengthy monologues, often studded with actual wit and insight, albeit slurred wit and beery insight—often trash-talking bands (an extension of his sports-heavy upbringing), including his own, sometimes when members of those bands by chance are in the audience—between songs. So popular have these bits of between-song banter become among the faithful that a comedy record comprising a few choice morsels has been assembled and released, called *The Relaxation of the Asshole,* featuring a photo of Bob passed out on a couch, but that's not the true origin of the phrase. The true origin of the phrase is that when you are driving around the streets of Northridge drinking beer (also known as "Freedom Cruising") and listening at full blast to whatever songs Bob has just recorded, and he has to piss, you pull over to the curb and he swings his legs out the passenger door and pisses on the sidewalk, sitting down. "The secret to pissing sitting down," he will tell you, "is you have to relax your asshole." Thus: and so.

The band did not take the stage until around 11:30 P.M., after a brief movie featuring a montage of still photographs from all stages of the band's career intercut with images of bucolic splendor—butterflies flitting across sunlit meadows, a hawk sailing across a canyon—set to a Muzak version of "Windows of My World," a song from the very last Guided by Voices album forever. You would not think the movie, titled *Memories* and deliberately constructed to leach the show of sentiment, would instead have the reverse effect: We've watched this little montage six or seven times now and it never fails to induce both smiles and, well, yeah, what might be construed as tears. Opening the set with the first track off 1992's *Propeller,* a song called "Mesh Gear Fox/Over the Neptune," which Guided by Voices had not played live for some time, the band went on to play shoulda-coulda-been hit after hit, until the witching hour, also by tradition the point at which balloons are released and people hug and kiss. And so balloons were released, and people hugged and kissed, band members kissing other band members, band members kissing wives and girlfriends who came out onstage, audience members hugging and kissing other audience members. Doug Gillard may have played an impromptu solo version of "Auld Lang Syne" on guitar, wearing a top hat and a bright red Ex-Lion Tamer's coat he'd saved for the occasion, but here memory fails. An enormous bottle of champagne—technical term for this particular size: "Nebuchadnezzar"—a present from Matador Records, home sweet home to many Guided by Voices records, including its last, was toted by unflappable tour manager Rich Turiel and maybe two other guys onstage and uncorked. Plastic cups were placed under the foaming mouth of the bottle as Bob attempted to pour, which is when Tobin Sprout wandered onstage looking for his cut, in the minor incident related above.

At this point show business resumed, and continued until you would have to guess at least 3 A.M.; you'd have to guess because even those wearing watches were in no shape to interpret their mysterious glyphs by that time. Other things of note happened during the set, including the mysterious delivery of a mass of hot dogs, quickly devoured; the presence of longtime GBV "associate" Trader Vic onstage, where he had rigged up a fairly spartan bar featuring shots of tequila or whiskey, for which he had the temerity to set up a tip jar (full by the end of the night—we did say that Guided by Voices members are generous); the return of the neon sign "The Club Is Open" which had formerly adorned many stages at many shows and which was a reference to a line from a song called "A Salty Salute" from the album *Alien Lanes;* and the unfortunate and sad and complicated absence of Manager for Life Pete Jamison, for reasons to be explored later. Also sadly missing were two of Bob's earliest and longest-serving (if you count the years of obscurity in which the band nevertheless toiled like squirrels saving nuts for the Big Winter) bandmates, drummer Kevin Fennell and (more crucially/mysteriously) guitarist Mitch Mitchell. Kevin had wanted to come, but had called unreasonably late in the day and asked to bring four or five extra guests, which, considering the already bursting-at-the-seams guest list, and the fact that extra tickets were being scalped on the Internet for hundreds of dollars, was a simple mathematical impossibility—upon being told which, Kevin with characteristic petulance simply decided against going. But Mitch—Mitch had disappeared. He and Bob had fallen out years ago, in fact seven years ago, and now even had Bob tried to proffer an olive branch, no one knew where to find Mitch. Rumors abounded: that Mitch was a short-order cook at an undisclosed restaurant, that he had moved out West to go to truck-driving school, that he was in fact a truck driver. A trip to his house, where the band had spent long hours practicing back in the mid-'90s (as much drinking as practicing, but despite its sloppy rep, GBV had always worked hard on Bob's songs), just after the epic storm, produced no answer despite repeated knockings at his door which would have roused a ghost, if Mitch by some process of transmigration, doubtless induced by the veneration of the league of Guided by Voices fans, had passed into the spirit world. But nothing. No reply. And so his presence in this book will remain one of spirit rather than substance, just as he was present tonight in spirit, because some of the guitar parts on the older songs were his parts, and further because rhythm guitarist Nate Farley had been Mitch's protégé, introduced to the band first in the role of roadie, and only later as a kind of Mitch Jr. Which is not to slight Nate's contribution in the slightest, because in many ways he surpassed his mentor's antics both on and off-stage, and was all things said probably a better guitar player, "better" being a word that's difficult to quantify in this context but probably true.

It's particularly appropriate that one of the celebrity guests on the last night of a three-show New York stand near the end of the last tour was Michael Imperioli, who plays Christopher on the HBO series *The Sopranos,* because in many ways Bob has played for twenty-one years the part of a Mafia don, with an extended "family" that consists of current and former band members (because you're never really out of Guided by Voices unless you've done something so egregious as to permanently offend Bob's strong sense of loyalty, in which case you really are dead to him), friends from elementary school and later, and actual family. There is never any doubt that Bob's the center of attention whenever he enters the rock room, or any room. A fact of which he is well-aware, and believes that he has earned.

Should you fail to pay him the proper respect in the rock room, your attitude will be noted. "The only people I hate more than people getting up my ass all the time at shows are people who think they're too cool to get up my ass," he says, only half-joking. But even those who have fallen out of favor for one reason or another over the years will eventually be forgiven and welcomed back into the fold, though with a certain distance commensurate with the severity of the original offense. "I forgive, but I don't forget," Bob said, many years ago. And he's got a memory like a large herd of extra-smart elephants.

Bob's also a big fan of *The Sopranos,* and GBV tour manager/webmaster Rich Turiel remembers watching an episode with Bob and a few other members of the inner circle, and the episode was one where Tony Soprano made a joke and everyone had to laugh and you could tell the laughter was forced. "And Bob kind of looked around at us, and we quickly had to say, 'No, no, Bob, you really *are* funny.'" Because one of Bob's most endearing traits is that he's a very funny guy, and more than that, a consummate storyteller, which may help elucidate why he understands structure so well. A vastly misunderstood part of Bob's songwriting is that he *does* understand structure, and puts a lot of effort into the structure of both the music and the lyrics. While he's fully capable of writing songs that have no literal meaning, and often prefers it that way, just as often he will write songs with at least general meaning, some based on true stories that he transforms into music—into art, if you will.

Whether or not his talent for storytelling is part of the reason so many of his friends have remained close for so many years (i.e., because he's so frankly entertaining to be around) or whether he commands loyalty because he's desperate for an audience and underneath is still seeking the approval he was denied for so many years by so many people—that's something this book will try to explore. There's an undercurrent of melancholy, of bittersweet regret, that runs through so many of Pollard's songs that it's hard not to form an impression of a man who, despite his surface jollity, is at heart a sad and even lonely figure. But he hides it well. Earlier in his life that sadness often took the form of anger, and it still does, though time has softened his temper. He got in a lot of fights—physical fights, the kind where people can get seriously hurt—but he was brought up in a rough town, at a time when corporal punishment was a popular concept in child-rearing and emotions were most often expressed with fists. "My dad used to tell me, 'Don't give any shit to people, but don't take any either.' I took that to heart a little bit. I don't try to start fights, but I finish them," he says, though he points out: "Only when absolutely necessary."

By and large Bob's audience rarely sees that side of him, though there have been isolated public incidents, which will be addressed mainly because they're entertaining stories. The more prevalent public aspect of Bob, in terms of Guided by Voices, is his prodigious drinking, both onstage and off, though mainly on. Because a typical show ranges anywhere from two to three hours, and because Bob is often half in the bag by the time he hits the stage, the quality and coherence of the show deteriorates or improves, depending on what you've come to see and/or hear, over the course of things. There is famously a cooler of beer onstage at every show, and there is famously very little if any beer left in the cooler by the end of the show, which has often had to be refilled halfway through. Partly this is sleight of hand: Bob long ago developed a technique where he appears to chug a bottle of beer, but in fact he blocks the passage of liquid down his throat by pressing his tongue against the lip of the bottle, so that most of the beer flows harmlessly over his shirt and onto the stage, which requires frequent moppings by the tour manager to prevent accidents, of which there have been a few, some serious enough to do real damage to both equipment and personnel. Nevertheless, though Bob insists he has learned better how to gauge his drinking so that alcohol serves to enhance rather than detract from the quality of his and the band's performance, he is noticeably drunker by show's end than at the beginning. Sometimes to the point where, the next day, details of the previous night's performance remain fuzzy. In early days, when the scale and duration of the drinking was greater, there were occasions when he could not remember having played at all.

That is no longer the case, and especially not tonight, the Last Night, despite the extra-long set, despite Trader Vic's liberally distributed shots of hard liquor, despite the midnight champagne toast. By show's end Bob was able to stand, and talk, and hug, but not much else, and did not seem particularly cognizant of his surroundings. "I want to go out at the top of my ga-a-a-a-me," he slurred, gamely, as a joke, and then pinched his face with his fingers into a grotesquely funny mask. The same could be said for many others, postshow, even though they had not just spent nearly four hours jumping around and singing and drinking beer and champagne and tequila. On second thought, actually, most of them had; that's what you do at a Guided by Voices concert, that's the sort of behavior encouraged, sanctioned, and in fact engendered by the madcap revels you witness onstage. It's an elaborate hoax, of course, designed to make you believe that a moment of joy can be extended or even applied to the rest of your mundane life. What you rarely consider is the toll sustaining such an illusion takes on the performers. Part of that toll is evidenced tonight by the drained, weary, and above all relieved faces of the band members, surrounded by wives, girlfriends, family, friends, ex-bandmates, fans, management, record company guys, and strangers with candy.

"Not everyone can hang with Guided by Voices," said Kevin Fennell in an interview earlier that week. In another context, of course—Fennell was referring to the unusually high turnover in band members throughout the course of its course—but his statement could as easily apply to the legion of devoted fans who have matched, or tried to match, Guided by Voices: beer for beer and leg kick for leg kick, often shouting along to the lyrics with a fervor equal if not surpassing Bob's amplified delivery. The band's audience has been built to a degree on its Dionysian live shows, and though assuredly there were as many turned off by the onstage debauchery as turned on, those turned on were turned on for good, and often followed the band from city to city, in the hopes that the party would never end. With Bob as pied piper, Guided by Voices had morphed into a kind of Grateful Dead for the drinking set, and as long as there was another show to which to look forward, the party need not end.

But now the party *had* ended. The night had started with Bob singing these lines to the song "Over the Neptune/Mesh Gear Fox": "Hey, let's throw a great party today, for the rest of our lives." He sang those words for probably the last time, ever. The great party was finally over.

Back in Dayton a few days later, Bob seemed unusually ebullient for the sober hour of the day. We asked how he felt, now that Guided by Voices was over.

"How do I feel?"

He paused, and we thought we could hear him assembling a statement of mixed feelings, of relief and regret, of fear for the future and confusion about the present.

"I feel free," he replied. "I feel like a huge fucking weight is off my back."

"I am a new man."

"Hot Freaks"
R. Pollard
From the album Bee Thousand

THE SYNTHETIC RAINBOW

She hunched up
to scratch and bleed
a minute
a minor success
another one

We produce simple vibrations

In home museums of personal strength
mouse collaborations

R. Pollard

SPORTS

"Going up to Northridge was almost like going to Twin Peaks. There was kind of this obsession with sports and everyone was drinking."

— Don Thrasher

Robert Ellsworth Pollard Jr. was born on October 31, 1957, the second child and first boy for Bob Sr. and Carol Pollard. Bob Sr. worked for Frigidaire, a division of General Motors, and had shown some athletic talent at the high school level but had never progressed beyond his early promise. As a result, he transferred, to a certain extent, his athletic ambition to his sons, of whom Bob was the first, and consequently the first subject of his father's hopes. "He told me I had a 'golden arm,' when I was like ten," recalls Pollard. "But he was more encouraging than pushy. If I had a bad game, he always said, 'Don't worry about it.' He wasn't like one of those Bobby Knight dads."

Bob Sr. may also have been the source of whatever genetic musical talent his son inherited. "My mom and dad both were into Andy Williams and Frank Sinatra, and my dad was into big band music," says Bob. "He was into jazz. It was a musical household. And my dad could sing—he could sing like Nat King Cole; he had a good voice, so I'm sure that rubbed off on me a little. Just to be able to stay in pitch, to carry a tune—I guess you kind of inherit that sort of thing."

From an early age, Pollard would make up a cappella songs to entertain his family, particularly his older sister, Debbie. "The first song I ever wrote was called 'We Are from the Planet Mars.' I wrote a bunch when I was seven or eight years old. Debbie really liked 'Eggs Make Me

Sick'; that was my first hit. But Debbie and I used to fight a lot. She used to beat the shit out of me. She was the toughest fight I ever had."

Bob Jr. was followed in short order by sisters Judy and Lisa, and finally brother Jimmy, the last Pollard, born June 9, 1962. "Mom and Dad pumped us out, like a good Catholic family," says Pollard, though he adds that only he and Debbie were ever baptized, meaning "the rest of my family are assuredly going to hell—isn't that how it works?" Money was sometimes in short supply. For a once-a-month treat, the family would go to Marion's Piazza—pronounced "pizza," and a Dayton landmark to this day; its pies are served sliced into a multiplicity of two-inch squares, rather than the eight triangular slices familiar to most of the pizza-eating world—where the whole family would share one large pie. "Sometimes we'd get it to go, and we'd fight over who got to carry it in their lap on the way home, just so you could smell the pizza, because you knew you weren't going to get to eat very much of it." Bob remembers that he and Jimmy often ended up with only two or three squares apiece. "There were some people that had it worse, though," Bob's quick to add. "There was one family that their special treat, once a month, was that they got to eat good bread, meaning Wonder bread, and good bologna, meaning Oscar Mayer. The rest of the month they had to eat stuff from the Food Outlet or whatever.

"One time I saw a family having Thanksgiving dinner at Speedway," he adds, "which is like a gas station with a convenience store, like a 7-Eleven, right around the corner from my old house."

Dayton, Ohio—nicknamed the Gem City for obscure reasons—features the proud motto "The Birthplace of Aviation," and justly so, because of native sons Orville and Wilbur Wright, local bicycle shop owners, and incidentally the inventors of flight in 1903. Orville Wright's mansion still sits on a small hill in the southern suburb of Oakwood. Dayton also serves as home to Hangar 18, reputed storage site for the Roswell, New Mexico, alien crash remains; and to Wright-Patterson Air Force Base, where the Bosnian peace talks were held. Named after Jonathan Dayton, a U.S. senator from New Jersey, who in 1789 was one of four out-of-state worthies deeded the land—which occurs in the southwest corner of Ohio, about fifty miles north of the Kentucky border—Dayton was first formed as a township in the winter of 1796–97, and incorporated in 1805. The area had originally been settled by different tribes of Indians over the millennia, some of whom left elaborate and imposing burial mounds (most famous is probably the Serpent Mound in Adams County, concerning which all sorts of occult theories have sprouted) that exist, still. Prostitution was legal until 1915—the city's most famous madam, Elizabeth Richter, better known as Lib Hedges, died in 1923 and is buried in Woodland Cemetery alongside the cream of Dayton's crop. Plagued over the years by periodic flooding, the town raised two million dollars in the aftermath of the catastrophic 1913 flood (which was followed by an equally disastrous fire) to help construct a series of five dams. A series of canals were also constructed and reinforced, which helps explain the name "Canal Street Tavern," to this day one of the few places available for local bands to ply their rock.

In addition to the invention of the airplane, Dayton has contributed these several items to American culture: the cash register; welfare; ethyl gas; the portable electric generator; the electric ignition/electric self-starter; the original pop-top. Its skyline, such as it is, includes the Mead Paper building and one or two very old hotels. From the proper height, you can also see the town's two rivers, glittering darkly in the spaces between buildings or through notches in the low hills: the Great Miami River, which is not great and does not flow to Miami, and Mad River, which has been incorporated into at least one of Bob's songs. The satanic mills of Dayton include a corn oil processing plant and several General Motors factories. Driving through downtown late one night, Bob pointed to the Mead building, the tallest one downtown, unimposingly tall, and joked dryly, "That's where the fifth plane was headed on 9/11."

He went on to tell a story about how on that dreadful day an alarm was raised by the local citizenry concerning a plume of smoke rising high in the sky over Trotwood, a northern suburb of Dayton. "People had thought another plane had gone down there. Turned out it was a pig roast," Bob related, shaking his head. The incident serves to emphasize a particular point regarding the divisions between North and South Dayton. North Dayton, where Bob grew up, is largely blue-collar, hardscrabble, uneducated, and poor. South Dayton, on the other hand, is where the well-to-do, upper-middle-class, white-collar families live. North Dayton despises South Dayton. Northridge, the particular part of North Dayton where Bob was born and grew up and still lives, has a population of 21,848, which includes a total household figure of 8,988, of whom 1,079 make less than $10,000 per year. It is 87.9 percent white, and contains absolutely no one of Hawaiian or other Pacific Islander heritage.

Bob loves Northridge, obviously, but his relationship is tinged with a kind of helpless disgust at what he sees as the base ignorance of its residents, as exemplified by the Trotwood pig roast story. Turn now, if you wish, to the chapter entitled "Science," particularly to Bob's analysis of the song "Redmen and Their Wives," for a more complete examination of that attitude. Essentially, as Bob explains, Northridge is a kind of Appalachian community, peopled by rednecks, who are generally referred to—especially by themselves—as briars, the etymological derivation of which is uncertain, but which may refer to the type of backwoods mountain men (found in the movie *Deliverance,* for instance) more typically associated with residents of Kentucky.

"Bruce Horner [Monument Club founding member; see next chapter] used to say that's how Northridge was founded," says Bob. "That some briars from Hazzard, Kentucky, loaded up the bus and headed for Detroit and ran out of gas in Northridge. So they just settled here."

Whatever the circumstances of his upbringing, Bob had a relatively normal childhood. Or what passes for normal in a crowded house with a precocious, eccentric genius and very little privacy.

"My dad caught me once playing in the tub," Bob recalls. "I had these army soldiers, little plastic ones, and I was moving my legs in and out to make them float toward my dick. And I was yelling at them, 'Come to the King!'—the King meaning my dick. And my dad somehow saw me doing that, and he was like, 'What the hell are you doing?' So I said, 'What the hell are you doing watching me?'

"One time Jimmy was in the tub," he says, "and I was in the bathroom, too, sitting on the toilet, talking to him . . ."

". . . And he accidentally stuck his finger up my asshole!" finishes Jimmy.

"*Maybe* accidentally," jokes Bob.

"What were you doing in there anyway?" demands Jimmy.

"We were just bullshitting. I meant to frog you in the ass, and my finger slipped. Right up the asshole."

"We were brought up in a time when it was okay to hit your kids," continues Bob. "People didn't know any better. But the worst was, Dad had one of those hard yellow Wiffle ball bats, the thin plastic ones. Man, those fuckers hurt. I said to him, 'Just let me hit you once, on the leg. Just so you know how it feels.' He wouldn't let me."

But at the same time, whenever Bob got hurt for whatever reason, he'd get up and run as fast as he could back home. "I'd start yelling, 'Get my dad!' One time we were playing lawn darts and I got one right in the leg. I pulled it out and started yelling, 'Get my dad!' and I ran home as fast as I could. Because somehow I knew, or I thought, that no matter how bad I was injured, if I made it home to my dad I wouldn't die."

A naturally talented athlete, Pollard had good reason to nurse dreams of sports glory, and an environment—not just in his family, but in a part of Dayton where talented athletes were treated with an adulation usually seen only in Hollywood movies about high school football set in Texas— that encouraged a single-minded focus on sports. "I'd known Bob since grade school, but always as just the athlete," recalls Kevin Fennell. "Didn't know the musical side of his personality. I saw him in school, and that was pretty much it. It's not like we hung around together when we were kids."

"People thought baseball was my best sport because it's the easiest sport," says Bob. "Baseball's fucking easy. It blows my mind when I see what major league baseball players are asking to play nine-man stand-around. Of the three major professional sports, it's the easiest for someone my size to excel in. Basketball's tough because you gotta be either tall or super-quick. Football, you gotta be a bad-ass. But baseball, anybody can do that. My dad used to milk my arm down after I pitched. I'd hold up my arm and he'd kind of squeeze the arm toward my heart to try to get the circulation back in it or some shit. He called it 'milking it down.' That was his aspiration for me, to be a major league pitcher.

"I definitely had potential. If I'd had the right temperament and the right coach, someone who taught me to pitch correctly, I could have been in the majors, or definitely seen some minor league action. I've seen pitchers in the majors that can't break glass. I've watched them from down on the field. I'm like, 'Jesus Christ, I've faced better pitchers than that in high school.'

"My senior year in high school I won all four games in the postseason tournament and we went to the regionals and got beat in the first game. We were getting close to winning the state; we had a good team. Then I went to Wright State. I was a relief pitcher my freshman year. We had a really good team my freshman and sophomore years, we had really good players. Wright State was all walk-ons at the time. By my junior year they started giving out scholarships. So they gave out nine or ten scholarships a year—but the best players were now juniors and seniors, my class, and we weren't on scholarships. So all the people on scholarships were sitting on the bench.

"My junior year my record was one and four. My only win was a no-hitter. But my ERA was under two. We just had a shitty team. My senior year I had the best record on the team. I was kind of the ace. But I had developed a bad attitude. Me and this other guy, Jeff Jacobs, we used to walk out to practice and kind of wave it off and go out to our cars. Because we weren't on scholarship, and to me it was kind of a waste of time. I hung out with freshmen and sophomores who smoked pot. I had a bad attitude for four years at Wright State. I still have recurring nightmares of fighting with the coach.

"My junior year, when I pitched the no-hitter, I got into a fight with my assistant coach, Bo Bilinsky, who was a police detective," says Bob. "It was probably not a good idea. My coach had taken me out and said to me, 'When you learn to pitch, then you'll be a pitcher,' which pissed me off because of course when I learn to pitch I'll be a good pitcher; one would certainly hope so. I got off the field and I was talking to Jeff Jacobs, and he goes, 'What'd he say?' and I go, 'He gave that "when I learn to pitch then I'll be a pitcher" shit.' Then Bo Belinsky comes over and says, 'You can't stand out there with your thumb up your ass, Pollard,' which I probably *was* standing out there with my thumb up my ass, but I said, 'Fuck you, Bo.'

"I got up to walk around at the edge of the dugout, and I heard *pow-pow-pow-pow*—footsteps. He came up behind me and grabbed me and dove on me and we went down. And it's funny, when we went down fighting—I was pissed, I was cussing—I heard all these tinging noises coming from the metal bleachers where another team was waiting to play next, and they were all running down the bleachers to come watch. I could hear all these cleats hitting the bleachers.

"We fought for a while, then they broke it up. The athletic director was walking with me, trying to calm me down, but I was going 'I quit' again!

"I've always had a big fear of failure. I wasn't that good a student, I wasn't that smart, so I really had to work my ass off. I always went to class, I always took notes, because I just—I can't fail. The worst I ever did in college was first quarter of my freshman year. I had three Cs and a D. I was pretty proud, too, because that was the hardest I ever worked in my life. High school, I don't remember having to do anything. I don't remember ever doing homework in high school."

Much to his father's eventual dismay, he was the primary instrument by which Bob first became hooked on post-Beatles rock. "I'm old enough to remember The Beatles on Ed Sullivan, I think I was about seven, and my sister Debbie used to buy 45s of British Invasion stuff, Beatles and Herman's Hermits and later on The Monkees and The Hollies and early Bee Gees," Bob remembers.

"But my dad started me in record collecting. He signed up for the Columbia Records club, twelve LPs for a penny, and he let me pick the twelve. He didn't mean to, but he got me into weird music, too, because I didn't know what to buy. I'd never bought an LP; all I bought was 45s. So I based my selection on what the cover looked like and the best band names. So I got King Crimson, and Moby Grape, and Ten Years After, and I didn't even know who they were.

"Then I got addicted and he tried to get me to stop, because I was spending all my money on records. And I continued to spend all my money on records, until . . . well, I still do. I used to take money out of my mom's purse and buy records, and they would ground me until I admitted that I did it.

"I was lucky enough to be a child of the sixties, not old enough to worry about Vietnam but old enough to dig the music. There were so many great songwriters, so many great songs in the sixties. So even though I really liked sports, and my dad wanted me to be an athlete—both me and my brother—secretly I really wanted to be in rock."

Because of Bob's burgeoning interest in music, and consequent perceived bad influence, his parents banned Jimmy from Bob's room, which posed a slight logistical problem in that the two brothers shared a room. "How am I supposed to stay out of Bobby's room if it's my room, too?" asked Jimmy, plaintively, to no effect.

His deep and immediate connection to the music he began collecting did not help his growing animus toward sports—despite the fact that in high school he was not only a star pitcher, but quarterback of the football team and shooting guard for the basketball team.

"I just was a bad sport. Sports brought out the worst in me. I fucking fought, I fucking cussed, I fucking cried, I was a fucking big baby. I'm glad I don't play anymore. I developed a really bad attitude about organized sports, and coaches. When I was invited down to tryout camp by the Reds at Riverfront Stadium or wherever, I saw these eighty-year-old men in Reds uniforms just yelling at people. And I was like, 'Fuck these guys. This is baseball! It's fucking nine-man stand-around!' I think they ought to get rid of baseball. It's fucking boring. To me it's just been around too long, it's become obsolete. I wouldn't be hurt if they didn't have it anymore."

For several years in Northridge, during the period of younger brother Jimmy's subsequent basketball ascendancy, the most famous Pollard in Dayton was not Bob but Jimmy. "Jimmy was God back then," says his older brother. "And when Jimmy was God, I came up with this T-shirt idea, that he would wear a T-shirt that said 'God,' and I would wear one that said 'God's Brother.' When Jimmy played basketball, I worshiped him; he was my fucking hero. He was good at baseball, too. His senior year, when he led the state in scoring in basketball, he also led the Dayton area in hitting. He batted like .540. He didn't throw quite as hard as I did, but he was a better hitter. That's because he had to bat off me all his life. After I'd pitch to him, he'd go down and face these other little kids and it was like they were lobbing it to him. He'd smash the ball."

Jimmy was more than just Bob's hero. He was a hero to many area basketball fans, which is not surprising given the astonishing track record he established while playing for Northridge High.

"In 1980, Jimmy was the leading scorer in the state of Ohio in basketball," Bob recalls, showing again the extent and specificity of his memory. "He averaged 36.1 points per game. He had the single-season record for points scored, which I think was 887. He had the record for the most points scored in a single game, which was 57. He would have averaged much more than that—at one point he was averaging 41 points a game and teams started stalling the ball on him, to keep the score down. He was fucking phenomenal. And that was before the three-point shot. A lot of his points came from downtown, too. I'd say with the three-point line he might have averaged six or seven more points per game. But Jimmy says, and I kind of agree with him, that he might have averaged less. Because since they've incorporated the three-point line people have been scoring less. Before, they didn't worry about it. Now they're out there laying on the motherfucker, trying to get the three. They're not as creative anymore. Jimmy was creative, and he could score in a lot of different ways. He'd drive, and he'd shoot from outside. But a lot of his points came from twenty-five to thirty feet."

After such a distinguished high school career, it wasn't surprising that Jimmy scored a scholarship to Arizona State University, one of the country's collegiate basketball powers.

"He got a full ride to Arizona State. His freshman year they were third in the nation. He played with Byron Scott, Lafayette Lever, and a lot of guys that went on to have careers in the NBA. He was about the eighth man. He didn't start, but he got in a lot of games. I think his high game might have been 10 or 11 points. He had a chance to maybe start in a couple years. But then he hurt his knee. He came back to Dayton for the summer after his freshman year, and we played in a basketball league out in Fairborn. That's when he fucked his knee up—he actually hurt his knee in a recreational league. He probably shouldn't even have been playing, but you have to keep yourself in shape somehow."

"I played my freshman year, it was fun and everything," relates Jimmy Pollard, "then I blew my knee out, rehabbed for six months, I played three days, blew my knee out. Rehabbed, blew my knee out, rehabbed, blew my knee out. And after a while the doctors were just like, 'Hey, you're gonna have to quit.' It was a fucking relief! 'Well, fuck it, good.' I tried for two fucking years to rehab my knee. It's like someone knowing they're gonna die for two years. It was brutal. The last two and a half years out there all I did was rehab, play a couple games, blow it out again, rehab, get it operated on, rehab, blow it out again, get it operated on, rehab. You start to come to grips with it a long time before it's actually over. I still had hopes, but I could see the end of the road."

"I think my parents—especially my dad—were kind of disappointed," continues Bob, "because obviously sports, for us, was his dream. And if Jimmy hadn't hurt himself he had a good chance to be in the pros.

"He was bummed out, because he liked basketball, but at the same time, what can you do? I had the same problem in college. I fucked my arm up. My senior year in high school I was blowing people away. I was throwing in the nineties, I was just striking everybody out. I hurt my arm in American Legion ball over the summer; I fucked my elbow up. It just popped. For a long time I couldn't even throw the ball ten feet. My arm finally came around but it was never as lively as it was in high school. And my attitude was 'What can I do? Fuck it. Fuck baseball.' So Jimmy said, 'Fuck basketball.' But I'm sure he was disappointed."

"I got a letter, you know, that we got a new coach, and he said I wasn't working toward my degree," remembers Jimmy, "and so he was taking my scholarship. And I go, 'Fuck it, good, I've been here three and a half years and haven't even been to class.'"

"If he ain't gonna play basketball, he doesn't want to study," interjects Bob. "He studied anatomy," he jokes.

"I was ready to go home anyway," continues Jimmy. "And they sent my dad the same letter, so I'm sitting there and the phone rings. I answer the phone and it's Dad. And Dad says, 'So you blew it, didn't you.'"

Click.

Bryan Pollard, Bob's son, was born on March 17, 1981. He graduated from the University of Dayton in 2002 with a degree in philosophy. He currently lives in Portland, Oregon. Bryan kindly consented to write a few vignettes for inclusion in *Hunting Accidents*. This is the first of three.

"Jim, Jim, Jim . . . what about the counter? Yeah, yeah, yeah. Okay, Number 23 on two," Coach Bob said to a six-foot, hundred-pound twelve-year-old with a red mullet that dangled somewhere around the middle of his back and a face full of freckles and blackheads. The red-headed stranger jogged to the huddle, mouthing to himself, "Number 23 on two . . . Number 23 on two . . . Number 23 on two . . .

"Number 22 on three . . . no wait . . . um . . . Number 23 on two . . . Fuck, dude, just call a timeout, I don't remember what your dad said," he whispered into my ear as I ran my fingers through a row of blond locks that curled below my helmet. In his gray eyes I could see him picturing the spit-clad tirade that would inevitably ensue if Coach Bob knew that he had fucked up the play call. Luckily I remembered an episode from that morning.

I had woken to what F. Scott Fitzgerald would call "a fine fall day—football weather." The sunlight, which in early autumn was more of a blinding white glare, poured through our living room window, where our fullback, a twelve-year-old Italian kid with chest hair and a beer gut, and our best receiver sat on the floor playing Nintendo. I stood in the kitchen, listlessly hovering above my father. He sat at the table slurping coffee and fitting the eighty plays that would be used for our Pee Wee Football game onto a 5 x 7 note card. He wrote in surprisingly legible capital letters that perfectly covered the entire unlined side of the card (play No. 7 was never larger than play No. 32 and plays No. 75–80 never ran around the margins). The card always started with "1. Pro right 42 Dive" and ended with "80. Pro left quick pitch left reverse pass."

After each play that he wrote he asked, "Can you read that?" to which I nodded assent.

He asked something like, "Do you think Juice [our tight end, who swore that he was 11 percent Cherokee and 89 percent redneck and who ate grass while barking at the opposing team during pregame warm-ups] will remember that counter play we put in last Tuesday?"

"No," I said, hoping that he would agree. I only vaguely remembered the counter play myself.

"That's too goddamn bad! I'm sick of Juice forgetting the plays! We are running it to open the game."

When the card was complete he taped it onto my left wrist so tightly that I spent the rest of my Sunday afternoon playing Tecmo football on Nintendo with numb fingers and a stiff wrist. My friends, growing more and more nervous as game time approached, began asking Coach Bob questions like, "Does Tipp City hit hard?" or "How come we never run Neil A-Monster Rock [a double reverse throw-back to the quarterback]?"

I apprehensively called the counter play, the redheaded stranger shuffled nervously behind me, and nine sets of confused eyes stared helplessly back at me. No one except Coach Bob and Game-Day-Only Coach Jimmy (my dad's younger brother) knew how to run the play. I quickly pointed the running backs in their respective directions, told the linemen to just block straight ahead, and informed our slot back that he would be getting the handoff somewhere around the middle of the field. We broke with a clap and grunt and jogged to the line. Amazingly no one jumped on the second "hut" and after the initial whine and clap of ten twelve-year-olds colliding from a yard away, I bounced the ball off of my fullback's thigh, who had run through the two hole instead of faking a quick pitch right. The ball rolled around the linemen's clumsy, shuffling feet. It squirted and squirmed through about five people's hands before being picked up by the slot receiver, who, completely lost, was aimlessly jogging across the field praying that he had not fucked up the play. He ran it in for a 65-yard touchdown as an ecstatic Coach Bob followed him down the sidelines, waving his clipboard in enormous circles and slapping high fives with the row of kids who stood on the sidelines chewing on their mouthpieces, gawking at the giddy, hopping cheerleaders, or waving at their jubilant parents in the stands.

UNTITLED

I am forced to report
a new conspiracy
more performances
more horrors to build
it takes changes
and seek them out
for those who kill them
in cold blood
you can always try that

R. Pollard

GHOSTS

Geo: Hey what's goin' on, fishface?
Gibby: Geo, if you call me fishface one more time I'm gonna kick your ass.
Geo: All right, fishface. Take it easy.

You can invent nothing in "the mythological land of Dayton, Ohio," as Bob once introduced the band's hometown on stage, that Dayton has not already invented, and we mean that in the literal sense—Dayton, as previously noted, has, in its long and creative history registered more patents than any other town in the country—and in the metaphorical sense, as evidenced by the misadventures experienced by Bob and his friends moving from childhood to maturity in a place where blue-collar work is the means to a blue-collar end, a normative path Bob did his mighty best to escape.

When Bob was coming of age in the 1970s, drunk driving had not acquired the same societal and legal stigma that it suffers today. Bob remembers driving into a ditch off some back road, completely hammered, and when the cops arrived, the officer scolded him to be more careful with such a nice car. "He was more concerned about the damage to the car than about whether I was okay or if I was drunk and might hit somebody," says Bob. "He was like, 'That's an expensive piece of machinery, son. You have to treat it right.' But he didn't give me a ticket or anything. Back then it was just like, 'All right, get yourself home, you've had enough for tonight.' Now if I did that they'd probably execute me on the spot. But back then we used to drive down Dixie at fifty miles an hour and play this game to see who could hit a stop sign with an empty quart beer bottle."

Graduation from high school, and eventually college, brought the specter of maturity, which Bob, in the full grip of his musical obsession by now, having soured on sports (except in a recreational sense), regarded warily at best. He knew that he'd have to get a job, and he wasn't looking forward to the prospect. He decided on teaching, partly due to the fact that he could have summers off to work on his music, but mostly due to a recognition that he had to make a stab at growing up.

Even college brought its special horrors for Bob, beyond those related to the baseball team. "When I first got to Wright State," he says, "and I saw all these kids wearing backpacks and eating bagels, throwing Frisbees: I didn't come from that world. That was Big School or South Dayton mentality." What for some might seem an easy progression from high school for Bob proved a cultural canyon—stepping from the cloistered circle of Northridge into the labyrinth of the academy was a shock; he resented even the small cosmopolitan conceits of his fellow students, and felt out of place. For him, going to school was a necessary means to what at that time seemed a necessary working-class end: Keep your head down, work hard, graduate, work hard some more, die. What friends he did make were generally fellow North Daytonians, like Mark Greenwald, whom Bob calls his "artistic guru," and who later drew the nymph on the cover of Guided by Voices' *Sandbox* LP and still later provided cover art for the Hazzard Hotrods' *Big Trouble* release.

Bob did his best, within limits. After going out with Kim Dowler, a fellow Northridge High student, for seven years—"We were fifteen, we met before I could drive, so it must have been between sophomore and junior year in high school," says Bob—he married her in his senior year in college at twenty-one, settled down, bought a house on Titus Avenue in Northridge, not a mile away from where he grew up, started a family, and, most important, got a job.

"My job interview for my first teaching position—which was at a school where they sent all the really fucked-up kids that the other schools couldn't handle—consisted of two questions," Bob says.

"The first thing the principal asked me was 'if a student came up to you and said, "Mr. Pollard, my dad is fucking me up the ass at home, and I don't know what to do," how would you respond?'

"I was obviously taken aback, but I recovered. I told him, 'Well, sir, that's a tough one. But I'm from Northridge, so we're used to that sort of thing.' Whatever the fuck that's supposed to mean.

"And he kind of nodded, and said, 'Yes, I see your point.'

"And then he asked me, 'Are you related to The Man?' And I'm thinking—'cause he was black, so I didn't know if he meant, like, whitey, or what.

"So I just said, 'The Man? What do you mean?'

"'You know: Jimmy Pollard. The Man.' Because that was around the time Jimmy really was The Man. When he was breaking records in basketball.

"Yes, as a matter of fact he's my brother.

"'Well, Mr. Pollard, I can see you've made an effort—you're dressed nicely, wearing a tie. Can you start Monday?'

"That was all he needed to know," says Bob. "And he turned out to be one of the best principals I ever worked with, too."

The agreement Bob made with Kim when they married was a simple one, but in the end turned out to have a profound effect on the course of his life. "I said to her, 'We'll get married, but don't expect me to change from the way things are right now.' The point of which was to give each other some freedom to spend time with friends, and not be up each other's ass all the time. Basically, I promise not to fuck around on you if you promise to let me do what I want.

"Kim, though, was really a great mother, especially with all the shit she had to put up with from me. Our children turned out really well—I'm proud of them both—and that's mostly due to her.

"All I really wanted or asked for from her was space. And much to her credit, she gave me that. Or I took it. Either way."

WE DON'T NEED AN ID

Essentially, what Bob meant by "space" encompassed two things: making music, and the Monument Club. The Monument Club is an institution in Guided by Voices lore. If you are extended an invitation to attend—and it is unwise, unless you are certain of your place in the hierarchy, to attend uninvited, though you will not be turned away; but you will treated as if you don't exist, until you finally get the hint and leave, and then you will be viciously attacked in absentia by a jury of drunks—you have, at least temporarily, been granted a place in one of the closer circles of Bob's fiefdom. Bob is extremely tolerant of strangers, and welcoming—to a point. With Bob, everything is always to a point. The trick is to figure out when that point is approaching, a skill only longtime intimates have mastered.

A tip for would-be visitors: go late. By the onset of sunset, Bob will be sufficiently beerified that he will barely register your presence, and you will be hard-pressed to do or say anything he does not consider hilarious, or by his own sodden magic transform into hilarity. If you are lucky, you will catch him in a dancing mood, and he will demonstrate a dance he invented or claims to have invented (and Dayton, once again, is a cauldron of invention, so . . .) called the Pencil Sharpener, impossible to describe here except to say that it starts with a pencil-sharpening-like gesture of the hands, is followed by a kind of slide step to either side, and finished by a move Bob calls the coat hanger, which is a move that he saw Bill Cosby use in some seventies movie.

"We used to play basketball every Sunday at this place called Carpenters' Hall," explains Bob. "Basically most of the guys that are in the Monument Club now. We played ball together in school. We rented out the gym for a couple of hours and then we'd go drinking afterward. We'd go to Marion's or whatever and get hammered. Eventually, I converted my garage at Titus into the Monument Club—just so we'd have a place to go where it's cheaper—and we built the basketball court. And now it continues at my new house, although I haven't rigged up heat for the Monument Club area yet.

"Years ago, I was going through the drive-thru [a peculiar and fantastic feature of the Dayton area—like a fast-food drive-thru, but instead purveying beer and cigarettes: 'a candy store for adults,' Pete Jamison once described it] with Gibby [Mark Gibbs] and Forester Hickman. Hickman called himself the Great White Pelt-Finder. Which—you can guess what that means. He's nuts, a good guy, but sometimes over the top when he's been drinking. He can eat a shot glass. He did it for Doug Gillard. He bit me on the end of my nose one time, almost bit it off. Just fucking around drunk. He once said 'Fuck you' to me, and I said, 'No, fuck you, Hickman.' And he said, 'I said it first.' I said, 'Yeah, you did, you got me.' We were going through the drive-thru, and this guy Larry Pollard, no relation, asked us for our ID. So Hickman in the back goes, 'Fuck you, Larry, I'm a monument! We don't need an ID, I'm a fucking monument!' So we called ourselves the Monument Club."

Historically, the Monument Club has been a male-only enclave (Bob once described it jokingly as the He-Man's Woman Hater Club, after the clubhouse from the Little Rascals), but over the years, the rules have slackened, and honorary members or casual visitors unaware of the regulations (which aren't exactly posted) have brought along their significant others. There has been only one honorary female member: Back when Bob and Kim Deal were close friends, she was admitted without reservation, mainly because she was one of the few Daytonians Bob regarded as an equal, she was from North Dayton (Huber Heights, to be exact), and she could match most of the men drink for drink. (Obviously Bob's girlfriend, Sarah Zade, is an honorary member as well, in the way that when you marry a Canadian you get a Canadian passport; but since her exception does not prove our rule, we will pretend to overlook it.)

The only other long-standing imperative is that you do not show up beerless. Again, it's a rule that's often broken, particularly in the case of newcomers, and no one will throw you out should you arrive without the requisite twelve-pack of light beer, but you will be regarded askance. And you had better not drink the last beer, bub.

While there's sometimes a kind of governing rationale—say, if the Cincinnati Bengals are playing, or the Cleveland Browns (the Monument Club accommodates fans of either team)—there really is only one true purpose for the club. And that purpose is accomplished without fail, every time.

"Northridge has some drinking motherfuckers, and we've always been proud of the fact that we can drink people under the table," says Bob.

"I am a drunk. I'm not an alcoholic—alcoholics have to go to meetings. I know it's not good to be a drunk or whatever, but for a long time now I've been able physically to run rings around my peers, even those who don't drink. So fuck 'em. I'm a notorious fucking drunk. I'm a *famous* drunk. I'm proud of that. You can talk about dieting, you can talk about cutting back on smoking, but there is no option in drinking. You fucking drink."

The club meets every Sunday, beginning at noon, and in the days at Titus before Bob's divorce would include spirited pickup games of basketball. (Billy Corgan of the Smashing Pumpkins once stopped by when Lollapalooza was passing through town. Bob says he appeared perplexed that no one seemed to know who he was; but Corgan's tall, and his basketball skills, while ungainly, were not entirely lacking. He may have been taken aback, however, when one of the neighborhood kids, whom Bob often allowed to join in, commented on one of Corgan's jumpers: "That's a ugly shot!")

When Bob's son Bryan came of drinking age (Northridge drinking age, which is not the same as the legal drinking age in the Puritan States of America), he would sometimes attend, although an appetite for beer does not appear to have been handed down from father to son, despite Bob's best efforts (this is patently a joke—Bob would never, and has never, either encouraged or discouraged his children from following in his own lurching footsteps; free will is a thing granted both by God and by Bob, and like God, Bob will only smite you if you abuse the privilege).

An interesting parallel can be made between the core membership of the Monument Club, which has never changed, and the core membership of Guided by Voices, which has changed radically and often since its inception—by Bob's count there have been forty or fifty band members, though in fairness it should be noted that most of the lineup changes occurred in the early years, when nobody cared, when it was just for fun, and when Bob was much less tolerant of anyone who wasn't willing to follow his lead. Once the band had achieved some success, while turnover remained higher than in many bands, he never really fired anyone, except the members of Cobra Verde, which incident will be discussed in due course.

Bob's rock fantasy, never fulfilled, was that his band would be close-knit, and constant, like his heroes The Who, for instance, where, although the members fought constantly, the only changes were as a result of death. That fantasy has been fulfilled in the case of the Monument Club, however. The only way out is to die, and unfortunately, as time passes, so does the frequency of tragedy. Jack Garnett died suddenly of a heart attack in 1997, right around the time Bob composed his ode to fallen comrades, "People Are Leaving," on the solo album he released that same year. More recent, and somehow more tragic, was the death of Mark Gibbs, who in many ways was the heart of the Monument Club. Gibby, a lifelong heavy smoker, died of lung cancer, and though he may have been sick for a while, in his usual stoic style he never let on, and from the time he confessed his illness to the time he was discovered by his roommate, Billy Dixon ("That was a rough day," says Billy with typical understatement), lying dead, blood pooling from his mouth, only three weeks had passed.

"I used to envy people in Northridge who could drink really, really well, like Gibby," says Bob. "They were my heroes. Gibby used to get mad. I'd go, 'This is Mark Gibbs—he's the greatest drinker I've ever met.' He'd tell me, 'I'm not so sure you should be telling people that.' I'd say, 'He's the biggest drunk I've ever met. He's the king.' Gibby didn't like that. And it probably wasn't true. There was another guy from Northridge, American Legion buddies with Gibby, Steve Puchalski, who had like fourteen DUIs. That blows my mind. He's walking now. I see him walking, he takes buses and shit. He's the real king. He's the Freedom Cruise King. He's also, coincidentally, the uncle of Kid Marine."

But it was more than his capacity for beer consumption that made Gibby great. It was his kindness, his sense of humor, his mask of weary resignation, his willingness to help complete strangers at a moment's notice, his loyalty, and his inability to suffer fools gladly—and concomitant ability to put people, including Bob, in their place with his incisive wit—that made him special. He was a mess, there's no denying. A ruined, bloated, long-haired, sloppily dressed, chain-smoking alcoholic—all true. Of the core Monument Club members, excepting Jimmy Pollard and maybe Bruce Horner, he was the most open and least suspicious-minded. He will be sorely missed.

If brevity is in fact the soul of wit, then this exchange between Gibby and Jimmy during a Guided by Voices recording session at Cro-Magnon Studio (sessions were often attended by friends and family and other noncombatants, who usually outnumbered the musicians) might exemplify the best of the art of what in Northridge is called "cracking." As in, "You don't want to be cracking on me, Kevin. You don't want me to crack back in front of all eight of your fans." (Said by Bob to Kevin at a Brookwood Hall show featuring Kevin and Mitch Mitchell's side project, K.M.A.—Kiss My Ass. Clever!—after Kevin had addressed Bob as "Dorian Gray." This was five years before Bob even had any gray hair, he points out.) It is also sometimes referred to as "cracking my meat," with obviously phallic associations.

But we were speaking of brevity. Okay. It went like this, according to a reliable witness: Jimmy had just gotten a haircut, and it was really obvious that he'd just gotten a haircut. It was an obvious haircut, in other words. So as Jimmy gets up to leave, Gibby, in his usual position—slumped on the couch—says, in his usual sardonic tone, "Hey, Jimmy, Happy Haircut." To which Jimmy replies, in the same tone, scarcely taking the time to turn around on his way out, "Hey, Gibby, Happy Breath," referring to Gibby's difficulty breathing.

Should that exchange prove in any way illustrative to the casual reader of the comradeship and good humor of Mark Gibbs, then hurray.

If anything good can be said to have come of Gibby's passing, it might be that it prompted Bob to quit smoking almost immediately. What had begun as an onstage prop had escalated to a regular habit, but after seeing what happened to Mark, he cut back immediately. "I was smoking a pack a day, and I haven't completely quit, but I've cut way down," Bob says. "At first I quit completely, but now every once in a while, especially when I'm out drinking, I'll smoke one or two. Because nobody tells me what to do—not even myself."

WAS IT YOU WHO DRANK THE PISS?

"Remember at the old Monument Club where we'd piss into a piss bucket just outside?" recalls Bob late one night, surrounded by friends after a show. "And it'd be full of piss, Clorox, gnats. Bryan and all his friends were there, and—was it you, Jeremy [Myers]?—yeah, and they gave . . . how much did they give you? Fifty bucks? They gave him fifty bucks to stick a glass in there and drink that shit, do a shot of it.

"Jeremy's dad was Frank Myers," continues Bob, "who was a country songwriter from Northridge—he was one of my inspirations. We were the same age and I saw him play when I was young, and I was like, 'Goddamn, he's good.' He later went on to write or cowrite a couple of big hit songs. One for Crystal Gayle called 'You and I,' and another one that was actually recorded by some boy band, All-4-One, called 'I Swear' or something. So I'm not even the most successful songwriter in Northridge, never mind Dayton. They put him in the Northridge Hall Of Fame, no problem. Still haven't asked me, or Jimmy. Never will. We have a bad reputation."

A regular duty at Monument Club was emptying the piss bucket, which by the time it neared full was a two-man job, the urine slopping over the sides of the bucket as the two unlucky souls whose number came up carried the bucket—a big bucket, it should be noted—over to the far side of the basketball court and dumped its reeking contents onto the dirt. The job was made more difficult during winter, when the temperature was below whatever the temperature at which urine freezes, likely not much lower than that of water, since Monument Club members for the most part drank only light beer, and the older they got the lighter the beer, which is mostly water anyway. The point being that the urine had frozen solid, and stuck to the bucket, so that while there was no danger of slopping excess piss on your pants, you had to pound on the bottom until the frozen lump of urine slid out of the bucket onto the ground, where it sat like a giant piss Popsicle. By the end of a typical session the ground would be dotted with these slowly melting lumps, a landscape that, should a stranger have stumbled across that urino-coagulant minefield, he or she might be forgiven for believing in aliens, or monsters.

No more than fifty feet away from the Monument Club, just behind the basketball court, was an actual bar, then called Ridge Garden, now called the Whiskey Barn, serving actual liquor, but that bar a) was often crowded with people Bob either didn't know or didn't want to see, b) cost money, or at least more money than a twelve-pack of Bud Light at the Speedway gas station around the corner from Bob's house, c) did not contain a large-screen TV or posters of Guided by Voices, d) did not possess a stereo on which one could blast the latest Bob-related recording or (though this was rare) non-Bob-related music, and e) was not equipped with easy chairs and couches large enough to contain the gradually expanding bodies of many Monument Club members.

One time Bob and Jimmy did make the mistake of visiting the bar—remember, this is essentially in Bob's backyard, and he knew the bartenders, and they knew him and they knew Jimmy, too, and as with many Northridge residents who are not close to Bob but know him, they did not like Bob—with a couple of guests, and the bartender asked to see IDs, which were not readily available. "Fuck yous" were exchanged, and Bob and his party were impolitely asked to leave. So far as the historical records indicate, no one said, "We don't need an ID! I'm a fucking monument!" Which would have provided a nicely symmetrical ending to this part of the story, but, like the songs Bob hates most, that would be corny.

Core members of the Monument Club.

Criteria for inclusion in the core group: You have to be from Northridge, and you have to have known Bob since high school at least. You don't have to be alive. Thus, while there have been over the years many honorary members, including close friends and band members, these names have been excluded from the list by rule of law (apologies to Mike Lipps).

Robert Pollard as Bobby
Jimmy Pollard as Jimmy
Billy Dixon as Hunior
Mark Gibbs as Gibby (deceased)
Charlie Balderson as For Chrissakes Charlie
Jim Hamby as Bloodclot
Randy Campbell as Ranch
Dean Crabtree as Crab
Gary Phillips as Family
James Grigsby as 240 Scrigs
Daryl Deaton as Dink
Bruce Horner as Donkey
Tom Sitzman as Tommy Two Beers
Tony Conley as Tony Conley
Jack Garnett (deceased)
Tony Richison as Ratch
Geo as The Mascot

Each core Monument Club member has known Bob for longer than Guided by Voices has existed, and enjoys the familiarity and the intimacy that comes from such a long friendship. There is more or less nothing a core member can do wrong, no matter how egregious, like the time Gibby, on a freezing Northridge night, while in his cups, shall we say, dove into the club though the window, and passed out pissing all over himself. There are pictures, unsuitable for reproduction in, well, anywhere (*nihil nisi bonum de mortuis,* after all, and that goes double for pictures). But the point of the story is, the other guys pitched in, carried him into the house, into the shower, took care of him. Monument Club members—and you will find this is true of Daytonians in general, though nowhere more so than in Northridge—will perform feats of valor on your behalf should you find yourself in trouble. Especially alcohol-assisted trouble. But it has to be real trouble, not the kind former Guided by

Voices bass player and Bob's close friend Greg Demos always gets in when he drinks, where he's simply too drunk to move. "Help!" he'll bleat from time to time. "Help!"

In that situation, you make fun of him until you're ready to go, then you carry him onto Bob's couch or lay him out on the couch in the Monument Club and let him sleep it off.

Real trouble might be described as the time Jack Garnett—one of the older members of the Club, and one who had a tendency to get a little "red" (as Bob describes acting in an aggressively briarlike manner) from time to time—took his teeth out. He had a set of false teeth that were apparently precious to him, because on the occasion of which we're thinking, Jack was preparing to put the beat-down on some young punk (we're sort of improvising here), and he took his teeth out and with one quick motion threw them to Jimmy for safekeeping.

"And Jimmy caught 'em, too," remembers Bob. "Fucking disgusting." The occasion is commemorated in the song "Pantherz," recorded by Steve Albini, intended to be the first song on the *Power of Suck* concept album, shelved after it was decided that maybe the album itself might suck, which would be ironic in an unfortunate way. The song was eventually released on an import-only 7", and on bootleg vinyl. It's possibly not true that the album would have sucked, and later on we will try to reconstruct to the extent possible the original concept and the songs earmarked or written for inclusion, should readers wish to fashion their own homemade *Power of Suck*. In any case, in "Pantherz," Bob sings the line "I will have to take my teeth out," as a kind of threat to the song's protagonist, and, as we now know, as an homage to Jack Garnett, now sadly dead.

SHE'S MY PAYDAY

For the uninitiated, an encounter with Chris "Geo" Gianopulos can leave you with the impression that he's a perfectly normal, genuinely nice guy, which on one level is true, or that he's a slightly off-kilter, not-quite-normal nice guy, which is also true, and strangely on the same level. "Geo's our mascot," explains Bob. "He is from Northridge, which is why he's a core member of the Monument Club. He lived over by Mitch [Mitchell], on the street with Mitch and Charlie [Balderson]. But then he moved, he went to Meadowdale High with Pete [Jamison].

"This is what Pete says happened to Geo. I guess Pete and this other guy went up to Bowling Green one weekend for some kind of party. Geo's from an upstanding Greek family in Dayton; they're all lawyers and super-intendents and judges and shit. Geo's kind of the black sheep of the family. I personally think he's always been a little weird or whatever. But he's a very sweet guy, super nice. And he was the best athlete in that family, the Gianopulos family. They were all good athletes, but Geo was a great fucking football player.

"So they took Geo up to this party, and he told them he had to be back on Sunday for some real important family get-together. And Pete said they went up there and did acid and all kinds of shit and they left Geo and he never got back to his family thing, and after that he just kind of weirded out. I don't know exactly what happened, but that's the story Pete gives. According to him, Geo was never quite the same.

"He mows my lawn. He has a lawn-mowing service. He calls his service Amphibious Landing. He once told me, 'Bob, thanks for twenty-seven years of mow-jobs.' He's harmless, and he's the funniest fucking person I've ever met. He's the only person who can make me laugh until I'm crying hot tears. And he's persistent. He'll come around and he'll kind of be bum-ming me out, just bugging me, and I'm going, 'Come on, Geo, fuck.' But he'll just stick with it until finally I'm crying. He'll just keep doing some-thing fucking stupid until finally he's got me crying. It's insane. He gets on your nerves until you finally just give in, or you've had enough beers, and you just start laughing. He's more than the Monument Club mascot, he's Guided by Voices' mascot. It always says on the thank you section of our early albums: 'And Geo.'

"Mitch brought him around to my house. You meet Geo—and Geo's a hell of a nice guy; it takes a while before you realize there's some-thing a little bit different going on. There was a time when I used to go to bars with Geo. He was good-looking back then, he looked like a young Al Pacino. He still does look like Al Pacino but it's the way Pacino looks now. We were sitting in this one bar and these two really good-looking chicks come up to us. They're both interested in just Geo. And Geo's still talking to me, crazily, not even paying attention to these two girls who are standing there looking at him. They kept trying to get his at-tention and finally I said, 'Geo, do The Duck.' Which was this fucking crazy dance he does, anytime you ask he'll get up and start doing it. Just this ridiculous, finger-pointing, eyes-in-the-air dance. He jumped up and did The Duck and the girls left immediately and he sat back down and started talking to me again.

"Geo would do the shit that he does—you just tell him, 'Do The Duck,' or 'Do The Joker'—in front of any strangers. You tell him to do it in front of a stranger, he jumps up immediately, and they get weirded out. He has no self-consciousness. He'd do it in front of the president."

That lack of self-consciousness carries over into what you'd have to call Geo's musical endeavors as well. Geo's formed and named a number of imaginary bands, and though his band-name predilections betray an unsettling similarity to those of the purportedly sane Robert E. Pollard Jr. (not to mention that Bob has throughout his life invented many band names for bands that never have and maybe never will exist), there's just enough genuine craziness involved to distinguish between the two. Maybe.

> Representative Geo band names:
> The Quash Trippers
> The Suppository Oswalds
> Richard Flavor & the Flavors featuring Robert Flavor
> The Gibby-Geo Trio

> Representative Geo song titles:
> "Seashell Eyes"
> "Li'l Ol' Man," sample lyrics: "He talks with me and makes love
>   to me"
> "She's My Payday"—by which Geo means the candy bar, not
>   the day every blue-collar worker lives for

"He adds one song to his repertoire every two years," says Bob. "He also does covers. One time he did 'Hey Hey You You Get Out of My House.' He doesn't always listen carefully to the original lyrics. Another time he actually gave a performance at the Monument Club. He opened for Swearing at Motorists, which was Dave Doughman and Don Thrasher's band. I didn't think he was gonna show, he got so nervous. He can play guitar a little bit. The Monument Club was packed that night. Everyone was going nuts. I felt bad because after he played, most of the Monument Club went out to play basketball. Only a few of us stayed to listen to Swearing at Motorists. I wouldn't want to follow Geo. How could you?"

STEAK & EGGS

One of the more infamous stories in the Northridge Adventure Society book (and there was going to be a book, according to Bob, entitled *Black Ghost Pie,* collecting these stories, but there never was, though there may someday still be, because while this book will try, it can by definition never be that book) is entitled "Steak & Eggs." Bob's actually written a song about it, on an *Acid Ranch* album, but the song fails to capture the awful reality of the story, which is not only true but so true that we have been requested not to name the participants, who are not dead.

In any case, "Steak & Eggs" took place back in Bob's high school days. Two friends of his were at a party on a farm and took some acid, as was not uncommon in the 1970s, which was a pretty good decade for drugs and for drunk driving. (Bob himself experimented with LSD a few times, once with fruitful results, in terms of songwriting, as you will read in the chapter called "Science," and once that resulted in his simply stripping naked and answering the door that way. Fun!) It was late at night, and one of the two, whose personality was such that he might have done this whether tripping or stone sober, decided he was hungry. "I want some steak and eggs!" declared the instigator. His partner agreed: Steak and eggs sounded damn good just then.

Somehow they got hold of a machete (the 1970s were a pretty good decade for machetes, too) and headed for a nearby pasture, where a herd of cows peacefully stood sleeping and/or grazing. At the sight of these two lunatics approaching with brandished machete, most of the cows lumbered off, faster than the impaired duo could move. But the two finally managed to grapple one poor heifer to the ground, and began sawing away at the cow's neck—blood spurting everywhere, the cow bellowing pitifully. It is, however, apparently hard work sawing a cow's head off with a 1970s machete; in addition to which, one of the guys suddenly stopped, struck by an idea: "What are we doing? You don't eat the cow's head!" So the pair set to work instead on sawing off one of the legs, at which they had apparently made some little progress when the sun began to rise. "Fuck this, it's too hard," declared either one or both of the anonymous butchers, who then headed to Waffle House, where it is not reported whether they ordered and enjoyed a breakfast of steak and eggs, or even whether they ordered their hash browns "smothered, covered, and corn-holed," as Rex Bolander used to say, a joke which will be appreciated only by people who frequent the Waffle House, meaning Michael Jordan, at least. Hi, Mike! (Those baffled by this reference to basketball legend Michael Jordan should turn to the chapter "Love" and skim though until you come to his name. Which you assuredly will. Or you could just wait.)

HORNERISMS

Bruce Horner, whose nickname according to Bob is Donkey but who most people call Bruce, or Horner, or Bruce Horner, has a gift. He is one of the nicest people you will ever meet, but his grasp of the English language is, at times, less than firm. Which is not to say that he's stupid, because he's not. And often what comes out of his mouth, however mangled or initially mystifying, upon reflection turns out be either more entertaining than the correct phrase or curiously insightful. Had we world enough, and time, we could have assembled a more complete assortment of what have come to be known as Hornerisms. But this small sample, with accompanying translations, will have to suffice.

Sample Hornerisms (with translations):

I'm groovin' Mooch to be a magician. I'm teaching him to play Oregon. *(I'm grooming Mooch [Bruce's son] to be a musician. I'm teaching him to play organ.)*

You lie to your friends, I'll lie to mine, let's not lie to each other. *(No one's really sure what Bruce was trying to say here, but it does sound either profound or sad or sadly profound, or ridiculous, any one of which reasons may have prompted Bob to put the line in his song "Hey Mr. Soundman.")*

Fear and loafing in Las Vegas *(Bruce was trying to refer to the movie starring Johnny Depp based on Hunter S. Thompson's book* Fear and Loathing in Las Vegas.)

You're a good man, and I'm a damn liar. *(Think about it. No Zen koan matches the height of paradoxical wisdom contained in this phrase.)*

No beer here, no reason for me to be here. *(Basic Monument Club wisdom, often quoted by others in situations that have somehow become beer-free. Included because Bruce cleverly rhymes "here" with "here.")*

Out of bounce *(Out of bounds. Basketball term: The ball went out of bounds.)*

The Frank Sinatra Thee-ater *(Bruce was referring to the venue in Los Angeles where GBV was playing its last L.A. show, the Henry Ford Theater.)*

My son plays goldie. *(Goalie! Surely not Goldie the British musician/actor with the gold teeth and all?)*

I don't think I can top that off. *(I don't think I can top that one, i.e., do better than the joke Billy Dixon just told.)*

Look at that fucking bee-sting haircut. *(Look at that fucking beehive hairdo.)*

BOB IS DEAD

On December 3, 1979, a band called The Who, with which the reader might be familiar, played a concert at what was then called Riverfront Coliseum in Cincinnati. Bob made plans to attend, as you do, with frequent concert buddy Mitch Mitchell. Mitch stood him up, as sometimes happened with Mitch, who, though possessed of many virtues, could not count reliability among them. So Bob had to drive himself down to the show, despite dealing with a broken arm at the time (a non-Who-related accident). He made it into the Coliseum without incident, where he saw Mitch with some girl, thus explaining the standing-up part, but was unaware, as were most of the approximately eight to ten thousand fans inside said venue, that a tragedy of heretofore unprecedented proportions had taken place just before the show. Because the concert was oversold, and because the majority of the tickets were of the type called "festival seating," meaning unassigned seating, meaning that the earlier you got in the closer to the stage you could get, a crush developed at one of the entrances, and eleven ticket-holders died.

Sad, tragic, disastrous, catastrophic, heartbreaking, and here our thesaurus runs dry. But things got worse, when Bob's good friend Randy Campbell, watching breaking news of the story on TV, and seeing the bodies laid out under blankets by the entrance, where they had fallen, be-came convinced that he saw Bob's shoes on one of the victims. So convinced that he called Bob's mom and told her his theory. Which, as you can imag-ine, provoked a fair degree of distress in the Pollard household until Bob came stumbling in, very late but of course unharmed (except for the pre-viously mentioned broken wing).

"Nice job, Randy," Bob would like at this point to add, for the record.

BOB IS GAY

There's really only one openly gay man in Dayton, at least in what you might consider the musicians' community. His name is Tere Lerma, and he and his brother Luis, who's not gay but who does have some peculiar habits, like shaving his entire body when he showers, have been fixtures on the Dayton music scene for years. Bob even recorded a side project, Lexo and The Leapers, with Tere Lerma, and at one point signed Lerma's band, The Tasties, to Bob's short-lived attempt to expand Rockathon into a "real" record label.

Tere's not just gay, he's flamboyantly gay, and it's that very flam-boyance that renders him proof against the slings and arrows of Midwest homophobia. You can't call someone a fag if he calls himself one, and you can't make fun of someone's sexuality when he makes such an exagger-ated point of it, taking every opportunity to freak out the straights by flaunt-ing, in crude language, his appetites. As such, he's become tolerated, even accepted—even if that acceptance is accompanied by an undercurrent of uneasiness.

Which makes the following story all the more remarkable. "One time at the Monument Club, this guy came over," Bob recalls. "I eventually had to bar him because he was such an asshole. He was really drunk and in-sulting everybody. And Tere Lerma was there and he goes, 'That guy's a bigger fag than I am.'"

Later that same night, well past the usual closing hour of the Monu-ment Club, which generally shuts down—not by rule but by virtue of the fact that everyone has left, because most of its members have to get up and go to work the next day—sometime around ten or eleven o'clock (considering that things get started around noon, that affords plenty of quality drinking time), Bob was still going strong. After midnight, to quote by rote the pote. And the only other people remaining were Gibby and Tere Lerma. "Here's the scenario," Bob relates. "Gibby's passed out on the couch with snot hanging out of his nose, and me and Tere Lerma are slow-dancing. He asked me. I go, like, 'Whatever.' It was kind of sweet. It was very Lynchian."

ASPHYXIATED SPHYNCTER

Is it all good?
Wherever fear is clear
and ever enduring?

And is it coiled dormant
in black and white houses
where no zoom lens is permitted

R. Pollard

WALK

"There was this sense of, how the fuck did we not know about something this good, how could something this good exist and we didn't know anything about it for a decade?"

—Gerard Cosloy

"Congratulations, you're in Guided by Voices," said Bob when his family met Jimmy at the airport after he got bounced out of Arizona State in 1982.

"Which was kind of a joke," he continues, "because the band didn't even really exist. But I was serious at the same time, because I'd been in Anacrusis and I'd really dug being in a band, and I'd learned to play guitar a little bit and I was doing this sort of songwriters' guild called 86 with Nick Weiser and John Dodson. Also Kevin and Mitch and I had started to work on some stuff under different names, just trying things out. There's a tape under the name of Coyote Call called *Pissing in the Canal* that actually contains early versions of what later would become 'Hardcore UFOs' and 'Tractor Rape Chain.' That might be the first recording we ever made. It sounds like shit."

Actually the tape, recorded in 1982, which so far as we know remains in the sole possession of Kevin Fennell, sounds better than Bob remembers. There's an obvious R.E.M. influence on a few of the songs, but Bob's singing is confident and strong; the song structures are tight and imaginative; the lyrics, while more straightforward than those Bob would eventually come to write, are nevertheless intriguing; the drumming is inventive (possibly too inventive for Bob's liking); and Mitch, who played bass on almost all the early Guided by Voices stuff ("Mitch always played bass," says Bob. "He played bass up until '92 when we started playing live again.") provides not only capable, melodic bass-playing, but a surprisingly sweet harmony voice. There's a song called "Echoland," which despite its evident "Chronic Town" derivation, is as beautiful and melancholy a song as Bob has ever written. "Next stop Echoland, population growing," he sings.

The tape predated Jimmy's arrival, but the younger Pollard's lifelong enthusiasm for Bob's music was such that he hopped right on the Guided by Voices express (population growing). He'd been brought up not only hearing the catalog of Bob's youthful a cappella songs, but exposed—despite his dad's best attempts—to Bob's developing musical tastes. "It'd always been my dream to start a band," reiterates Bob. "In seventh grade we tried to start a band called Jello. The album was called *Jar of Jam, Ton of Bricks*. Because if you hold your tongue it sounds like 'Goddamn son of a bitch.' It didn't happen."

The fact that he could now hear a more fully realized version of Bob's vision only stoked the fires of Jimmy's enthusiasm. "I immediately bought a hundred-dollar guitar from Ed Jon [Captain Bizarre]," relates Jimmy, "which I eventually gave to Bob, who wrote six thousand songs on it. The buzzing one-stringer. It had this G string that for some reason—probably because we didn't know shit about guitars—we could not get to stop buzzing. You can hear it on 'Drinker's Peace,' some of the older songs. Even some stuff on *Bee Thousand*.

"I think for Bob my coming home was a relief," he continues. "He went through athletics, too, and knows the pressures of it. We'd get back together in the summers when I was in college, and as I grew older we grew closer—friends rather than brothers. And then when I left college, I think it was a relief: 'Hey, he's back for good.' We had a couple scuffles, but we became best friends instead of just brothers.

"It's pretty traumatic when a guy is fucking King Shit and goes off to a big college and blows his knee out and he's done fucking playing, and he comes home. You want someone going, 'Fuck that anyway, let's go play some music.' It was a nice outlet for me."

Bob's influence on Jimmy, still living at home after his ASU disgrace, was not well-received in his parents' household. "I immediately started letting my hair grow, got my ear pierced, then Dad really hated me," Jimmy relates.

"One time, my hair was getting long, and Dad's like, 'Help me hold up this shelf.' He was putting something up, and I had just made this weird fucking cross earring, and he notices, and he goes, 'I didn't raise a girl.'"

The genesis of Guided by Voices—just the years before the band even released its first EP, *Forever Since Breakfast,* in 1986—could easily occupy a book of its own. Because Bob has never lived more than a mile from the house in which he grew up, most of his early musical associates were fellow Northridge residents, people he'd known since childhood. Not that these were necessarily lifelong friends—even within Northridge, with its athletocracy, there were divisions. So that while Bob grew up within a literal stone's throw of some of his eventual closest collaborators, that doesn't mean he knew them. Or liked them.

"I used to see Mitch [Mitchell] and Kevin [Fennell] in my neighborhood," Bob remembers. "Kevin lived right around the corner from me. And Mitch used to come and see Kevin. They were in the same class; I was two years ahead of them. And they'd see me down the street and they'd fucking run. I didn't like 'em. There was a separation at the time between jocks and freaks. Kevin and Mitch . . . I don't know if Mitch was a freak— he did have long hair—but Kevin was the epitome of a freak, and we just didn't like freaks too much at the time. We'd see them all the way down the street and we'd say, 'There they are!' and they'd run. But they played music. Kevin and Mitch had a band—I think they were called Ambush. They were probably ten or eleven. Blue Mist was another one of their names. I saw them play a couple times. They were pretty good for that age. Thing is, they never really improved with age, the way they should have, until the early to mid '90s. That doesn't make sense to me. Starting so young, shouldn't you be a fairly accomplished musician by your late teens? Don't get me wrong, they did eventually blossom, at least rise to the occasion when it arrived. Something of which I was quite proud."

According to Kevin, "Bob said it ate him alive to watch us up there playing. Because he wanted to do it, and obviously his parents wanted him to play basketball, play football. That band nonsense? Forget it. He was very envious that Mitch and I, we had our hair long—he didn't have long hair. We wore holey jeans—he had to wear nice clothes. He wanted that. And later, he talked about that, a lot."

"I *did* want to have long hair and play music," replies Bob. "He's right, but . . . don't misconstrue that I was jealous of Kevin. I was jealous of the concept of being able to do what you want. I always used to go, 'Man, I wish my parents would get divorced so I could do whatever I want.' I'd live with my mom, and I could do whatever I want. That was the case with a lot of kids who could do what they wanted: They came from single-parent households. But the only thing I thought was cool was the fact that they played music. I went to see them a couple of times. I always wanted to be in a band, but it couldn't happen at the time—no one played. It was all just make-believe. We did album covers and T-shirts when I was a freshman, in art class in high school, but we couldn't get a band. We wanted to but no one knew how to play.

"I joined Anacrusis freshman year in college," says Bob. "Up until that time I really didn't know Mitch very well, other than 'There he is, the little kid with really long hair.' Mitch was also a good athlete, so I knew him through sports. But we were never friends."

Anacrusis was a heavy metal cover band comprised of Northridge musicians. All it lacked was a singer. According to Bob, "Anacrusis knew I could sing because I always sang out loud, all the time, anywhere, anytime I wanted. Everybody knew I could sing. Or at least would make an attempt." Significantly, Mitch Mitchell was the bass player. "[Band members Tony Conley and Wendell Napier] called me on Monday night and said, 'Do you want to be in our band? We have a show on Friday night,'" says Bob. "And I go, 'No, there's no way, that's impossible.' They called me again the next day and said, 'So, do you want to do it or not?' And I said, 'Okay, man, you must have something if you're gonna be that persistent.' I practiced on Tuesday night with Mitch and one of the guitar players. On Wednesday night I practiced with another guitar player, Tony Conley, and our drummer, Bruce Smith. On Thursday we had a full band rehearsal and because everybody knew their shit, we had like twenty-five songs. We had them down in one practice. We played the show on Friday night, and there had to be three or four hundred people there. We did all covers, we did UFO and Cheap Trick and AC/DC, and kicked ass. Everybody from Northridge thought we were great. It was the most fun I've ever had onstage.

"All day long at school I was nervous to the point where I wanted to throw up. There was a band that opened for us, called Birth, some other Northridge guys, and they completely fucking blew it. They came out with

'Johnny B. Goode,' then they went into some Lynyrd Skynyrd song and they fucked up in the middle of it and started arguing and fighting for like twenty minutes. The guy that sang—he had a T-shirt that said 'Tits & Wieners'—he came over and said, 'Man, there's a guitar player we know out in the audience, please let us have one more song.' The crowd was getting restless, booing and shit, and I go, 'Okay, whatever.' They got this guy to come up who was actually the singer and guitar player for Mitch and Kevin's band Ambush when they were kids. They did 'Green Grass and High Tides' for like forty-five minutes. I was pissed off. But I started getting this surge of confidence because I was thinking, 'We got twenty-five songs that are pretty cool and we're gonna kick ass.' The crowd kind of went nuts. That's when I really got the fucking bug. I realized: I *need* to be in a band. That was about 1976.

"Right around then, I got rid of a bunch of my records because I decided that music was evil. I got scared. Devo caused that, really. Devo and some of the postpunk stuff that was going on I thought was really negative—at the time I still was not quite sure philosophically what I believed in—and I thought music was going into a negative place. Then I realized, no, it's just pointing out that there's a lot of bullshit in the world. What punk rock was doing in general—I thought it was an evil thing, I thought it was just a 'fuck you' to everyone. Which it was, but it was breaking things down. It was a call to arms. A back-to-basics movement, and the message was 'Get out of the fucking way. We need a new reality.' Once I realized that, I loved it, but at the time I thought, 'Man, this is devil rock.' A result, partly, of my Midwest semipuritan upbringing. I gave a bunch of records to Mitch and then about three days later I go, 'Can I have my stuff back?' I even joined the Devo fan club. I started to really dig their stuff—they became my favorite band, almost my religion.

"Mitch and I really started getting into punk and postpunk, and we started trying to incorporate that into Anacrusis, which was a heavy metal band. They kicked us out. Then they said they'd like to have me back in the band, but not Mitch. I said, 'No—Mitch is my partner.'"

For his part, Kevin Fennell had quit high school in tenth grade and left Northridge, moving to Huber Heights, a neighboring North Dayton suburb that bills itself as "The World's Largest Community of Brick Homes." Kevin recalls, "I no longer saw those guys until much later. And the cool thing is, I heard about Anacrusis, and I went and saw them. But I didn't go in, because I didn't want them to see me seeing them. So I kind of peeked, and they were pretty fucking good. So I wanted to be in *that* band. I was like eighteen or nineteen by then."

Kevin never ended up in Anacrusis, and didn't reconnect with Mitch or Bob until a few years later, when he met and married Bob's sister Lisa. "Bob invited me down to his basement, to the Snakepit," which was the room where Bob stored his vast and growing record collection and continued to write and in a primitive way record songs. "So I saw his record collection, and I was like, 'Holy shit.' And I told him I'd seen him in Anacrusis, and I asked what he was doing now. And he said, 'I'm really not doing anything. There's this guy Nick Weiser, and we have a sort of songwriters' guild called 86.'

"It wasn't a band," recalls Kevin, "it was just a few guys kicking around ideas. They didn't play out or anything. Of course, Bob was light-years ahead of those guys. I wanted immediately to put together a band. I pushed him real hard."

Bob was hesitant—for quite some time he remained insecure about both his songwriting abilities and his general musical skill. "He was always like, 'I don't know. I don't know.' He wasn't very confident," says Kevin. "I'm not a songwriter, but I would imagine people criticizing or not understanding what I was trying to do—that's pretty risky stuff. He was especially uncomfortable with his singing voice. He thought he sounded too Southern. He always heard it sounding kind of twangy. I didn't hear it. Of course, I'm from here."

The encouragement of Kevin and Mitch Mitchell wasn't quite enough for Bob, who was reluctant even to let anyone hear his songwriting efforts, much less start a band. He received a crucial shot in the arm when he met the man who would become Guided by Voices' Manager for Life, Pete Jamison. Pete had attended Meadowdale High, and gone on, like Bob, to be a schoolteacher. He first met Bob "probably in 1980 or '81—we played softball together in the summer with all the teachers," recalls Pete. "We were called The Vacationers. I'd heard about him in high school, the name and everything. I went to Meadowdale and our school boundaries touched each other—if you went across the street you were in Northridge. When we met we were both teachers, but at different schools."

The two struck up an immediate friendship, based at first on the fact that "everybody on the team was married and stuff except for me, and Bob was married but he never acted like it. We'd get some beers and go over to his house and he'd play me R.E.M., Wire. . . . We'd go down to the Snakepit and he'd DJ and talk.

"That's where he introduced me to all these eight-tracks he had. He'd made them back when you could get recordable eight-tracks. These were from when he was in high school, and he couldn't play guitar at all: He would have one string going *dong dong bong bong,* and he would just sing over it. You'd look at these eight-tracks and at first I thought they were real—they looked completely professional, with band names and cover art and song listings and even label logos—until you looked closer and saw they were drawn in crayon. Rex Polaroid was one of the fictitious artists. He had a boxful of them. It was just him hitting strings on the guitar. But you could hear the vocal range, and of course the songwriting."

Within a month of meeting Pete, Bob felt comfortable enough to play some of the eight-tracks for him. "I picked Pete because I knew he didn't know anything about music," says Bob. "I wasn't intimidated by him the way I would have been by people that knew something. And his immediate enthusiasm and encouragement, just the way he would push me to do more—without Pete, there is no Guided by Voices, and I'm always going to be indebted to him for that. He's the first person to have confidence in me."

"He was always singing," says Pete. "I'd be like, 'Who's that? That's pretty cool,' and he'd say, 'Oh, that's one of mine.' When he finally cracked open this big box of tapes, started playing me stuff, I was blown away— out of three songs one would be great, one would be awesome, and the other one would still be good. I was like, 'Dude, are you still writing?' And he'd go 'yeah,' but he was very reserved about it. He's like that—he won't do anything until he knows that you're totally enthralled. I came over one day after that and he was playing his guitar—he was much better by now— and he played a song for me. After that it would turn into a weekly thing where we'd go over and listen to records, and then put on one of his eight-track things. When you think of some of the great songwriters—like Dylan, or John Lennon—I could tell he had that in him. When he played just on guitar it was great, too.

"I kept saying, 'We need to get this out, let people hear it.' But he kept stalling. I knew how competitive Bob is, so I decided to use that. I said, 'I just can't believe this,' and he goes, 'What? What?' I said, 'As a football player you're probably one of the greatest quarterbacks I've ever seen.' And in basketball he was great and he was a professional-quality pitcher. 'If you're sitting here playing these songs for me, I can't believe you can't do this in front of other people. I think you're afraid.' I pulled his tail. 'If you don't have confidence in your guitar-playing,' I said, 'you can probably get a guitar player.'

"Not a week later he goes, 'Man, I got a band together.' So we planned two parties at my house on James Street, and both times the guitar player left town the night before the show. The first one they were called The Geese and the second one they were The Crowd. Mitch and Kevin were in the band, too. Bob was really depressed. I go, 'Dude, you can do it. You don't need another guitar player. I've seen you play.' About two weeks later he was like, 'Hey, you want to come to band practice?' Like it was football practice. I said, 'What band am I gonna see?' And he said, 'My new band.' It was him on guitar, Mitch on bass, and Kevin on drums. I go down to Kevin's basement and they had taken Bob's acoustic guitar and drilled a hole in it and taped in a little pickup. And that became Coyote Call.

"This time I didn't plan a party; they got a show at the Greenleaf, which was on Dixie, right near Bob's house. That was their first show and they made a poster for Coyote Call. It was supposed to be Coyote Call in big letters, then Bob's name a little further down, then Kevin, Mitch in smaller letters. But when they got the posters they had misspelled his first name 'Booby' . . . Booby Pollard. Oh, he was pissed."

"It did *not* say Booby," counters Bob. "Pete and his brilliant fucking memory. It said 'Boby Pallard,' which was bad enough. We were called a bunch of different names: Beethoven and the American Flag, the Instant Lovelies. We played a show as Coyote Call, and we played a show as the Instant Lovelies. The Dayton amateur night at Canal Street. We only played for about twenty minutes. Me, Mitch, and Kevin. Mick Montgomery, who owns Canal Street—he's a big supporter of local music, but he can be kind of uptight. One time Mitch and I were there watching some acoustic thing, and we were drunk and singing over them. One of the barmaids, who I later found out was Nate Farley's mom, kicked my feet out of the aisle. I said, 'Don't ever fucking kick me.' So Mick comes over and says to me, 'You know, for a musician, you're an asshole.'"

To which Bob immediately riposted, "Don't ever call me a musician."

"I couldn't play very well," he continues, "but I could play well enough. I started writing really structurally complicated songs just to fuck ourselves up. So really, in the early days, when people said we sucked, we kind of did suck. But it was interesting, because we played complicated songs—badly. It was almost postpunk, like Pere Ubu, but not nearly as cool."

"After that, they didn't play out all that much," recalls Pete. "Partly because they were too loud. Bob had to have everything loud as hell. Everybody was complaining, and the crowd was expecting, like, country music. He played all originals. His friends from Northridge were like, 'You can sing, Bobby, but you gotta sing something different!'

"When I went to maybe the third practice, Bob looked at me and said, 'You wanna be our manager? It's for life; you're not quitting on me!' I didn't care about that—I knew he'd leave me by the wayside. At the time I was unemployed; I had my unemployment check, I went out and got two microphones that I thought were great—they were probably fucking horrible. I set up some sort of thing they could sing through. I had these big metal horns like the ones at outdoor drive-ins—not at the car but on the screen. You could hear them from a mile away, but it was real tinny and metallic, and incredibly loud. It'd just ring in Kevin's basement—this was when Kevin was still married to Bob's sister.

"The next logical step was, let's record something," Pete continues. "I had a cassette tape deck that took quarter-inch jacks in the front. They could record practice. Hang some mics somewhere decent and record some songs. They would record the music on a cassette and then Mitch would put it in the stereo, then Bob would sing over it onto another cassette. Kind of a lo-tech two-track. I left the machine down there for a year, so of course it got destroyed. Some of that stuff off the Coyote Call tape may have been those recordings."

"When we got together and just fucked around in the basement," says Bob, "just Jimmy and Mitch and me, we made up some pretty cool shit. We might jam out something and I'd try to learn it, and then add parts to it."

Going to the basement after Jimmy's return from college was a vital step in the evolution of Bob's songwriting. The hundreds of tapes that Bob, Jimmy, and Mitch—with help from a constantly changing cast of supporting members—recorded down there constituted the bulk of what would later become famous as "the suitcase," a repository of complete songs, fragments, and raw ideas that Bob did then and still does draw from, some of which were released on the appropriately titled *Suitcase* box set in 2000. But the one hundred songs on that compilation represent only a tiny fraction of the actual number of songs on the basement tapes recorded from 1983 through roughly 1990.

"It wasn't actually a suitcase," says Bob. "It was a hard vinyl carrying case used to hold shipments of detonators for machine guns, for the military. I worked at a place called Freund's Precision one Christmas break in college, and I assembled them. A really tedious job. I think they gave me a case."

"Instead of trying to write songs for a band, when he didn't really have his own identity," says Jimmy, "we would just fuck around, come up with crazy ideas. Which actually helped him find his identity. It gave him confidence that he could use his own weird shit and make it into pop songs."

Style points, as always, counted for something as well. Bob was interested from the beginning in making an impact as a live band, even if that impact was wasted on the unappreciative patrons of the bars of Northridge. "One time The Needmores were supposed to play this place called Lucky Buck's, on Needmore," recalls Bob, "which was just around the corner from my house. So the plan was, we'd meet at my house literally like ten minutes before we were due to go on. This was when Jimmy and I were on the outs [see below], so it was just me, Mitch, and Mike Tomlinson [best known as the guy who yells 'Is anybody ready to rock' at the beginning of 'Mesh Gear Fox/Over the Neptune' on *Propeller*]. Mitch showed up, and he'd been doing coke, and he was freaking out: 'I can't do it.' We calmed him down. We walked outside, nice summer night, all dressed up, ruffled shirts, wearing our guitars, and Mike had his sticks. We walked across North Dixie, stopped at the traffic light. Mike was playing his sticks on the pole. I don't know what people thought we were doing. Then we got to Needmore and walked across straight into Lucky Buck's, through the club, and onto the stage, without stopping, plugged in and immediately started into a choreographed version of 'Gimme Some Lovin'.' People were like, 'They finally have their shit together.'"

Needmore Avenue, the thoroughfare behind Bob's house on Titus, looms large in Bob's mythology. Not only did he name his publishing company Needmore Songs, he formed at one point in 1985 a side project called The Needmores, which had the distinction of being a) the first and only band that Jimmy Pollard ever played live in and b) the direct cause, related to section (a), of the only really serious physical fight between the two brothers.

"We were practicing for The Needmores down in Mike Tomlinson's basement," recalls Jimmy. "And I had new strings and they kept going out of tune and I kept tuning them but they wouldn't stay in tune. Finally Bobby's like, 'Dude, you're gonna have to learn how to get your guitar in tune.' I'm like, 'I don't know how.' Tensions were rising and shit. Finally Bobby pulls his guitar off and says, 'Man, I've been wanting to kick your ass for a long time anyway.' So I got mine off and go, 'I've been wanting to kick *your* ass. For fifteen years!'" The two went at each other hard, falling to the ground, wrestling and punching, crashing through piles of junk and rolling over dog shit, and ended up in a tiny space where there wasn't any room to maneuver.

"Eventually we just gave up or whatever, but Jimmy was still hot," says Bob. "And Tomlinson's girlfriend, who always hated me anyway, says to Jimmy as he's walking out, 'I'm glad you did that, he needed that,' and Jimmy goes, 'Fuck you, too!'"

Bob and Jimmy did eventually reconcile, and with Jimmy back on board, The Needmores played a party at Pete's house; no one seems to remember exactly when. But Jimmy never overcame his self-consciousness with regard to his technical ability. "I played a couple fucking strings here and there," he comments sardonically. But he has always been, and will always be, the most important nonperforming member of the band, and has still cowritten more songs than any regular member. Most important, he's one of the few people Bob trusts to give sound advice.

The issue of playing live became moot not long after Jimmy's one-off appearance with The Needmores anyway, as Guided by Voices, as they were named with some finality (twenty-odd years' worth, anyway), were about to call it quits for six years as far as playing live, in order to concentrate on the far more pleasurable pursuits of writing, drinking, and, occasionally, when they could scrape together enough cash, recording.

"Bob would talk about what makes a band, and he was saying you're not a band until you put out vinyl," recalls Pete. "Bands can play out and stuff but . . . He was starting to practice in his basement a little bit with different people. I think that's when Captain Bizarre was around, maybe.

Between Coyote Call and actually recording was when he went through all those people like Captain Bizarre."

The saga of Captain Bizarre [real name: Ed Jon. Nicknamed by Mark Greenwald, Ed was a slightly heavyset fellow who wore a top hat and a trench coat when playing out. On the back of the coat, spray-painted in white letters, were the words "The Winkler." The nickname becomes clearer when presented with these visual aids] is representative both of the reason for the extraordinarily high turnover of players in the early days of what would become Guided by Voices and of the native strangeness with which Bob had to deal while trying to forge his musical identity.

"Captain Bizarre was a good guitar player, but he was always trying to change things, and he whined. He was a big baby," says Kevin Fennell. "'We need to do it *this* way!'"

Bob adds, "He would say stuff like, 'Bob, you said we were gonna do some Gerry Rafferty.' No we're not, Ed. What on earth would make you think I'd want to play Gerry Rafferty?"

"As you can imagine, that didn't last very long," continues Kevin. "He was pretty tough to tolerate. Bob took out a lot of his frustration on Captain Bizarre. Then again, Captain Bizarre allowed himself to be humiliated. He kept coming back for more. I felt bad for the guy, after a while. Everybody took a shot. Back then, even in the early days, there was a lot of beer being drunk. Captain Bizarre was a good guy to pick on—he made a good scapegoat.

"The last straw—it started just by him not being in tune. Bob would stop the song and say, 'Hey man, you need to tune up.' At a certain point, Captain Bizarre said, 'I *am* in tune. I'm in tune with myself.' That's all it took. Bob was like, 'In tune with yourself? That doesn't even make sense! Either get in tune or get the fuck out.' So he pretty much got the fuck out. Never to be seen again. The last anybody ever saw of him he was pushing his amp down the sidewalk in the snow. Crying." Bob says that Ed Jon is in fact now dead.

"Bob was spitting on him. He head-butted him, too. I didn't think that was very nice, but fuck it. He's the kind of guy that probably deserves to be spit on. He was such a pain in the ass. He could play, but . . . Early on, the only people Bob could tolerate were me and Mitch. He couldn't tolerate anybody else. That's why we went through so many band members. He could somehow tolerate me and Mitch, I guess because we pretty much went along with him. What Bob said went. It was not a fucking democracy. It was a dictatorship, and if you're gonna be in the band, you have to play by his rules. And I didn't have a problem with that. But I saw a lot of people come and go. There were people who couldn't hang for a week, much less years. Bob used to be brutal. He got better once we got some success. He mellowed out a lot."

"We were driving around," recalls Pete, "and Bob said, 'I think when we're ready to record I'm gonna be Guided by Voices,' and I said, 'Oh man, that's awesome.' I told him, 'If we do one record then we have to do three.' I knew the first one would not capture the greatness of what it could be, and I thought that by going through three records it would give Bob more motivation than to try to put all his expectations on one record, and if it was horrible . . . So when he committed to three to me, I knew that no matter what he thought of the first one we would do another one and another one."

"Pete's dreaming," replies Bob. "There was never any three-record plan—maybe in his head. The fact is, we made a record because The Highwaymen made a record. Before that point we had no notion of how to make a record. We didn't think it was possible. We thought it was for people on Warner Bros. or RCA. There was obviously a lot of indie shit going on, but I wasn't that familiar with it. We started thinking about it in '85, and we did *Forever Since Breakfast* in '86. We did an EP because The Highwaymen did an EP. We put it out on I Wanna, a local Dayton label run by this guy, Jim Carter, who had a radio show on WYSO, this little college station. He called himself 'Reverend Jim Cool.' We put ourselves on I Wanna—we didn't ask permission, we just did it. That pissed 'Rev Cool' off a little bit. He put out a compilation a couple years later of I Wanna bands. He didn't include us."

"We recorded in a studio down in Crescent Springs, in Kentucky," says Pete. "Group Effort Studios. And we just split the costs. There were five of us. So instead of four hundred bucks per session we each put in eighty. But Mitch and [drummer] Peyton Eric, who everybody called Tim, [and who, according to Bob, 'was going back and forth with Kevin Fennell as to being in the band or not; Tim just happened to be in at the time'] never had their money. So guess who covered that little bill." (Editor's note: Was it you, Pete?)

The Highwaymen were a rival local band—the closest thing to a rival, at least, that Guided by Voices faced back in the mid-'80s, when Bob briefly tried his hand at public performance. Eventually The Highwaymen changed their name and moved to Austin. The feud between the two bands, according to Pete, "came to a head in 1986 or '87 when one of the guys from The Highwaymen was organizing a show of local bands at Brookwood Hall. Bob thought he should have a certain slot. And this guy from the Highwaymen said, 'Well, you can have fourth or you can have fourth.'"

"So I go to the guy," says Bob, "'That's because you're [singing, throatily] *The Highwaymen!*' Because they actually had a theme song, like [singing again] *'We're the Highwaymen.'*"

"I was not happy with *Forever Since Breakfast*," he continues. "We let the guy in the studio pretty much dictate what had to be done and I thought it sounded sterile. But I was still amazed that we had actually made a record—something you could hold in your hand, a physical product, just like the ones I combed through at the record stores. I remember when Mitch and I went to pick them up. We couldn't wait to tear the boxes open. We wept, I believe."

After a while the euphoria wore off, especially when friends and family—to say nothing of the public at large—failed to respond with the good vibrations Bob felt even his tentative first steps deserved.

Which led to one drunken night over in a warehouse space where Cro-Magnon Studios was also situated, just off West Third Street downtown, which was often used as a practice/performance space for local bands. Bob and Mitch were invited to attend the practice of a band called The Scam, featuring Dave Poneman, who would eventually move to New York and carve out a niche in the lucrative solo singer/songwriter market. At the time, Poneman was one of the few local musicians to express his admiration for Guided by Voices.

"Me and Mitch were drinking, and we had brought a box of *Forevers* to give away to people, and eventually, I don't know why, probably because we were drunk, we started throwing them against the wall," says Bob. "We must have smashed up about fifteen or twenty. Some local promoter called us 'schmucks' for destroying our own records. We didn't even know what that meant. If you're gonna insult us, at least use a word we can understand. I felt like, 'Fuck you, they're our records, we paid for 'em, we can do whatever we want with them.' Of course, looking back now, they would be worth five hundred bucks each. So I guess we *were* schmucks."

"We did a second record," Bob says, "but I said—and this became the Guided by Voices aesthetic—'I'm gonna put whatever I want on the fucking record. Because obviously we're the only ones listening.' So whatever I liked, no matter how it was recorded, was going on the record. Whether it was recorded into a boom box, or on a four-track, or in a studio, it's going on the record."

"My thought was, 'Do the first one and see who's in and who's out,'" says Pete. "The second one—the struggle of going down to Kentucky, spending so much money, people not having their parts down, not being ready—I didn't want a repeat of that. Plus Bob really didn't like not having control over the recording process. A friend of mine had told me about Steve Wilbur's eight-track studio right around the corner from me, in his garage. We go in there and record and it's only fifteen dollars an hour. We were spending two or three hundred dollars a night in Kentucky, we could go over to Wilbur's for a whole weekend for that much."

"Originally it was gonna be called *The Future Is in Eggs*," says Bob. "I had the concept in my head. I knew this guy in high school art class called Paul Preston, who could really draw, detailed drawings. He had a head shaped like a pear. I called him Pearhead one time in class. I thought it was pretty clever. So he goes down to gym class and he says, 'Hey, have you guys seen Pearhead?' And he meant me. So that became my nickname, even though I made that nickname up for him.

"Anyway, I had decided for the cover. . . . I had a painting of a cockfight, maybe in colonial times or whatever, with a bunch of guys standing around watching, and I go, 'I want this to be the cover, but I want you to make it contemporary, I want there to be bikers and businessmen and shit,' and it was gonna be called *The Future Is in Eggs*. But I couldn't find him—we had a deadline for the artwork and he disappeared. So I go to Mitch, 'We gotta come up with the cover quickly. We gotta get a picture of Big Daddy.'"

Big Daddy was a rooster Bob had originally bought for his son Bryan as a pet. But the pet proved unmanageable as it grew, and moreover, vicious, so Bob gave Big Daddy to his neighbor Nana, an old woman who apparently loved animals. Bob had a history of animal trouble while living on Titus. Another time a neighbor let one of his pit bulls loose in the streets, prompting Bob to take his "Tennessee Thumper," as he called his baseball bat, to his neighbor's house and threaten to bash the dog's brains in if it ever came loose again. It wasn't the only time the Tennessee Thumper was used in a threatening manner. But it's the only time we can at the moment remember.

"By that time Nana had put Big Daddy in a pen, because he was fucking with me. I called the cops on Big Daddy. So Mitch was trying to take a picture through the chain-link fence, and Big Daddy was trying to attack him. That's why the picture's all fucked up. So we ended up calling it *Devil Between My Toes*. Because Big Daddy was fucking with me, I go, 'Man, I got a devil between my toes.' It's got a subtitle, too: *What Makes Big Daddy Happy?*

"We put that record out, and once again nobody gave a shit—except my assistant principal where I taught, I think his name was Bruce Rahn, went out and bought [*Devil*] and told me, 'Man, that's really good.' He really dug it, and there weren't too many people saying they dug my shit at that time. I was happy with [the record], just with the fact that it was all over the place. I still wasn't really happy with my songwriting. Some of it was okay, some of it was embarrassing. I was getting more experimental."

Another important connection Bob forged during that time was with Tobin Sprout, who headed up his own band at the time, called Fig. 4 (pronounced Figure 4—Toby, though a Daytonian, was a graduate of Ohio University's art program and an accomplished photorealist painter). "The 4," as Toby sometimes referred to his band, would play local clubs, such as they were, and Bob and Jimmy and Pete would often be in attendance.

"I think the first time I noticed [Bob and Jimmy] was probably in 1983, at the 1001 club [on Brown Street; renamed Walnut Hills some time later, and currently renamed something so awful we can't bear to print the name]; we were kind of the house band," recalls Toby. "It was me and Dan Toohey and Jon Petersen. There weren't a whole lot of people in attendance, but I remember Bob and Jimmy and Pete would show up, and they'd kind of stand in the shadows, and they had these dusters on; at least Bob did. Eventually, at one of the shows, Pete came over and said, 'There's somebody over here that wants to meet you,' and took me over to Bob."

"He really was a rock star even back then. Even when I used to see him in his early bands, and there was nobody paying attention to him, I was like, 'This is amazing, this is the coolest thing I've ever seen, and nobody gives a shit.'

"He wasn't as much of a performer at that time, partly because he played guitar—but it was the music that just struck me right away. It hit on the sixties, but there was something new there.

"You also felt that even though nobody gave a shit then, it was going somewhere. It *had* to go somewhere because it was so unique, and good. You knew just looking at Bob—even if he didn't know it. You could see history before it happened."

At the time, Bob was devouring everything he could get his hands or his ears on. He and Jimmy and Mitch or some other combination of comrades constantly scoured record stores and attended dozens of shows, traveling up to Columbus or down to Cincinnati to see indie-rock bands that had no place to play in Dayton. One memorable trip was to Cincinnati to see R.E.M. and The Replacements at Bogart's, a club Guided by Voices would later headline. While walking past the back entrance, dressed in their dusters and Cuban heels, the stage door suddenly opened and the club manager yelled at Bob and Jimmy and company, "Are you The Replacements?" Without a moment's hesitation, Bob said, "Sure," and he and the rest were ushered backstage, and then proceeded to sneak out front and watch the show for free. (This story may not be exactly true down to its smallest detail, but it harbors seeds of truth, and we very much enjoy the symmetry of Bob's pretending to be The Replacements and then later, according to some rock theorists, in essence replacing The Replacements.)

More often, Bob and Jimmy and Mitch perfected the art of heckling. "One more!" they'd yell at a band after the first song of the set. "Please! Just play one more!" Other times they would bring cheese to throw at the band. "We proclaimed ourselves 'the real punks,'" says Bob. "This was right around when the mosh pit, or slam-dancing, started to happen. Me and Jimmy and Mitch went to see Hüsker Dü down in Cincinnati, and this band called Squirrel Bait was opening. We never did get to see Hüsker Dü. We got right down in front, like we always do, and these kids started that slam-dancing shit, going around in a circle, knocking into people. I told Mitch, 'Don't hit anyone, we're just gonna stand here.' You don't tell Mitch not to hit anyone. He clotheslined one of the mosh pit guys, and security was all over us. I'm like, 'We're allowed to stand here and watch the show.' But they kicked us out, which I didn't mind because I thought Squirrel Bait was awful. They were just kids. Later I listened to their record and it was good, but live they sucked. As we were leaving I heard one of the Squirrel Bait guys go, 'That's right, get those bikers out of here.' The funny thing is we asked for our money back, and they gave us more than we paid. So we turned a profit.

"Then we proceeded to go to a strip club, a real nasty one in Newport, just over the bridge in Kentucky. On the way back, Jimmy was driving, and he got pulled over by the cops. We were surrounded: There were like three cop cars. We were waiting in the car, trying to figure out how to get back, because we thought for sure Jimmy was cooked. He was hammered; they were putting him through the whole field sobriety test. Then Jimmy comes back and gets in the car. 'I guess I passed,' he said. He said the first question the cops asked him was 'What kind of boots are you wearing?' Jimmy said, 'Beatle boots,' even though they weren't true Beatle boots—they didn't have Cuban heels. Maybe the cops were Beatle fans."

"After *Devil*, we made *Sandbox*," says Bob, "and we went right back into the studio. I thought *Sandbox* was overproduced, and after that I said, 'Fuck that, I'm not ever going to do that again.' And I don't think we ever did. Well, no, we did, after we signed with TVT and did *Do the Collapse* and *Isolation Drills*. Because I always wanted to make a good, big, proper-sounding record. At that time, we had no idea how to accomplish that. I don't think, to be perfectly honest, that the band—and this includes myself, obviously—were really capable of doing that then, even under the best of circumstances. But the funny thing is, people say we sold out on *Do the Collapse*—no! We sold out on *Sandbox*. I even put that corny fucking photo of us on the cover. I thought it would be our power-pop record, like The Raspberries or Big Star. I thought it would get us recognized."

Not that anyone even had the opportunity. "Bob didn't want to let anything out, and I couldn't send out anything for him. He wouldn't let me," Pete recalls. "He was ashamed of it. He didn't want anyone to go, 'Why'd you waste your money on that?' He was doing it for himself. Plus his mom and dad would say, 'You made another one?' Every single thing that he was doing, he wasn't getting any positive feedback. People that he loved wouldn't even say, 'Nice try, it's getting better.' Because he didn't have much feedback he wasn't sure it was actually any good."

One early advocate was Byron Coley, whose influential fanzine *Forced Exposure* championed many indie-rock heroes well before the mainstream caught on. He also wrote an underground column for *Spin* magazine, in which he mentioned Guided by Voices, likening their genre-hopping style to "a field of kangaroos."

"Some guy in Delaware wrote about them and Jimmy [Johnson, coeditor of *Forced Exposure*] and I got in touch with Pete, probably right after *Sandbox*," recalls Coley. "Technically those records were so homemade-sounding, but unlike garage bands at the time, it was a guy that was obviously grappling with vast ideas under the constraint of a limited vocabulary, or economics—it was difficult to tell. But there was a non-product-like quality that was refreshing."

In order to pay for the pressing and cover art for *Sandbox*, Bob, Pete, and Jimmy took out a loan using the Teachers Credit Union. "This is the beauty of my plan," continues Pete, still under the impression that he'd masterminded a three-album deal with Bob. "I go, 'Bob, this is the last one. We'll go over to Wilbur's and record everything like we've been doing and then when it's done, we're just gonna have to get a loan to get it pressed immediately.'

"We thought it would be easy to get the loan but it wasn't. We were actually turned down. But it so happened that my mom's signature was on file at the bank, because of the mortgage on her house, so I went back to the manager and I said, 'What if I had my mom's name on the loan, as a cosigner?' Luckily, the manager was in a local Dayton band herself and she pushed it through. She was fired like a month later. I don't know if that's why, but we got the loan for *Sandbox*.

"I knew Bob well enough to know that he's not gonna want to stop with *Sandbox*," says Pete. "But the great part is, once you pay down the loan, you can go back and knock it back up to the original amount, maybe even a little more. So the next year it would be a little more. It got to maybe a couple thousand at its height. And when we got to *Propeller*, that's when we realized we had gotten more use out of the vehicle than we intended. It's like the rover on Mars—we thought it would last for ninety days and it's a year and a half later. So we just said, 'We'll do *Propeller* and that's got to be it. We have to pay off the loan and put it to bed.'"

During the recording of *Sandbox* Bob came across another kindred soul, one who was to have "a profound influence on the direction of the band for years to come," according to the manual of rock clichés we were issued by our editor as an aid in writing *Hunting Accidents*.

"We had this band called the New Creatures," recalls Greg Demos. "It was me, Don Thrasher, and Bill Hustad. We did a gig at Brookwood Hall in I'm guessing 1986.

"Hustad broke a bass string, and he had to restring the whole bass, and we're sitting there with our thumbs up our asses and so I just started playing 'Nature's Way' by Spirit and I'm in the middle of singing that and all of a sudden I start hearing a second voice or harmony and at first I thought something was reverberating or someone had put echo on or something and I look over and there's this dude standing up onstage just nailing the harmonies. Which was how I met Bob.

"And Jimmy was there, too, so after we got done, we started talking and that's really how we met. We would stop by when they were recording *Sandbox,* and then in the summer of '87 we were recording the New Creatures record, also at Wilbur's. Bob and Jimmy were there a lot at the studio and I think we just started hanging out."

"It was exactly a garage," says Don Thrasher of Steve Wilbur's eight-track garage studio. "We'd never been there. Bob had been recording there, and we kind of got interested in what was going on, so we went and checked it out. Toby was actually doing the Fig. 4 record there at the time too. It made sense to us—we had been doing four-track stuff too. Wilbur's seemed like a cool alternative. It literally was a two-car garage. The door was sealed off and there was shit everywhere.

"He had an eight-track reel-to-reel and a board and a little isolation booth that was separated with glass. He was a heavy metal guy and there were club lights and all kinds of junk. He didn't really know quite what the New Creatures were doing, but *Sandbox* was pretty straightforward. He enjoyed it, but it wasn't really his thing.

"Bob always had friends hanging around, like he does now, and they had no concept of what he was doing musically, and they didn't really even care—they still thought he was King Shit just because he was Bob. If you were getting ready to record, they'd always be around, shooting hoops and drinking beer."

In the wake of *Sandbox*'s inevitable failure to bring fame and fortune—it's probably the weakest record the band ever made—Bob decided, once more, that he was going to forget about trying to achieve any kind of success, and simply do what his growing songwriterly instincts told him. He tried to make another record at Wilbur's in 1987, titled *Learning To Hunt*, but shit-canned that before it got to the pressing stage. Songs from that abortion can be found on *Mag Earwhig!* and on the *King Shit and the Golden Boys* disc from the Scat Box. We have not been given permission to tell you the names of these songs. But the one from *Mag Earwhig!* you can probably guess.

Bob decided to do exactly what he wanted. And what he wanted was eclectic, and weird, and noisy, and badly recorded, and as often unlistenable as it was breathtakingly beautiful. The results of which were both filed away in the suitcase and released on two subsequent records, *Self-Inflicted Aerial Nostalgia* and *Same Place the Fly Got Smashed*. On these two records, you can "really hear Bob start to come into his own," again according to the rock cliché manual, to which we are probably overresorting. He began to develop the characteristics that would produce, via *Propeller*, an aesthetic capable of connecting with a much wider audience than the faithful few in Dayton.

By the time the band got to *Same Place*, Kevin and Mitch had tired of not playing live, and so had left the band to start another project, called alternately Fathom Theory and K.M.A. Their departure left a hole Greg Demos and Don Thrasher were only too happy to fill, with the help, as always, of Jimmy, and—unexpectedly, as they were finishing a song called "Blatant Doom Trip,"—Tobin Sprout, who had moved with his family to

Sarasota, Florida, for a couple of years, but who returned in time to put a guitar solo on the song without ever having heard it before.

"Greg and I produced *Same Place*," recalls Bob. "It was his idea to do the panning, if that's what it's called [Greg tried to emulate the sound of certain '60s records by hard-panning the basic tracks to one side and the vocals to the other], and after he did it I thought it sounded like shit. But now I think it's cool. It's part of the concept, it's a dark concept; Drinking, destruction, murder, and madness. But ultimately salvation [laughs]."

"I just remember trying to record as fast as possible," says Greg. "It took three or four days to record and I tried to mix it in like two hours. If I'd had more time, it could have been better, but I'm still a believer in doing things as quickly as possible."

However pleased/displeased he may have been with *Same Place* sonically, Bob was more displeased with his situation financially. Each album had incurred a loss, to little apparent effect. In fact, he was under considerable pressure from his family to "quit doing that stupid shit," as his dad put it during one heated discussion.

"The thing was, they were sort of right," says Bob. "It was just out of fear that I was throwing my life away, wasting money for nothing that I'd need for the kids' education. That I wasn't living up to my responsibilities as a husband and a father. And to some extent, they had a point. Which is why I decided to pull the plug. It was time to stop kidding ourselves, grow up, pay down the loan, act like adults."

But not before one last go-round. Pete remembers getting an excited call one morning. "We were putting out *Same Place* and we were dealing with the loan and stuff. And I get this call from Bob and he goes, 'I got it man, I got it. You're not gonna believe this.' I think he said it came to him in a dream or something—you know, one of his inspirations. 'We're gonna call the album *Propeller* and it's gonna come out on Rockathon—just like a danceathon, it never stops. Right through till the end.'"

BRYAN POLLARD—VIGNETTE #2
IN A LIMITED EDITION OF THREE

It was a Saturday morning in early February and a ceiling of shadeless gray spread across the sky. A sheet of frost covered my neighborhood in a glittering crust of ice and the ubiquitous Midwestern cold engulfed everything, from the scattering of bare trees and the lifeless garden of frozen dirt chunks and bulbless stems that girded my house to the hardened dog shit that dotted my backyard. There was not even the slightest breeze.

I had been in the backyard practicing my three-point shot for about an hour. My cheeks, fingers, and toes were numb and I had not made a single shot in fifteen minutes. Amidst frustration, I turned to walk back into the house and quit basketball forever when my father came strutting across the backyard.

"Wanna get a quick game in?" he gruffly mumbled.

"Um, yeah sure, I guess we can."

He indifferently grabbed the ball, then heaved up a dozen or so impossible bank shots and high-arching, perfectly rotating twenty-five footers, pumping his fist and yelling, "Ohhh! Get down!" every time that he made one. When his pregame routine was complete he slung a bounce pass at me.

"Ready?"

"Uh-huh," I said, wiping the bottom of my shoes and underhanding the ball back to him.

Immediately he jab-stepped left and dribbled around me for a simple right-handed layup. He smiled as he playfully slung the ball off of the backboard so that it bounced a centimeter over my outstretched hand and right back to him for an open jump shot; he giggled as he cradled the ball at his side and flung up some sideways spinning reverse layup that rolled around the rim for at least ten seconds while I stood underneath, hopping up and down, before it dropped through the cylinder for one point. I shot seven or eight off-balance bricks and air balls and once dribbled the ball off of my foot so that it pitifully rolled over six mounds of hardened dog shit before coming to rest in the center of my back lawn. With a 5–0 lead, my father cheerfully retrieved it. He figured that the game was over.

Suddenly my shots started falling. I hit a few two-pointers that prompted him to calmly mumble, "Nice shot." I miraculously lobbed a one-hand leaner over his outstretched hand, banked in a twelve-foot fadeaway push shot from the hip, and casually rolled in a left-hand layup after he bit on a fake spin move. He stopped smiling, stopped giggling, and began to try and muscle me down low so that he could put the game away Charles Barkley style.

Clearly, he sensed that the momentum had shifted. Those baby hooks in the lane that he never missed started spinning off of the rim and into my hands; his quick leaning jump shots started missing to the right and careening out of bounds. Suddenly the score was 9–7, my lead, and I had the ball. He checked and immediately charged me, slapping at the ball so that he could get a quick score off of a steal. I could see competitive spirit mixed with a bit of worry spreading across his cheeks in the form of two rouge-colored wings.

I turned my back and slowly tried to nudge him closer to the basket; he pressed his right hand into the small of my back and gently pushed me so that I stayed around half-court pointlessly dribbling the ball behind me. I faked a spin move to my left and quickly turned to my right, where unbeknownst to me, my father had lunged for the steal. Our heads collided with a dull thud. The ball rolled to the right as we both stumbled backward. I confidently barked, "Ball," and waved my hand at him. He jogged over to the ball, punted it about forty yards into the parking lot behind our house, and hissed, "You can get the fucking ball," as he marched back into the house and slammed the back door. It was the most satisfying ball retrieval I have ever experienced on that court.

When I entered the house he was sitting in the kitchen with his leg slung over the corner of the table, rotating a collage he had just pieced together from the dozen or so *National Geographics* strewn across the linoleum floor. Without looking up, he said with a wry, sorry-I-lost-my-temper smile, "You had me fucking beat. I don't understand why you faked the spin move instead of just walking to the basket for an easy layup. Still can't beat the old man, I guess." It was the only time he has ever mentioned that game.

PIG DOGS '88

Off and running
on a microscopic race track
on a weekend maneuver
on a hunch
we were the fun bunch

To get going you go
and wouldn't you know
one by one
we got it on
like a power plant
with Arena Rock Alarm Clock
the welcoming committee

We know these things
and one time looked alike
and we looked around
a lot
to notice
seize control
and smash down any blockades
trying to fuck our parade
trippin'
and we don't stop for nobody
including Gizmo's ass

R. Pollard

TIME

"The music was better then, I think. Not that it's not good now, don't get me wrong. But it was better then."

—Kevin Fennell

By 1991, Bob's rock 'n' roll fantasy seemed to be deflating like a punctured blimp. He was in debt as a result of self-financing the previous five records; Jimmy and Pete were also in debt. Mitch and Kevin had gone off to do their own thing, and though his songwriting and general musical aesthetic had progressed in an objectively obvious way, at close range it was difficult for Bob to see that any real progress was being made. For a long time he really had been doing music only for himself, and as selfish as Bob can sometimes be, that simply wasn't enough. So he made a decision. He'd record one last album, throwing on the best songs he could muster from his catalog of unfinished business, and venture into a real studio once and never again.

Before he did so, he wanted to make it clear to his band, or more accurately, to the loose collective of players operating under the banner of Guided by Voices, that *Propeller,* jokingly so named because in Bob's words it would "propel" them to the top, would be the group's last record.

"Right as we were finishing up *Same Place,* Toby moved back into town," says Don Thrasher, who served as drummer for most of the record. "With *Propeller* it became me, Bob, Jimmy, Greg, and Toby. All of them were playing guitar. We rehearsed the songs, and Bob was still writing songs like mad. *Propeller* changed a lot—the whole second side is stuff that he came up with as we were recording, and even after we recorded it."

This was a feature of Bob's restless pursuit of perfection that became standard over the next several albums—*Bee Thousand, Alien Lanes,* and *Under the Bushes Under the Stars* went through myriad changes, both in terms of songs and even titles (for instance, *Alien Lanes* was originally called *Scalping the Guru,* and was intended to be a double album; *UTBUTS* started out as a concept album called *Power of Suck,* also a double album; and *Bee Thousand* was eventually, in 2004, reissued in a Director's Cut that extended over three vinyl albums).

"He had decided he didn't want to do it at Wilbur's," continues Thrasher. "He wanted a bigger feel for the studio stuff. We did it at Encore in the Oregon District. Again it was a guy who totally had no idea what Bob was doing. Bob was in there laying down a guitar part for 'Over the Neptune' and the engineer came rushing into the booth, saying, 'No, no, stop.' He said the guitar was completely unintelligible, just noise. In fact it was perfect, it was exactly the way it was supposed to be, and the guy just had no concept. We soldiered on, and it turned out well. We got time to mix it and Bob kind of punched the guitars up a bit more. It still doesn't have quite the big studio sound that Bob was going for, but it definitely has a different sound than the other stuff on the record, the four-track stuff and boom box stuff that Bob added later."

Toby's involvement on *Propeller* proved a matter of relative happenstance. "I think they were getting ready to go over and do a session and I might have called Bob," he recalls, "or maybe I just went over. They were all playing basketball. And he asked me if I wanted to do some recording and of course I said yes.

"He was saying it was the end of the line," confirms Toby. "He would say that all the time. One night we were practicing, and Bob was on the same rant, you know, 'This is my last album and I'm done.' The next morning at like seven o clock, bright and early, he calls up all excited and has to come over right away, and runs through 'Exit Flagger' just on his acoustic. We went downstairs to my basement and threw it together. He played drums and I played pretty much everything else. Most of the stuff that we did basswise at the time was on guitar.

"The four-track seemed like a natural progression. It evolved by itself. I had the four-track back with Fig. 4, so we started using it in Guided by Voices more and more. We liked the sound a lot, and we realized—

why do we have to deal with idiot engineers and costly studio time when we have this machine that lets us record with immediacy and doesn't cost anything except a cassette tape?

"'Exit Flagger,' 'Weed King,' 'Lethargy,' and 'Large-Hearted' were some of the first things we did on four-track. '14 Cheerleader Coldfront' was actually the only song that Bob and I sat down and wrote together, ever. I came over with the music and some sort of melody and my acoustic, and Bob goes, 'What's that?' and he ran upstairs and grabbed some lyrics. I had I think maybe a verse and a chorus and we recorded it right away, on a boom box."

Greg Demos provided many of the more elaborate guitar leads, as he was at the time probably the most accomplished musician in Guided by Voices. Though he moved to bass when the band started playing live again, he was an accomplished guitar player, and the only one who could really shred on lead.

"Greg would say to me, 'Blow some melody smoke,'" remembers Bob, "and I would. I'd just sing him an approximation of what I wanted the part to sound like, and he'd reproduce that."

"*Propeller* was really a bunch of separate projects," says Greg. "Boom box, four track, studio, and snippets." This variegated approach to assembling an album, created partly out of financial necessity and partly out of a desperate search for the right sound, or mix of sounds, became the working aesthetic for the next few Guided by Voices albums. After the band was signed to Scat Records, and then Matador, and began to release more albums that sounded, by commonly accepted norms of recording quality, like shit, the process that Guided by Voices had developed and adopted organically was labeled "lo-fi" (because, one supposes, "sounds like shit" isn't really useful as a catchphrase), and the band was lumped in with several other bands (Pavement, Sebadoh, Grifters) whose idea of Perfect Sound was not the relatively high-gloss, high-cost production dominating the airwaves even after the advent of punk-derived product like Nirvana and Green Day.

Bob decided to extend the homemade aesthetic of the album to the cover art as well. He had the albums printed up in five hundred blank white sleeves, then assigned batches of twenty or so sleeves to each of the band members, reserving the largest batch for himself. "It took like a month to get them all done," recalls Bob. "Jimmy did a lot of the coloring; he was really good at that." Though one of these handcrafted items recently sold on eBay for the staggering sum of $6,200, the sleeves weren't exactly labored over. "I worked really hard on the first hundred, but after that it became a chore," says Bob. "We were just throwing anything on them." By the time the group neared the end of the run, ideas had run short. A crushed six-pack carton was glued and shrink-wrapped to the front: done! Pete Jamison claims to have that copy, still unopened, which he threatened to bring to the Final Show in Chicago and open, but he didn't come to the show, and there are good reasons to believe that he had no plans to come to the show. But we'll broach that topic later.

"We divvied up the finished results between band members, who took I think ten or twenty each," says Bob, "and friends of ours as well. I offered ten to Gibby, but he said, 'No thanks, man, I don't even have a turntable.' He was pretty bummed when I told him that I sold one for sixty-two hundred dollars, not long before he died. He could have used that money."

Propeller was, in fact, not the curtain call Bob had intended. As with most things that happen to Guided by Voices, the discovery of *Propeller* and the subsequent launch of the band into the limelight was a product partly of Bob's reluctance and partly of his pride, or ambition, or whatever you want to call the secret drive that pushes an artist to succeed long past the point where most ordinary mortals would have given up.

The short version of what happened is that somehow the record fell into the hands of some influential tastemakers in New York—Matt Sweeney, a well-regarded and well-connected musician who made a mission of championing GBV to scenester/tastemakers like Sonic Youth's Thurston Moore, himself an active advocate of lesser-known worthwhile music, and Mark Ibold, bass player for Pavement and an avid record collector. Some of these people, most notably Sweeney, wrote Bob fan letters, and received in return the entire Guided by Voices catalog. Bob was immensely flattered by the attention, but at the same time confused at how anyone might have gotten hold of a copy of *Propeller.* Unbeknownst to him, Pete Jamison had sent a few to fanzines and distributors, unwilling to let such a gem languish in obscurity, but afraid to let Bob know that he'd taken such a bold step.

And then, one day, came the call that changed Bob's life forever. [Editor's note: all rock biographies are required to use this sentence, under the Albert Goldman Act of 1985. Sorry.]

"Ron House [late of Great Plains and Thomas Jefferson Slave Apartments, two very fine Columbus bands of the '80s and '90s] was working at Used Kids, kind of the main indie record store in Columbus," recalls Scat Records owner Robert Griffin, "and he told Bob to send me a copy of *Propeller*. Bob was going into the store buying stuff at the time and he had just come by, and I talked to Ron later that day and he asked me if I'd ever heard of them. I said no, and he was talking them up a bit. He said next time Bob came in the store he would tell Bob to send me one. And he did.

"All I knew about Bob was Ron's exact description: there's this weird guy from Dayton, been in the store every weekend, buys a ton of records, and he's got a band. Given that, I didn't have really high hopes for the record. But I figured if Ron said I should check it out then I should.

"Doing the distribution for Scat myself at the time, I was totally swamped with records, so I put it on at some point while I was packing orders. And I dug it and I just kept putting it on and then it got to the point were I was listening to the record at least once a day and, you know, totally blasting it. It sucked me in. I called Bob at first just to sell some of the records for him, but the more I listened to *Propeller,* I was like, 'Shit, let's do some records.'

"I called him up and he's like, 'Well, man, the band broke up.' Then there was a pause. And he said, 'Wait, I think can put something together.' And seriously, it could not have been more than at the most seven days later, I got the tape for *The Grand Hour* EP."

"That's what made it so weird when it finally happened," says Bob. "When I was thirty-six years old, I mean—there's no way. My aspirations—I'd given up on that by the time I was in college. I thought there was no way you could do that. I still was in bands, I still did it, we still got together on the weekends and made music, but it was all just a joke. And the fact that it actually happened when I was thirty-six, it was kind of mind-blowing. I couldn't believe it. I thought it was some kind of weird cosmic joke. I thought I was gonna be like Buddy Love, you know, turn back into the Nutty Professor at his last performance.

"I guess it would have been about six or seven months later," continues Griffin, "there was that first show at CBGB at the New Music Seminar, in July of '93. That would be the first one they played. I really had to kind of talk him into it, to be honest, but eventually he agreed, and he pulled a band together somehow. I was there; my band Prisonshake was playing, too. Bob was shitting bricks he was so nervous. I think they all were.

"I had no idea what to expect at all, and by that time they had re-corded *Vampire On Titus,* but it wasn't actually released yet. But there were advance tapes going around, and that being the current incarnation of the band, I really had no idea how it would go over or what they would sound like or anything. So it was a big shock, but at the same time, it was so right. It was just, I don't know. . . . Everybody in the place could tell, it was just magic. It was amazing.

"I do remember that at the CBGB show a lot of people were like, 'They're old.' Which is kind of funny now, given that they've continued and done all sorts of other great stuff. People mentioned it in passing but it was like, at the time, 'Can they be good? They're old.' Which was obvi-ously kind of a dumb attitude."

The lineup Bob pulled together for the CBGB show in July 1993, and which continued intact through the end of the year, included Toby Sprout; Toby's longtime Fig. 4 bass player, Dan Toohey; Mitch Mitchell, who now moved from bass to extremely loud Les Paul-through-Marshall-stack guitar; and Kevin Fennell on drums. Bob decided not to play guitar himself, reason-ing that he would be either too nervous or too drunk to attend to the double duty of playing and singing. Mitch and Kevin, given the opportunity, quickly jumped at the chance to rejoin the band now that things were actually hap-pening. Kevin, however, wasn't really Bob's first choice for drums. In a pat-tern that would repeat itself throughout the course of post-*Propeller* GBV, Don Thrasher was approached to join full-time as drummer, but had to turn down the offer.

"I would have loved to join," says Thrasher, "but at the time my wife was pregnant with my son and I was working; there was just no way I could have done it." The problem with GBV's late success, especially in a town like Dayton, is that by the time things started to happen, many potential band members were at a stage in their lives where stability was an issue.

Ultimately, it would be this issue and not any perceived personality conflicts that would fracture what Bob still likes to refer to as "the *so-called classic lineup*." In point of blunt fact, however, Thrasher's decision to pass was fortuitous. Kevin was frankly a better drummer, though a more difficult personality. "In life," says Bob with a sigh, "there's always trade-offs." Actually, he never said that. But it's true.

Jimmy Pollard turned down the chance to play as well, but for a different reason—he didn't think he was a good enough guitar player. "It's fine for when we were just fucking around in the basement, I came up with a lot of weird noises and feedback and tremolo and shit," says Jimmy [failing to mention his patented "amp drop," where he'd drop a Fender Twin from about a foot high off the ground and the reverb coils (we're making that word up) would make a consequent reverberating sound]. "But I didn't have confidence that I could pull off playing in front of a bunch of people." (NB: Jimmy has asked us to refer to him as "the reclusive Jimmy Pollard" as a condition for being interviewed for this book. "I don't do interviews," he explains. Done.)

"When we went on, it was rapid-fire, like the Ramones," recalls Kevin. "We didn't give people a chance to even clap. I think we cranked out sixteen tunes, man. Bob would say the song title and go '1-2-3' and then bam! We had always practiced that way anyway, because of Bob's impatience, so we were used to doing it that way. We were nervous—Bob was really nervous; he kind of kept his back to the audience throughout most of it. Our game plan was to get in, perform, and get out. We were scared shitless."

Bob's memory of the event is more clearly focused on the long van ride to New York. "We stopped at this rest area in Pennsylvania somewhere," he recalls. "And there were these church ladies who'd set up a table with cookies and shit. They were having a bake sale. So Kevin, rock star that he already was in his own head, saunters over to these little old ladies and goes, 'What the fuck you got to eat?' We couldn't believe it. We tried to pretend we weren't with him."

"CBGB was packed," continues Kevin, "and the crowd response was great. I met some people—Beastie Boys were there, and Henry Rollins. A lot of people were there that night. Important people. Industry people. We probably stood outside the club for about two hours after the show, just schmoozing and drinking [Kevin didn't drink at the time; presumably he's referring to other band members, who did] and partying. Actually, Donna and I—my ex-wife—decided to smoke a little weed [Kevin was an AA counselor at the time, helping addicts to stay straight, having been in the program himself for twelve years]. That was fun.

"It wasn't so much that it was New York," continues Kevin, "it was that it was New York, and those people *liked* us. We played a lot of shows there in rapid succession, and people came out in droves. I just felt like they adopted us. They just took us in. They loved us. There was something about when people like you—because we weren't used to that—for me, it was scarier, once I knew that they were embracing us. Because it's like, 'Okay, now what?'"

For Bob, on the other hand, signing to Scat was a vindication of sorts. He was elated. He claims to have run up and down Titus—which (obviously) informed the title to the follow-up album to *Propeller, Vampire On Titus* (from a phrase by Bob's friend Jim Shepard, of the well-regarded but little-heard Columbus band V-3. Jim's now dead, a suicide, but when he was alive he called Bob "the vampire on Titus" one time, and hence, and so, and on we go)—yelling at the top of his lungs, "We're on Scat! We got signed to Scat! We're Scat Records recording artists!" The story is almost certainly apocryphal, or at least exaggerated, but it's true that after (more than) ten long years of absolute and utter neglect, Bob was feeling something he'd never felt with any real confidence: validation.

His family's response was somewhat more muted, as you might expect from people who hadn't ever spent their disposable income on records by The Mice, for instance. "At least you don't have to pay for it anymore" was his wife's reasonable response, but Bob wanted more than that.

He got it, but not in Dayton. He was treated with respect bordering on adulation on the band's first few trips to New York, and though he remained guarded at first, he could not help but feel a certain elation that his talent had finally been recognized.

"We went to New York one time, early on," recalls Bob, "and we stayed there for four days, and it was just a whirlwind, it was insane, and I forgot to call Kim, and she was pissed. Deservedly so—she should have been pissed. I tried to explain, 'You don't understand what just happened.' I tried to explain to people, 'Things will never be the same again—we just made it.' People didn't understand what I was talking about. We played this show and people went nuts. 'You don't understand what we just went through.' All of a sudden we're the critic's darlings, we're the flavor of the day or whatever. I tried to explain and she was like, 'Okay, we'll see.'"

The record deal with Scat and the reception of the live show in New York prompted an explosion of product from Bob. It's true that some of this was simply old material reworked, or things he'd written but hadn't had time or money to record—for instance, Robert Griffin's pretty sure that *The Grand Hour* EP consisted of material that had been left off *Propeller*—but suddenly everyone, not just Scat, wanted a seven-inch single or an EP or a compilation track, and Bob said yes to everything. Because at the time he really was convinced that everything was just going to vanish, go away, and he'd be relegated to obscurity once more; and so he was determined to make use of what he saw as an inevitably short window of attention to solidify the band's legacy.

The next full-length release, *Vampire On Titus,* was (if possible) the noisiest, messiest, most poorly recorded record Bob had ever done—it was recorded entirely on four-track, mostly with just Toby, Jimmy, and Mitch, and on several songs Bob played drums, except since he couldn't really play drums, he cheated by putting down a kick drum part and then overdubbing the snare part—and the songs were among the least-accessible Bob had ever written. At least at first listen.

"Okay, here's my big theory about art and music," explains Robert Griffin, "and that's that the key is suspension of disbelief. And I think one of the reasons why people like *Propeller* a lot, and *Bee Thousand,* is that they draw you in. Whereas with *Vampire* you really have to get used to it. At the time that Bob sent the tape, my first listen to it, especially stuff like 'Marchers in Orange,' I was like, 'Man, what the fuck is this?' But at that point I had been listening to the older records and I just thought this is a talented guy, he knows what he's doing, I'm gonna roll with it; he's somebody I want to work with and I'm not gonna fuck with it. But after I listened to it for a while, I remember—although I was taken aback at first—I had the master cassette and I had the boom box sitting on the toilet and I was listening to it, and I don't know if it was the sound reverberating off the tile in the bathroom or whatever, but there was a moment where it clicked, and I was like, 'Well, fuck yeah, this is a great album.' Once you get inside, it's a pretty big house in there."

Most reviewers agreed with Griffin's assessment. *Vampire* was repackaged by Scat with *Propeller* on a single CD, and the package was rated an extraordinary A+ by *Entertainment Weekly*. Suddenly, Guided by Voices was everywhere: MTV News did a piece on the band, Britain's *Melody Maker* flew a reporter to New York, and Bob started a several-year run as critic's darling. Certainly the fact that the band had toiled in the Midwest unrecognized for a decade, coupled with the fact that Pollard still held his job as a fourth-grade schoolteacher, lent Guided by Voices an authenticity and an unusual backstory that helped draw the attention of rock writers. But it was the music more than anything else that attracted notice, especially the obvious, and unusual, disparity between the eclectic and weirdly melodic, often very oddly structured and arranged records and the straightforward, almost classic-rock presentation of the live show.

"He wasn't in some major urban center where people had a certain way of doing things," says writer Michael Azerrad. "He was free to free-associate, basically, and he also knew there wasn't any kind of major label waiting, or that he had certain expectations that he had to conform to. So he just did whatever the hell he wanted. That's one of the great things about it. The other thing about the live show versus the records was that, in his own funny lo-fi way, he carried on the idea of The Beatles, meaning that the record is the record and the live show is the live show; he played to the strengths of each. In other words, you play with your effects and over-dubs and things like that when you're recording, and you kick out the jams live. That's what each context demands. He was very savvy about that, and he clearly knew what he was doing."

Not long after *Vampire* was released in 1993, Pollard set to work assembling what would become the band's most well-known (and to date best-selling) record, *Bee Thousand*, using for the most part the lineup he'd assembled for the live show (although Don Thrasher did play drums on a couple of songs, and as was his wont in recorded situations Bob played a good deal of guitar), except for—obviously—Toby and Mitch's contributions. Jimmy Pollard also remained an active contributor, especially when it came to contributing ambient noises, and ideas.

Bob recalls, "Jimmy came up with a title, *Zoo Thousand;* I think there's a marker on the highway that says Z-1000 or something like that. Later, I saw on a drive-in marquee a listing for the movie *Beethoven,* about the dog. They had used a U instead of a V, and it looked like *Bee Thou-sand.* Also, if you hold your tongue and say *Bee Thousand* it sounds like 'Pete Townshend.'"

Titles always have been and always will be important to Pollard. He often uses them as starting points in his songwriting: "I Am a Scientist," one of the better-known songs from *Bee Thousand,* was simply a title in a long list of titles in a notebook before Bob decided to turn it into a song. Byron Coley notes, "He's really good at making lists," which may be a key to his prodigious output. Bob never stops making lists. Out drinking, he will often delegate someone to make notes of the titles he comes up with. While he may forget the titles themselves, he'll never forget the fact that he delegated you to keep track of them, and you can expect a phone call, maybe days, maybe weeks, maybe even months later demanding that you produce the contents of the list from that night.

"*Bee Thousand* was almost completely comprised of shit that I'd writ-ten, bits and pieces that I threw together before I was ever in Guided by Voices," says Bob. "I would always try to salvage things. There was some stuff taped, but a lot of it wasn't, so I'd go back and try to remember what were the good parts, that I can now go back and work on. I'd think of an old song that we used to do live, and I'd work on that and make it better."

"I just knew that was gonna be a record that sold forever," says Robert Griffin. "And that's what gave me the courage to challenge Bob about the sequence and what songs he chose to be on it, because I knew, if the right songs and the right sequence were there, that it was a record for the ages.

"The thing that people really connected with on *Propeller* was, you can turn it up loud and there are all these songs that just totally get your adrenaline going, and amazing hooks, harmonies—it's all there. It seemed to me that if we could open up *Bee Thousand* with four or five, just boom boom boom boom boom, you know, just knock people right over the head with it, we'd have them right from the beginning."

The record was released in May of 1994, although advance copies had been floating around for weeks and even months before that. During the fall of 1993, Bob had become friends with fellow Daytonian Kim Deal, an ex-member of The Pixies and now leader of The Breeders, whose album *Last Splash* had been released only a few months earlier and had already sold nearly half a million copies (it would go on to reach almost double-platinum status), and was an album Bob genuinely admired. Kim asked Bob if Guided by Voices would play at a show she was putting together at Dayton's Hara Arena in March of 2004 featuring The Breeders and the Afghan Whigs. Naturally, Bob said yes. Playing Hara Arena was in some ways the fulfillment of a lifelong dream, considering the many shows Bob had attended there: AC/DC, Cheap Trick, Alice Cooper and now Guided by Voices. Determined to live his arena rock dreams to the fullest, he asked the good-natured Breeders tour manager if he would lead the band onstage in the darkened arena with a flashlight. That may have been Bob's favorite part of the show.

Sometime during the next day or two, Bob and Jimmy and Matt Sweeney—in town to watch the show and drafted as a last-minute impromptu lighting director/soundman for GBV, who hadn't thought such details necessary—visited Kim's house in Oakwood with a cassette of *Bee Thousand*. The album knocked everyone out, especially after they got stoned, and for likely the first time in his life Bob felt a sense of community and acceptance in his hometown. Kim's example proved that you don't necessarily have to move out of town to achieve success, and her enthusiastic embrace of his music was doubly gratifying because she came from Dayton—and North Dayton at that. Although she had since moved to the more affluent south part of town, her house was modest, and messy, and her basement was full of musical equipment. Bob immediately recognized in Kim a kindred spirit, which made their eventual falling-out all the more sad.

But for the time being, things were swinging. Guided by Voices played a surprise birthday gig at Walnut Hills, a downtown bar, for Kim and her twin sister, Kelley, in June, just before leaving on the band's first real tour. Bob had even learned a Breeders song, "Invisible Man," on guitar, which at the end of the night, on Toby's borrowed Telecaster, he proceeded to play solo, and very drunk—so drunk, in fact, that he thought something was wrong with the guitar; he was strumming the strings but producing nothing, no sound. "Guitar's broken," he mumbled into the microphone, at which point Toby reached over from his seat in a nearby booth and turned up the volume knob on the guitar. The results can be heard as a hidden bonus track on the *Crying Your Knife Away* bootleg LP (but not on the CD version).

The lineup that night was not the same lineup that had played only months before at Hara Arena, owing to the departure of Dan Toohey, whose spoken vocabulary consisted, seemingly, only of the phrase "That's weird, man," and who consequently had to resort to letter-writing to make a point of his complaints to Bob. "There were three main complaints. I can't remember what they were," recalls Pollard. "I think one was he wanted more time between songs onstage. And more time between songs in practice. And I forget the third one but I'm pretty sure it had something to do with time."

Exit Toohey (Bob doesn't take complaint letters well), enter, again, Greg Demos, who had finished studying for his law degree at Ohio State and was ready to rock, which is a legal phrase. Bob had initially wanted Greg on bass anyway, but at the time of the first few shows Greg was still in school.

"I took the bar in February 1994 and then started playing solidly," remembers Greg. "I did the Insects of Rock tour, Lollapalooza. That was ridiculous, playing during the day; it was like a hundred twenty degrees on stage. Not to mention that I may have been overindulging in alcohol at the time." His face used to turn a shade of red so bright you would fear for his health, but he never slowed down or stopped spinning around the stage like a dervish.

"Those first six months seemed to me the most fun, before it became a business," recalls Greg, who had to make a difficult decision to leave the band after the midsummer stint on Lollapalooza's second stage. "For me, I was very torn. But what it came down to—it was just two completely different competing interests. On the one hand I was lucky, I was living a dream, but I had to balance that against the harsh realities of life. Living in an ideal world where you could do what you'd always wanted to do, I would've stayed. But I'd accepted a job at a law firm that started in September. It was a hard decision but it was the only thing I could do. It's uncool, but it really came down to money, and security," he adds, using a reasoning that would become familiar for departing band members in the coming years. Demos's ambivalence was very real, as evidenced by the fact that he would come in and out of the band from time to time, and Bob never stopped trying to persuade him to become a full-time member. "It's funny about the decisions made," says Jimmy Pollard. "His decision could have possibly waited. If you're a lawyer, you're always gonna be a lawyer. He was younger than the rest of us. He had time. But whatever."

Greg brought a new level of energy to the already explosive live show; his trademark move consisted of a (mostly) controlled spin, bass held high over his head. There were times when that spin was not so controlled, just as there were times when Greg would drink himself nonfunctional. He fell off the stage more than once in his on-again off-again stint with the band, but quickly established himself as a fan favorite, particularly because of his pants, strange to say. He had shown up at one of his first GBV shows at Canal Street Tavern in blue jeans, and was immediately sent home by Bob to change into something more appropriate to a real rock band. When he came back, he was wearing a pair of ridiculously tight striped white pants. The look was perfect, if not entirely functional: On a few occasions thereafter, the pants split open. Once, during the band's two-show stint on the Lollapalooza second stage in July of 2004, the split exposed at least one of Greg's balls, a fact he tried to hide with his bass, though he kept turning around to the side of the stage to show Jimmy and Pete what had happened. And another time, much later, during one of his frequent, if brief, return engagements with the band, during a show at South by Southwest in Austin, Texas, in support of *Do the Collapse,* the pants just gave out entirely. There's photographic evidence of this incident, which we are particularly pleased to include in the photo section of *Hunting Accidents.*

Another time, during Lollapalooza, Wayne Coyne of the Flaming Lips came by the band's van to say hello, only to catch Greg in the middle of changing out of his rock pants and into civilian clothes. His eyes fixated on Greg's underwear lying on the floor of the van, featuring "the biggest skid mark you ever saw," claims Bob. Wayne turned a pale shade of green and walked off hurriedly. It should perhaps be noted that Bob's request that Greg don the striped white pants for the final shows in 2004 went unfulfilled— only because a now slightly heavier Greg could no longer fit into them. He claimed he could only get them up to about his knees.

It should also be noted that when we say "the band's van," at this point in time we are referring to Mitch's van, a rust-riddled, graffiti-covered death trap featuring a bumper sticker with a pot leaf and the motto "Inhale to the Chief," no heat, no seating, but with the singular advantage of a rust hole toward the back of the van down which one could pour beer and dispose of joints in the event Mitch's driving, or the van, or a combination of the two attracted the attention of the police. We would ask the reader to keep in mind that for much of the time the band was on tour during the days in which Mitch's van was the primary mode of transport, Mitch was on parole for selling pot, meaning that not only could he not be found in possession of pot himself, but he was not supposed to be found in the company of anyone smoking or possessing pot. Not to mention what would happen if he were found to be driving drunk.

One time, early on, heading back to Dayton at probably two or three in the morning after a show in Bloomington, Indiana (possibly; no one involved remembers exactly), Mitch—who had, of course, been drinking—made a wrong turn on a one-way street, or committed some similar traffic law violation, and was pulled over by the cops. The single thought running through the mind of each band member, as they frantically poured beer though the rust hole in the back, was "We're going to jail." Because, let's face it—a drunk driver on parole with a bumper sticker that says "Inhale to the Chief" and scraggly long hair and several visible and unpleasant-looking tattoos is not exactly a picture of civic responsibility.

But Mitch, as was his wont, simply leaned out of the van window as the officer approached and asked, in a very pleasant, coherent voice, for directions to the highway. And the officer, without so much as a cursory glance at the huddled masses in the back of the van, proceeded, very politely, to give Mitch directions. It was neither the first nor the last time God would protect the fools and drunks of Guided by Voices.

We mention the van at this point mainly to point out that during the band's brief adventure at Lollapalooza, security required Mitch to move the van a safe distance from the venue grounds, as a visible gasoline leak from its undercarriage was creating an unacceptable fire hazard. Which is not to say the band didn't blithely drive back home in the van. Safely.

Insects of Rock, a package tour featuring other Scat bands—most important (for future reference), on at least one or two shows, label-mates Cobra

Verde—represented the first time the band had ever been out for an extended period of time (GBV rented a van). It was the beginning of Bob's learning curve on the economics of the music business.

"It turned out as they were traveling around," recalls Griffin, "they were wondering why we didn't split the money up every night. And given it was the kind of tour where we played in Hoboken and then the next show was in Seattle, I was paying for everything and I figured whatever was left at the end, we would split it. I think that's where the seeds of any kind of weirdness between me and the band were sown. Because I wasn't giving them the money after each show, their feeling was 'Well, what's he doing with it?' But none of them said anything to me. I would have been glad to make some other kind of arrangements."

Bob freely admits to a certain paranoia when he first began dealing with labels, both during the Scat years (encompassing *Propeller, Vampire On Titus,* and *Bee Thousand*) and later when dealing with Matador and the vagaries that attend signing a manager, who by long-established (though not necessarily just) tradition takes 15 percent of a band's gross income.

But paranoia is "not an entirely misguided attitude to have in this business," says Robert Griffin. "The first big problem was that I had done a distribution deal with Matador for Scat, and it got to the point where I think *Bee Thousand* came out in May of 1994 and by December or January I still hadn't gotten paid by Matador. I've got a record that's sold at least twenty to twenty-five thousand copies already and I haven't gotten dime one.

"The whole Matador experience was difficult. To their credit, they eventually made good. But at one point when I had done a complete audit of all the expenses that had gone against my account, there was seriously like sixty thousand dollars that was charged back against my sales that had nothing to do with me whatsoever. Like Blues Explosion posters—you name it.

"I don't think anyone had done that purposefully. I think that was more a symptom of how overextended the staff was. But I can totally understand how at that same time when I'm like with Matador, 'Where's my money?' Bob's doing the same thing with me.

"Over the years, the sticking point, moneywise, between us was that once I did finally get everything straightened out with Matador—I subsequently ended the deal because things were not changing—when all was said and done and I paid the band their royalties there was still about twenty grand I owed them. But it was money I'd never had. I've slowly chipped away at that, down to like twelve grand. Over the years I've paid Bob a quarter of a million dollars, or pretty close to that."

Partly as a result of his frustration with Scat and partly out of a desire, which would manifest itself over and over in the ensuing ten years, to simply progress—that is to say, to have access to larger recording budgets, better promotion and distribution, and just more options generally—Bob began to entertain interest from other record companies, which were drawn to Guided by Voices by the overwhelming critical acclaim that greeted *Bee Thousand.* Chief among his suitors were Warner Bros. and, ironically, Matador, which was already distributing *Bee Thousand* as part of its deal with Scat.

"Probably the first person to play the records for me was Johan Kugelberg," recalls Matador co-owner Gerard Cosloy. "I think he was playing them in the office—and I know Matt Sweeney was responsible for turning a lot of people onto the records in the office and elsewhere.

"Johan was bringing these records into work and we were listening to them and the songs were spectacular. The recordings were obviously rough, but based on the other records we were listening to, that was the last thing that was going to bother us."

"The first show I saw was at CBGB and I think it was maybe the second CB's show. I went into it very skeptical, because the fact that everyone I knew was raving about the gigs just made my bullshit meter go off. And they really blew me away. I *was* surprised at how old they were. The thing about the records—the songs were great and obviously there was that raw, lo-fi thing going on, and it was coming from this kind of classic-rock songwriter perspective. But when you saw them live, it was just so fucking powerful; it rocked so hard, it was physically powerful. I was expecting something way more low-key, like the records, so that also just kind of blew me away. I was already kind of getting sold on the notion that the band was Bob's vision, and as much as that may have been true in the past or present, the band was fantastic. So that was my initial impression: 'My God, as great as these records are, they don't even hint at how fucking awesome they are live.'

"My interest at that point was purely as a fan—we didn't even discuss anything else. I made no effort to establish any kind of rapport with them. After the CB's show I spoke briefly to Mitch, just to tell him how great I thought they were. Then Geoffrey Weiss from Warner Bros. started chasing them, and I don't remember at what point we began to think about pursuing a more serious relationship. Robert Griffin had already done that, for one thing, and Matador had a P&D [production and distribution] deal with Scat, so we already indirectly were dealing with them.

"I have to say, I've always felt weird about signing them away from Scat. Like it wasn't maybe the right thing to do. Because we've had that happen to us, where we'll work our asses off to bring a band to a certain level of success, and then a bigger label swoops in and reaps the rewards."

In fact, the decision to sign with Matador was not an altogether easy one for the band. Warner Bros. went all out, flying Bob and Jimmy to Los Angeles, where A&R man Geoffrey Weiss—who'd previously gone so far as to visit Dayton to meet with the band, taking in, as luck would have it, a show at Canal Street Tavern during which Mitch was in jail, as sometimes happened, so that the show wasn't all that great, with Toby forced to single-handle the guitar duties—picked up the band and drove like a maniac through the Hollywood Hills, pointing out important tourist sites like Madonna's house and the "Hollywood" sign. He then took the guys on a tour of the Warner Bros. offices, where Bob and Jimmy met people with impressive pedigrees, difficult-to-pronounce names, and visible disinterest in yet another goddamn rock group. The moment that sealed the fate of Warner Bros. was when Bob walked into the office of the head of the publicity department, a genial fellow who tried to lighten the inevitable tension by relating how the first cassette dub he'd received of what was then called *Scalping the Guru*, the album after *Bee Thousand*, had been somehow messed up, and was playing at the wrong speed or something. "This lo-fi shit's gone too far!" joked the poor publicist. Bob's face turned rigid.

Nothing Geoffrey could do after that—an avid record collector, he took Bob and Jimmy to his house and let Bob browse his vinyl; an avid gourmet, he took the band to the most expensive and exotic restaurants in Los Angeles, not realizing that anything more complicated than pizza or burgers makes Jimmy sick—stood a chance.

So they flew back to Dayton, drinking Scotch and Cokes, because that's what The Beatles had drunk on their first tour of the U.S. ("They tasted awful," remembers Bob.) One of the conditions Bob had set to which-ever label chose to sign him was that it would have to release *Scalping the Guru*—which had been recorded much the same way as *Bee Thousand*, al-though the band had borrowed an eight-track recorder for some of the songs, so that it was not an entirely four-track deal, and it had been mixed down onto a cassette (later taken to Cro-Mag and transferred to DAT, which enabled Bob to cross-fade certain songs and smash others right up against each other, giving the twenty-eight-song album the intentional im-pression of being one giant melodic blur)—exactly as presented, with no rerecording or messing with the sound other than mastering. Bob didn't really know what mastering did, but he knew that it was necessary before a record could be pressed.

In the end, what became *Alien Lanes* was mastered by Bob Ludwig, a very famous engineer. When Toby called him to discuss the technical as-pects of the mastering process (Ludwig generally worked alone, somewhere in Maine, and mailed off the results), he asked naively if Ludwig had ever mastered a four-track recording before. "Well, I did do Bruce Springsteen's *Nebraska*," answered Ludwig, which was good enough for Toby.

Before signing with a label, Bob wanted to sign with a manager, for the simple reason that he did not want to talk to anyone from the label or the booking agency or the lawyer for any of the other industry people who were now suddenly clamoring for his attention. He chose to go with Gold Mountain, the company that represented Nirvana, Sonic Youth, Beastie Boys, and, most important for Bob, The Breeders.

The band then went to New York to visit with Matador. At the time, Matador had a P&D deal with Atlantic Records, which was run by Danny Goldberg. By way of contrast to the band's reception by the executives at Warner Bros., Goldberg was flattered that GBV wanted to meet him, saying that "Steve Malkmus [from Matador label-mate Pavement] refused to meet with me." Bob expressed his desire to have a wall full of gold records "just like Kim Deal," and Danny expressed his desire to help Bob achieve his desire. Goldberg also admitted he knew next to nothing about music, but was surrounded by people who did, upon whom he relied with something approaching blind faith. Then a guy named Val Azzoli, Danny's second-in-command, walked into the room. Val was a real old-school music biz type. He'd started out managing Rush. He looked old-school, and he talked old-school: meaning crude and to the point.

"You guys should enjoy this part of the process," said Val, "when everybody's tryin' to blow you."

Without missing a beat, Bob replied, "I'm tired of blow jobs. I'm ready to get fucked."

Bob made the decision to sign with Matador soon afterward. The official signing took place on his birthday, Halloween, 1994. The deal, by indie-rock standards, was a good one—one of the more expensive in Matador's history. The advance for *Alien Lanes* was close to a hundred thousand dollars. The cost for recording *Alien Lanes,* if you leave out the beer, was less than ten dollars. Bob took 40 percent and split the remaining money evenly among the band members, who each received a check in the neighborhood of ten grand, before taxes.

Once more, Bob tried and failed to convince Jimmy to join the band full-time. Jimmy's confidence in his ability to play live had not improved, and further, as he explains, "When it came down to getting signed by Matador, I'd just gotten married. I started a family, bought a house, and was working at GM with great benefits. . . . It just came down to, this is a little more secure. We weren't making any fucking money. I quit my job, and what am I gonna do for money, really? We just got nine thousand dollars each for our advance, or whatever—how far would that go?"

"At the time, when there was bad blood between me and Bob," recalls Robert Griffin, "the thing that was upsetting to me was like, 'Matador might give you good advances but I will bet any money that the statements that you're getting are not accurate and you're getting dicked by packaging deductions and this, that, and the other thing.' Our statements have on them every single expense, every single sale, and I always said to them: 'Audit me anytime.' Because I'm not pulling any punches. On the [Scat] box set, that was a fifty/fifty deal and Bob makes probably I would say eight bucks on each one. On [Matador's box set] *Hardcore UFO's* I would be amazed if it were even half that."

Despite the move to Matador and the consequent upgrade in promotion, and the increased touring the band undertook at that time, *Bee Thousand* remains the band's biggest-selling album, at least to date. "It's probably right around sixty thousand," says Griffin, "and I imagine there are probably another five or ten thousand because I licensed it to Matador for manufacturing in Europe. Only in the last year have I gotten paid on those—ten years after the fact. It sells at least a thousand or two a year, maybe more. Whenever there's a new album, there tends to be a spurt of sales. But that one, more so than any of the other records, keeps going."

For whatever reason, *Alien Lanes* was not, at the time, received quite as rapturously as *Bee Thousand*. It sold well, and over time has come to be regarded as a fan favorite, but there was a palpable sense of disappointment on Bob's part that the record didn't take off in the way he'd hoped. He was of course justly proud of his latest creation, and many of the songs from *Alien Lanes* remained in the set list until the band's breakup. He especially liked the extrapolation from *Bee Thousand*'s use of short songlets, which he dubbed "snippets," into the guiding aesthetic of *Alien Lanes,* which despite its twenty-eight tracks clocked in at just over forty-one minutes.

During a typical session for *Alien Lanes,* the band would meet in Kevin Fennell's basement, where they were practicing at the time before complaints from the neighbors forced them to move to Mitch Mitchell's (unheated) garage. Bob would have written another song he wanted to include on the album (*Alien Lanes,* like most Guided by Voices LPs at the time, threatened to become a double album at one point, and its sequence would change on an almost daily basis); let's use as an example "Game of Pricks," a late addition. Bob would run through the song on guitar with Kevin on drums once or twice, until he felt Kevin had a sufficient grasp on the structure. He'd then record the results. A bass part would be immediately overdubbed, and then Bob would lay down the vocals. Toby would place cheap Radio Shack microphones where he could—the main criterion being to avoid knocking over the half-full beer cans that littered the garage floor—and operate the cheap Tascam four-track machine, which recorded on cassette. By "operate" we mean, in essence, turning all the bass knobs down as low as they would go and the treble knobs as high as they would go, which explains the tinny, hiss-ridden sound of both *Bee Thousand* and *Alien Lanes,* a sound Bob particularly liked because it reminded him of the way songs used to sound when he listened to them on transistor radios as a kid. Toby would then mix down the results onto another cassette, and the song would be finished. Total time: maybe half an hour.

* * *

The release of *Alien Lanes* introduced Guided by Voices to their first extended bout of touring: first an extensive U.S. tour in the fall of 1994, coheadlining with The Grifters, an excellent band from Memphis; then shorter U.S. tours during the spring and summer of 1995, after an aborted session at Easley Studios in Memphis; and a stint in Chicago with Steve Albini in winter and spring.

The spring tour that took the band through the Midwest and all the way up to Vancouver, with a planned southerly course down to San Diego, was notable for a crisis that occurred offstage. The night after the Vancouver show, Toby discovered that his wife, Laura, had gone into labor with their first child, about a month earlier than expected. He made plans to head out the next morning on a plane back to Dayton, leaving Bob with the prospect of canceling the entire West Coast swing—until, that is, then–guitar tech/roadie and eventual full-time GBV member Nate Farley stepped in.

"I was the roadie," recalls Nate. "Mitch brought me in because we were friends. I just laid low, did my job, stayed out of people's way, didn't try to act like I'm part of the band. We're going across the country, and every single night—I learn by ear, I can't read music or anything like that—I would check out the set, and I was loving it, because I got to see GBV play every night.

"So we get to Vancouver, and Toby found out his wife was going into labor. And Bob was like, 'We're gonna have to cancel the West Coast tour.' And I finally gathered up the balls to say, 'I could learn the songs.' And Bob looks at me and goes, 'You could learn all these songs.' At that point I think there were only like thirty-two songs in the set. He didn't know that I was paying attention, I don't think, or knew them by heart just because I loved them.

"The best part of this story is he goes, 'All right, when we get back to the hotel, you're gonna come up to the room where me and Toby are at, and you and Toby and Mitch will go through the songs together.' So me and Mitch were getting out of the elevator, and from down the hall I could hear Bob's voice. And it wasn't a happy Bob's voice; it was a worried, angry, doubtful Bob's voice. I think there were phrases like, 'These songs ain't fucking "Johnny B. Goode." He can't learn all these fucking songs, how the hell's he gonna do this? We gotta call off the tour.'

"And it's getting louder and louder the closer I get to the door. Finally I get to the door: knock knock knock. And then there's quiet. We go in, and Bob's sitting there with his head in his hands. The first thing we started out with was 'Tractor Rape Chain.' And I ran through that with no problem. I think we did 'I Am a Scientist' after that, went through that with no problem. I could slowly see Bob looking up and starting to get into it, like, 'Whoa, wait a minute, he can do this.'

"I was like, 'I already know these songs: I can do "Motor Away," some of the simpler ones, but there's stuff like "Evil Speakers," where it never goes back to the same thing twice. These are the things I really need to work on. The other stuff, don't worry about it, I already know it in my head.' And I think we spent an hour and a half, two hours in the room that night, and the next day I had time to practice the songs at the Canadian border.

"The first show was at the Crocodile Café in Seattle, and I was really nervous, and I got one glass of Jack. One short glass of Jack on the rocks, and I walk up to Bob, and he's like, 'Dude, are you sure you should be drinking before this?' And I'm like, 'I got to, or I'm gonna flip out.' I didn't want to get drunk, but I had to get a little drink in me. Things went perfect. And every other show after that went perfect. I got a little cocky after that, because it was me and Mitch, with our dual Les Paul assault. At a certain point I told Bob, 'You know, I know Toby's harmonies, if you want I can sing those,' and he goes, 'Why don't you just do everything—sing all the songs, do the whole show by yourself.' I was like, 'Okay, now I know where the boundaries are.' I got paid to play guitar and to roadie, so I think I made more money than anyone else on that tour.

"There's a bootleg of my first show. Bob goes, 'This is Nate Farley. He's our roadie, and Nate's an angel.' I think that's the first and last time Bob's ever called me an angel."

Following that, there occurred an extensive European tour, the band's first ever, which was remarkable for a couple of reasons—the extent to which it exposed Bob's xenophobia, and the beginning of Kevin Fennell's sad decline back into alcohol and drug abuse.

The European tour started in Germany. "When we got to Münster, for the first show, our hotel was a kind of tiny inn or something, and we had these tiny European rooms, with slanted ceilings so you couldn't even stand up, and there were no bathrooms, and no phones. I got so depressed. I started crying," Bob remembers. "I was like, 'What the fuck are we doing here?'"

He pulled himself together quickly, of course, and continued through a brutal schedule that included several shows in Germany, Holland, Belgium, France, and finally a week of shows in Britain, where the band met up with Kim Deal's side project, The Amps, which included two future members of Guided by Voices: Jim Macpherson and Nate Farley. The sight of hometown faces cheered Bob considerably.

For the first time the band was equipped both with a tour bus and a professional tour manager, a nice guy from Sheffield possibly called Manny, who also served as driver. Inexperienced in dealing with tour managers, and not quite understanding Manny's role, Bob kept insisting he fine band members for showing up late to the bus, by withholding their per diems. Manny tried to explain that disciplinary actions were Bob's role, not his, but Bob wanted someone else to play the bad guy. This became especially apparent after the band took the ferry from France to England in order to get to the Reading Festival, and Kevin boasted about smuggling a piece of hash in his shoe across the border.

"I've got a wife and kids," remembers Toby Sprout, still angry after all these years. "If he gets busted, we're all busted. It was an incredibly reckless and stupid thing to do."

Bob was furious, and demanded that Manny do something, fine Kevin or fire Kevin (of course, he couldn't really fire Kevin, because the tour was only half-way through). But Manny kept insisting that Bob would have to confront Kevin, something Bob seemed to feel a) was beneath him and b) he was too angry to handle properly. Eventually, Pete Jamison was delegated to deliver the admonition, and Kevin apologized to the band. But it was only the start.

When the band got to Glasgow, Scotland, Bob remembers sitting at a bar with Kevin, drinking a British lager, which he liked much better than the heavier European stuff.

"That looks really good," commented Kevin.

"It is good," said Bob.

"I wish I could try one," said Kevin.

"Well, maybe you can," suggested Bob. "You've been sober for twelve years. You're a different person now. Maybe you can handle it."

And that was all it took. Bob to this day feels responsible for Kevin's relapse, but the truth is—and Kevin agrees—that an alcoholic chooses to drink or not to drink. And Kevin chose to drink. The very next morning he was up bright and early in the hotel bar, downing Guinness after Guinness—"breakfast of champions," he told a horrified Bob. Kevin also claimed that the magician David Copperfield was sitting in the lobby. Seeing Kevin's condition, Bob was doubtful, but when he turned to look he said, "Goddamn, that *is* David Copperfield!" Unfortunately, Copperfield's magical presence was insufficient to prevent Kevin from plunging, steeply and irretrievably, into the maw of addiction.

What Bob didn't know was that everyone in the band felt responsible for Kevin's backsliding. He'd approached the other members separately throughout the tour, complaining that he "didn't feel like one of the gang" because he was the only abstemious member. And each member responded the same way Bob did. In truth, Kevin was only looking for reassurance for a decision he'd already made.

Back in the States, Kevin held it together for a while, mostly due to the influence of his wife, Donna, but it was really only a matter of time—specifically, until the next tour, in support of *Under the Bushes Under the Stars,* the follow-up, eventually, to *Alien Lanes.*

UTBUTS took an unusually long and tortuous road to completion, though in the end most of the songs on the version that was released were recorded in one hectic week at Cro-Mag in Dayton. But originally, the follow-up to *Alien Lanes* was intended to be a concept album called *The Power of Suck,* a semiautobiographical version of the Guided by Voices story, chronicling the rise and fall of a fictitious band called at first Pantherz (when they sucked) and eventually King Shit & the Golden Boys (when they "made it"). Modeled loosely after The Who's *Quadrophenia,* the plan was to include a short story, as on that album, giving the broad outlines of the concept. The story was in fact written, but no one seems to have thought to retain a copy.

Bob's relationship with Kim Deal had only grown closer since the two had first met. During Lollapalooza, while GBV was playing the second stage, The Breeders were playing the main stage, and included in their set was a fiery version of "Shocker in Gloomtown" from GBV's *Grand Hour* EP—a song that so enraptured Kim she would play it over and over on her turntable for hours, as if trying to unlock its sonic secrets. So when Kim asked Bob to come up during their set and sing his song, he naturally agreed, though he was nervous at the prospect of singing in front of twenty-five thousand people. The Breeders' version was much faster than the

Guided by Voices' version, and as a result, in concert with his nerves, Bob fucked up his own song, coming in on the second verse too early. Despite the fact that very few in the crowd probably noticed—musicians are in general far more conscious of their mistakes than the listening public—Bob fled in embarrassment back to The Breeders' dressing room, where only the administration of a large glass of whiskey and the constant reassurance from Jimmy enabled him to overcome his temporarily shredded self-confidence. That, and kicking the Beastie Boys' ass at basketball without even trying: Bob and Jimmy against one of the Adams and Mike D, on the portable hoop the Beasties had brought along on the tour to show off their skills.

So when Bob asked Kim Deal if she would produce his next record, she agreed without hesitation, and offered to work for free. Bob had decided (once again) he'd like to make a stab at a Big Studio record, a hard-hitting rock gem along the lines of his favorite albums, *Who's Next* and the first Cheap Trick album, and recognized that Kim's years of experience in Big Studios with The Breeders and before that The Pixies were likely to help him realize this goal. He recorded a set of twelve demos that he can no longer find, and has managed to reconstruct only partially through the cracked lens of his memory.

PARTIAL RECONSTRUCTION OF *THE POWER OF SUCK:*

1. Pantherz
2. Debbie X (I Am Decided)
3. Drag Days
4. Trader Vic
5. Bughouse
6. He's the Uncle
7. Sheetkickers
8. Pink Drink
9. Why Did You Land?
10. Don't Stop Now

Many of these songs have been released either on bootleg, or on *UTBUTS* itself, or on *Suitcase,* or in other versions on other records, and as the band rehearsed the songs in Kim's basement in preparation for going down to

Memphis to record at Easley—Pavement had just finished recording there, and had recommended the studio to Kim and to the band—Bob would add songs, and change the lyrics to some of the original demos, so that as usual by the time recording was set to begin there was a double album's worth of material to wrestle with, including eventual *UTBUTS* tracks "Official Ironmen Rally Song," "Redmen and Their Wives," and "Big Boring Wedding."

The band first went to Chicago to record for two days with famously iconoclastic engineer Steve Albini, who despite his prickly reputation turned out to be practically the nicest guy in the entire world. (One of his quirks was to call everyone "Senator" when they were overdubbing: "You all set, Senator?" "You want to try that again, Senator?" He also referred to mistakes as "balloons": "Couple of balloons on that track, Senator, how about another run-through.") His collection of microphones was impressive— he had a German microphone from the 1930s he called the Hitler mic, and a Russian one from the '40s which, you may have guessed, he called the Stalin mic. He worked without an assistant, running from the control room upstairs to the recording space downstairs to adjust a mic or tune a drum: he was particularly adept at tuning drums, and at inducing fantastically huge, booming, drum sounds. He paid least attention to vocals, preferring a dry, untreated sound—though he did accede to Bob's request for some Lennonesque slapback echo on one song, which, being Steve, he insisted on creating the way it would have been created by George Martin, through some archaic version of actual, physical tape-looped delay.

The band finished "Pantherz," "Sheetkickers," "He's the Uncle," "Superwhore," and had time left over to improvise an instrumental, which Bob later put lyrics on and called "Girl From the Sun," and which appears on the fan club album *Tonics and Twisted Chasers,* as well as on the *Daredevil Stamp Collector* EP or his Fading Captain series as an instrumental. Toby and Bob stayed in Chicago an extra day to mix, and the rest of the band drove down with the equipment to Easley, where Kim and engineers Doug Easley and the other guy began the process of setting up the equipment, placing microphones, and adjusting levels and EQ or whatever it is people do in recording studios.

Problems arose when Bob's famously impatient style of working clashed with Kim's famously patient style of working. Bob had never entertained ideas like making sure the backing track was right before proceeding to overdubs, or doubling and even tripling vocals. Kim also had ambitious ideas with regard to arrangements and instrumentation that involved bringing in string players and such, ideas that Bob enjoyed in theory, until he realized how fucking long it can take to put down a string part.

The true breaking point, however, came when Kim suggested that they fly in [Breeders' drummer] Jim Macpherson to play drums. She didn't feel that Kevin was capable of giving the proper performance on a couple of the more important songs, and knew that Jim, an experienced studio drummer and moreover a powerful, solid player, would make a meal of those particular parts. Bob balked.

"He used to be my brother-in-law—I can't fire Kevin," he said.

"I'm not suggesting that you fire him," Kim replied, "just that we try Jim on a couple of the songs. Otherwise they'll never sound right."

The next day, Bob announced that he was cutting the session short in order to get back to Dayton in time to see his son Bryan's basketball game—an obvious lie, of course, but such was Bob's respect for Kim that he couldn't bring himself to tell her the truth: that he was fed up, that it was taking too long, that he didn't like the way things were sounding, that he didn't understand why he had to spend so much time (and money—because Bob always had one eye on the budget, and even though Kim had volunteered her services, the studio costs were mounting), and perhaps most important, as always with Bob, that he was homesick.

Years later, with the benefit of experience, Bob realizes that the problem was not so much with the process, but with the players.

"[Easley] didn't go as well as I would have liked," he says. "You get in a big studio and you want to make something that has balls, you've gotta have some people who can pull it off. And that includes myself. I think I've gotten better. I can play rhythm, but . . . I've always wanted a lead guitar player. I like indie rock, and postpunk, but . . . I like rock and roll, and rock and roll has always had a good lead guitar player. Any great rock band, with the exception of bands that operate as a band, like Wire or R.E.M., has always had a great lead guitar player, and I think that was the missing ingredient in Guided by Voices at that time. Although Kevin had become an outstanding drummer, we needed a power drummer. A caveman."

So the band left, with maybe half an album's worth of unmixed material. The songs that ended up on *UTBUTS* Bob then took into Refraze Studios in Dayton to remix, or more accurately, mix. The results of the

Refraze session, while not exactly *Who's Next*, were satisfactory to Bob—but when he got back from Europe, he realized that he'd written fifteen new songs on tour, and that he liked those fifteen new songs a lot, and that moreover he wasn't too crazy about the *Power of Suck* idea anymore. He also was unsatisfied with the vocal sound on the Albini recordings, and doubled his vocal on four-track on those songs, after first asking Steve's permission, which was granted, albeit reluctantly.

But before he could get back in the studio, there was a tour opening for Urge Overkill to contend with. One word: disaster. Urge Overkill was a formerly great band who'd made a successful leap into the major leagues with their previous album, *Saturation*, then had been boosted further by having their cover of Neil Diamond's "Girl, You'll Be a Woman Soon" heavily featured in the movie *Pulp Fiction*. But they were promoting a new album, *Exit the Dragon*, which was truly dreadful, and, against his better instincts, Bob was talked into supporting them by his management. From the start, things went badly. Kevin Fennell threw out his back a couple of weeks before the tour, and Nate Farley recommended his friend Craig-o to fill in. He didn't have time to learn the songs properly—unlike Nate, Craig-o had not started out as a die-hard GBV fan—and so early shows were often a mess. UO's crew treated GBV like an unwanted intrusion, as professional road crews have an unfortunate habit of doing, even after it became quickly clear that the majority of the paying audience were there to see the opening band. Things came to a head in Toronto, when after the set proper was finished the crowd loudly called for an encore, and Bob tried to step back onstage to oblige his fans. He was then attacked by a combination of the Urge Overkill road crew and the venue's bouncers. Fists flew briefly, and Bob was hustled off to the back office, where he was told that he was banned from the club.

"I didn't know someone could kick your ass and carry you off at the same time," Bob joked later, but at the time his temper got the best of him, and he threatened to pull out of the tour then and there. After a flurry of back-and-forth calls between Bob and then-manager Aaron Blitzstein at Gold Mountain, Bob agreed to continue for at least a few more dates, to see if things improved; and in fact, for a while things did improve—the guys from Urge, who were going through an internal crisis of their own, started hanging around with GBV, and relations warmed considerably between the two camps. But not enough: Bob couldn't get over the fact that he was being forced to play a shorter set when from his perspective Guided by Voices was pulling in the majority of the crowd—he felt that he was shortchanging his fans. Finally, he could take no more, and decided to pull the plug on the tour in Philadelphia, much to the dismay of Urge Overkill and of the promoters for the upcoming shows, of which there were several.

But no matter—Bob, still uncomfortable touring, returned home and almost immediately began recording what became the final version of *Under the Bushes Under the Stars*. The bulk of the songs were done at Cro-Mag, with five or six hangovers from the Easley and Albini sessions.

The album was released at the end of March 1996, with a headlining tour scheduled to kick off at the South by Southwest conference in Austin, preceded by a warm-up gig in early March at the Southgate House in Kentucky. The supporting act for that gig was Kim Deal's Amps, and an incident at that show proved a permanent rupture in the two friends' relations. Already angry at what she saw as her peremptory treatment during the Easley sessions, Kim was infuriated by what she felt was Bob's thoughtlessness in using up all the sound check time at Southgate. After The Amps' set, she stormed through the backstage area, looking for Bob, and took out her frustrations on a conciliatory Pete Jamison by punching him in the stomach. Hard.

For his part, Bob couldn't understand the fuss, partly because he put little stock in sound checks himself. "It wasn't a deliberate slight," he explains. "We didn't know what the schedule was, or how much time we were taking. We just don't pay attention to stuff like that." Which was exactly Kim's point—that Bob was thoughtless, and should have been more respectful toward Kim after all she'd done to help Guided by Voices: covering "Shocker in Gloomtown" both live and on an EP, putting the band in the video for the cover of that song, boosting the band's rep in every interview she gave, and finally offering to produce GBV's album for free.

Bob's view was that Kim, with The Amps, was trying to duplicate (i.e., rip off) GBV's lo-fi aesthetic—that Kim was essentially using Bob for his indie-rock cred. At the end of the day, though, the breakup was due simply to a clash of two alcohol-fueled egos, and was probably inevitable. The Southgate House incident was simply the final ingredient in a long-simmering cauldron of resentment. Add to that Bob's confession, some months later, that he had at one point actually "been in love" with Kim, though he of course would never have acted on his feelings, and it's not hard to see the flip side of a mutual attraction turning ugly.

But Bob had bigger problems to face. Kevin's battle with alcohol and now drugs was beginning to take its toll on his performance. At a show in May at Moe's in Seattle, he nodded off before the set, and had to be hauled into the dressing room shower and dosed with cold water to be revived. Even then, he was groggy and seemed unfit to play. Word spread that the drummer for a novelty band called the Presidents of the United States of America was across the street and had volunteered his services, but without hesitation Bob said no.

"I'll always be grateful to Bob for that," says Kevin, though it remains unclear whether the gesture was out of loyalty to Kevin or out of horror at the thought of having someone from such an awful band fill in. In any case, Kevin recovered in time to play, a pitcher of beer at his side the whole set, and depending on who tells the story, he played either better than he'd ever played or a bit slower than usual. The two versions are not necessarily incompatible.

In June, after a show in Washington, D.C., Kevin went out in the middle of the night, took a taxi to the wrong side of the tracks to look for crack, and ended up getting stabbed. The wound wasn't serious, but the situation was.

By now Bob was beginning to tire not only of the problems with Kevin but with the whole "so-called classic lineup," as he really does like to say. In late summer, Toby told Bob privately that he was leaving the band. He simply couldn't balance raising a family and playing in a rock band, especially one as turbulent and unstable as Guided by Voices.

"Looking back, I don't understand what my problem was," admits Toby. "A lot of it was, I felt like, 'I'm in my thirties and what the hell am I doing; I've gotta get my life together—what am I doing out here?' So it was a conflict I had with myself. And the touring was tougher then because we didn't have as many hotel rooms and you ended up sleeping on the floor around pizza boxes."

Toby's decision helped Bob make his own, very difficult decision, which he hadn't quite made when Kevin was arrested two days before a show at Dayton's EdgeFest in September 1996 for shoplifting a five-dollar bottle of wine. Once again, Craig-o was called on to fill in. And that was that. "I didn't fire Kevin, he fired himself," says Bob. "I called him and told him, 'I always said you were in the band until you fucked up, and guess what? You fucked up.'"

In fact, the breakup of the classic lineup, portrayed by the press as Bob's up and firing the whole band on a whim, wasn't entirely Bob's idea. Toby had quit, Bob had yet to find (and never would) a permanent bass player, and Kevin had simply bottomed out. Only Mitch remained, and Bob didn't fire Mitch. He wanted to keep him.

"We needed to progress somehow or it was gonna go down," says Bob now, looking back. "We had to become a better rock band. We're Guided by Voices, we're quirky, but I don't want to continue making records on four-track and dropping amps and shit. I want to become a real rock band and be taken seriously. I had to make some changes in the personnel in order for that to happen. Toby was already going to quit anyway. I had to get Jim Macpherson in my band. Goddamn. If he's available. And Nate, and then Doug came out of the Cobra Verde thing. But the main thing is that I wanted to get Macpherson in my band. And I tried really hard to get Greg Demos in the band for good, and he almost joined at one point. I offered him a pretty good deal, more money than his law firm was gonna offer him, I think, but he decided to go with the law thing. Same with my brother, too—I wanted him in the band. He was more into the security of family and a job. But that's the thing: Guided by Voices in my mind has always been like a guild or a club, more so than a band. You might go, but you're never really gone."

PRE-MED'S A TRIP

(after you repeat life report back for further instructions)

And in the beginning
God saw us crying
you were crying
fully exposed

Pre-med's a trip
I learn nothing
of heads and compound eyes
distinct shape of thorax
the breath and smell

this is how up I've come
how?
into the company of one

R. Pollard

Dennis Cooper is a poet and novelist best known for his beautifully written explorations of the darker aspects of human relationships (see Closer, Frisk, Try). *His was the last contribution to* Hunting Accidents, *a fact he blamed on two broken wrists ("slipped on the ice in Moscow"; likely story) and the intimidation factor of writing something about someone he admires as much as Bob. And then he reinjured his wrist playing Resident Evil 4 (a very likely story). The following, therefore, is the product of a great deal of suffering.*

When I was in high school in the late '60s and early '70s, English teachers routinely assigned a book called *The Poetry of Rock*. It consisted of lyrics by popular rock stars of the day laid out on the pages like poems and subjected to thumbnail analyses by self-styled literary critics. The teachers' assumption was, first of all, that we spent a lot of time pondering the lyrics of the songs we liked—and in those days, we sort of did—and, second of all, that if this assumption was correct, we would have to agree that writers like Frost and Cummings and Dickinson were cooler since their poetry didn't need the crutch of a musical sound track.

Still, all that effort notwithstanding, poetry has remained the world's most unpopular great art form, and the tactic was wrongheaded for all sorts of reasons. Chief among them was the fact that the lyricists anthologized in that particular book—Dylan, Simon and Garfunkel, Jim Morrison, Leonard Cohen, et al.—actually read poetry and considered themselves poet troubadours whose songs were intended as contexts for their meaningful musings. In other words, "Lucifer Sam" and "I Can See for Miles" and even "I Am the Walrus" weren't deemed poetic enough to make the cut. The establishment, as we used to call people like teachers and critics, has always mistaken quasi-literary lyrics for great ones. Truth is, the real genius song lyricists know either consciously or intuitively that great songs can't be subdivided into words and music without murdering both in the process. The greatest rock songs aren't poems in a sonic blanket or pieces of music littered with rhyming bits of conversation, but rather the equivalents of sonic sculptures or works of architecture. The less distinguishable their components, the more perfect the results.

By those standards, Robert Pollard is easily one of the great rock lyricists. Personally, I think he's the greatest rock lyricist of all time, period. Actually, I think he's the greatest living artist in any medium, but that's another story. His songs are positively enjambed with an almost insanely comprehensive knowledge of what a rock song has been in the past and could be on a regular basis now if songwriters believed in rock as a form and dedicated themselves to using all of it to give fans the most startling and pleasurable experience possible in a span of thirty seconds to seven or so minutes. I can't think of another artist working with the English language (poets included) who has his appreciation of the fucked-up beauty of the lazy, accident-prone, anti-exalted way Americans speak and write. Nor is any artist more capable of devising exciting examples and patent-worthy reinventions. Apparently, Pollard is not much of a reader or art history buff, but you could have fooled me, because, strictly in terms of style and tone, his lyrics juggle techniques associated with surrealism, the absurdists, realism, conceptual and postconceptual art, art brut, and on and on, creating a kind of history-of-aestheticism montage aspect to his work. At the same time, he tosses off ideas and metaphors and similes with such seeming spontaneity that his lyrics function equally as a random, crazy energy that jitters inside each song like lightning in a bottle. Pollard does this so consistently and voluminously and variously that it would be impossible to try to prove my point by deconstructing a few exemplary songs from his thousands of mind-boggling masterpieces in every known rock genre—often two or three genres within the same track. That proof would take a whole book in and of itself. All I can suggest to you is that as a hypercritical language Nazi (see: my novels), my being debased into a superlative-spewing zealot by Pollard's massive genius is some kind of proof. Or to paraphrase a poem by a real poet, Bill Knott, the only correct response to a child's grave is to lie down on it and play dead.

—Dennis Cooper

SCIENCE

"As a dog barks at the moon, to no purpose are your sayings; take your heaven, let them have their money."

—Robert Burton, *Anatomy of Melancholy*

There's no real point talking about the meaning of any of R. Pollard's songs. The lyrics, while crucial to the sound and sense of the song, are not the main argument—only a part. The argument of a Guided by Voices song is the melody/rock mix crossed with those sense fragments that evoke a response in the listener. The way these three elements work together in the context of a song like "The Best of Jill Hives," for instance, is to produce a reaction (dependent, as always, on the individual listener) of pure melancholic joy capable of clearing whatever clouds of doom might have enveloped you on any particular day. The song's lyrics might mean nothing in any conventional sense, but when paired with the chord structure, the melody, the singer's delivery, and the band's performance, your heart cannot help but leap from its constraining cage.

Having said that, many of Bob's song's do have a lyrical intent—that is to say, he wrote them for a specific reason, or to express a specific point, or even to tell a story. He's always been reluctant to discuss his motives or purposes with regard to specific songs, but by asking him to do so, we were able to produce some surprisingly cogent results. Occasionally, we hit a stone wall, because occasionally Bob's songs really don't have any particular motive or purpose, but for the most part—bearing in mind that what follows represents only a fraction of the eight-hundred-plus songs he's recorded, never mind written—when pressed, he can come up with at least a reasonable explanation.

The extraordinary thing about this experiment is that Bob was not told in advance which songs he would be asked to discuss, and yet did not need to resort to a lyric sheet or any other mnemonic device to produce his responses. Which, depending on your opinion of his songwriting, either means he's gifted with an extraordinary memory, or he's insane. We report, you decide.

One minor structural note: the songs are arranged in rough chronological order, and for the most part come from Guided by Voices releases rather than solo or side projects. A few exceptions to this loose rule are tacked on to the end, simply because we were curious.

OLD BATTERY

That's kind of writing about mortality. At the time I was in my twenties, but still . . . I don't know exactly what it was about, but . . . the fear of getting old. I played that album for Toby, and he made me play that song again, immediately. That was one of the first songs I was happy with the recording of; I just thought it was a weird song. And the chorus was "Die hard," and I think that was pretty much around the time of Bruce Willis's *Die Hard,* I believe; I think it was. "Die hard"! It's mainly about fear of growing old, and I think it was inspired kind of by my grandmother at the time. How you become kind of religious at the end of your life, just in case. You think you can do things ritualistically that will get you into heaven.

HANK'S LITTLE FINGERS

It's about a guy I know named Hank. I knew him through his cousin, and I asked his cousin, "Man, I got a song, it's about Hank, it's called 'Hank's Little Fingers.' Do you think Hank would mind?" He goes, "Yes—so don't tell him." Hank inspired me actually to play guitar. He was born with a birth defect—he had really, really tiny fingers on his right hand. I don't even know how to describe it. I'd see him and I'd see this other guy, Charlie "Guitar" Watson, they would play acoustics under the highway, under the overpass. I'd go down there and I wanted so badly to be able to sit with them and jam when they did Stones songs or whatever. But Hank especially inspired me. He'd strap a rubber band around his wrist, and somehow he attached a pick to it, and he could play really well. I go like, "I've wanted to play guitar for so long, and I'm too lazy to do it—and it's a tough thing, to learn how to play guitar." But he inspired me to do it. One of the earliest incarnations of the band, Hank was gonna be in it. I thought that would be cool, and kind of weird.

Part of it's also about hunters. "Lepus, canine, cat, and reptile." *Lepus* means "rabbit." Northridge, where I come from, is really a kind of Appalachian community, and Hank came from that kind of household. There's a lot of kids that live down by the river. There's a lot of rivers, and railroad tracks, and a lot of them have guns and are into hunting.

PORTRAIT DESTROYED BY FIRE

It's about spousal abuse. Yelling and hitting and that sort of thing. "Rings of gold and rings of blue"—those are bruises. It could be about family abuse, just physical and verbal. When I was young, it was commonly accepted that you could whip your kids, that you could discipline them in that way.

TRAP SOUL DOOR

It's about not being able to get along in a relationship. "Just one spark makes a hell of a fire, I'm still wrong but you're still a liar." Not being able to come to an agreement, just out of pride or whatever. Most of it probably had to do with my inability to get along with people. I've got a pretty bad temper; I try to control it. I do better now that I don't play sports. I'm defensive— I don't try to start arguments.

I still lose my shit, though. I gotta do better. If I can't find something: "Goddamn! Where the fuck is it! I just put it fucking down!" No one's around when I do that except maybe Sarah [Bob's girlfriend]. She has to suffer that, trying frantically to help me so I'll shut up.

PAPER GIRL

That's Greg's favorite. He made me play that on acoustic all the time. "Paper Girl" is just about nothing. It's just a groovy sixties pop song. It's corny. Play "The Pape"! That's what they used to call it: "The Pape." I like the structure of that. The first really good songwriting session I had was down in my basement. We had a PA down there and my amp, and I wrote a shitload of songs that later came up on a lot of different stuff. "Paper Girl," "Liar's Tale," "Echos Myron," all that shit. They weren't called that then.

CHIEF BARREL BELLY

I really don't know what that's about but it's maybe kind of about me versus organized religion. I think. I've got a problem with organized religion and just the ritual of religion. And the fact that people go to church and they're saved and right after that they go and gorge themselves at Cracker Barrel or whatever. Although there was no Cracker Barrel at the time I wrote that song. So my thing was that one day a week you go do this, and the rest of the week you can do whatever you want. I don't have a problem with conviction to a philosophy or a belief, but just—like, three Hail Marys and that's it, you're cool after that. I guess confession's okay, but the idea that a single person can be ordained by the divine to have that power to forgive you blows my mind.

DRINKER'S PEACE

That is pretty obviously about drinking to a point where you kind of just don't give a fuck anymore. It's a love song to alcohol. "Life was too real till you got here." Some people think it's about a person, and that's the thing about lyrics or poetry or whatever: It's whatever you think it is. People come up and tell me what they think a song's about, and it kind of sheds new light on it for me. Like, "Yeah, maybe you're right." A lot of my songs start as poetry. The more melodic ones start as music. It's harder to fit words into melodies.

PENDULUM

Those are my favorite lyrics I've ever written. In fact, *Same Place the Fly Got Smashed* is my favorite lyrical record. But "Pendulum" is just about . . . I started getting into grunge. *Same Place* was inspired by grunge, although it doesn't seem like it. But it was. And "Pendulum"—that's another drinking song. "Come on over tonight, let's put on some Cat Butt": that's grunge.

A few years later some guy from Cat Butt actually wrote me and said thanks for mentioning Cat Butt. Jimmy used to come over, and Mitch, and we'd get fucked up, listen to grunge, and then we'd do some ourselves. "The pendulum swings, it cuts, yeah, we'll be swollen and infected but so what?" That was kind of prophetic. Because now, hey—we're still doing it. We're still middle-aged children, we're fatter than we were, nobody gives a shit. Who cares? I was dyeing my hair for a little bit. I just thought, "I'm still in rock, I don't want to look like The Moody Blues, or Kenny Rogers or some shit." So I thought, "I better dye my hair." Then I thought, "Fuck that." I saw some of my friends that were dyeing their hair and it didn't look good. With me, sometimes it looked too dark, sometimes it looked all right. It was never consistent. The reason I did it, we were signing with TVT, there were still aspirations from TVT that we could have a hit, so I better play the game and look like I'm younger than I am. Even though I quit dyeing it, I still look pretty young for a fucking drunk.

14 CHEERLEADER COLDFRONT

That's probably my favorite title that I came up with. I was at a high school basketball game, a tournament; I think it was in Centerville. And they had so many cheerleaders. I counted fourteen all the way across the court, facing the crowd. They were all really pretty and you could see that they were obviously kind of stuck on themselves, they were just staring—the point is that it was obviously all about them; it wasn't about the game, it was about them. And that's when I said, "Look at the fourteen cheerleader coldfront." I had to write that down. Then Toby—it was actually Toby's song, but it needed some lyrics. In fact it was the only song that Toby and I ever sat down and worked on together, truly cowrote together.

WEED KING

It's just . . . obviously.

EXIT FLAGGER

I think it's about going through life confused and not certain of what's going on, because of all the bullshit involved in it. Until you get to the point where—you die. The "Exit Flagger" is the Grim Reaper.

QUALITY OF ARMOR

Defense mechanisms that you develop through your life just because of situations that piss you off or scare you. You're being bombarded from so many different angles by lies, and things you need to do, and things you're not quite sure you should do, but they say you should do, or be, and you just develop this shield against that. How's your armor? Can you deal with it?

The lyrics are ridiculous. Just overrhyming and forced in my opinion. But you get the gist of what I'm trying to say. That was the first song I brought to 86, the songwriting guild with Nick Weiser and John Dodson. It was the first song I wrote on guitar.

"Montezuma Halls." Don't ask me why I threw that in there. I guess I was trying to throw war imagery in there too.

SHOCKER IN GLOOMTOWN

That was when we first kind of broke. So that was about the years we played in obscurity, and were you there to witness it happening, the birth of Guided by Voices. Kind of about the Dayton scene, in general. Baring our ass for all to see—that's about us; now people will be able to see what fucking buffoons we are. "And no one got to kiss it." It's almost about the brevity of being in a band. When we first broke I didn't think it was gonna last very long. It was like, "Okay, here's our fifteen minutes of fame or whatever, and we'll bare our ass and no one will get to kiss it."

MY IMPRESSION NOW

It was originally called "Tire Pressure Down," but I changed it—I didn't think that made any sense. Now I wish I'd kept it; I like that title better. I was kind of questioning what I'm doing. I had to make a decision about rock versus teaching. What people had told me, what people are telling me now, where I'm gonna go. All those songs—"Game of Pricks," "Gold Star for Robot Boy"— kind of had similar themes. Solutions that don't work. The answers to life, and how many different answers there are, and the confusion of it, how hard it is to swallow, but you kind of have to—that's the thing, you're trying to create your own philosophy, and yet they shove religion down your throat.

DUSTED

That was another kind of religious song. If certain aspects of Christianity and religion in general are true, then why is it so mysterious and symbolic? Why can't you just let us know? Tell us, man, don't give us fucking free will, we don't know what to do with it. If we get, by our own free will, either heaven or hell, and most of us are failing miserably, wouldn't it be better to *make* us do the right thing, take away free will, so we can all go to heaven? It's free will, but you gotta make the right choice. Now, when I say, "Why don't you just tell us what to do," I don't believe that. I don't believe in the fundamentalist Christian concept of heaven and hell anyway. The song's about the whole banality of that worldview. Like that movie *The Passion [of the Christ]*. I don't want to see that! I don't want to see a man butchered up—for us. Because basically it implies that we all have to do the same thing. That's a sad picture. Why such sadness? Why are we here for such sadness? What have we done? What the fuck have we done for it to be this bad?

IF WE WAIT

That's just a prissy song about my friends and me getting drunk. It's almost like my "Happy Birthday, Mr. President." I'm singing it in a female voice, even. It's just a goofy song. Another getting-old song. Let's drink and make rock. "If we wait for our time, then we'll be dead." That was written in that same really good session with "Echos Myron" and all those other ones. The midsection was inspired by an acid trip.

The other song I wrote on acid was "Goldheart Mountaintop Queen Directory." I was looking in the mirror, and my face turned into my son's, into Bryan's. I just got all goose-pimply and I fucking cried and I wrote that song. I don't know what it has to do with. But that's what inspired me to write it.

NON-ABSORBING

It's kind of self-explanatory. It's kind of about independence and identity. Trying to find out who the fuck you are and who the fuck other people are. And it's about judgment. You know how people sit around and talk about other people, like I do all the time? 'Cause it's fun. It's not necessarily such a good thing to do. I don't know what makes that fun; I guess there's just nothing else to talk about but each other. It's kind of fun to talk about your own bullshit, too, your own fuckups. It's more fun to laugh at yourself. It's harmless, but it's not. It's something that you say consciously to yourself, "I don't want to do that anymore," but then you get drunk, and it's too much fun. I feel bad about it, and it would be better not to do that, but . . . that's what people do. I'm not saying it's right. You go out, you sit and you talk about events and you talk about movies and music, and you talk about your friends and sometimes it's good and sometimes it's not so good.

When I was a teacher, and parents would come in for parent-teacher conferences, in order to say something about an area of improvement that a kid needed, I would always start off by saying something good about the kid. And then it's easier to let 'em down. So even when you're talking shit about your friends, it's important to say something good about them, too. We're all in it together. We're all fuckups.

BUZZARDS AND DREADFUL CROWS

Another fear-of-the-unknown song. Just of death, or evil, or whatever. The things that are constantly bombarding you in the world that are negative. It's a song of negativity. I think of my albums as being movies, and my songs as being shorts. "Buzzards and Dreadful Crows" is a horror short.

YOURS TO KEEP

That's a weird song. I don't remember it being about anything in particular, but it's kind of like "My Valuable Hunting Knife" in the sense that one man's trash is another man's treasure. What's valuable to you? A necklace of fifty eyes? Is that something you'd like, to be able to see all over the place? It's also about acquiring things, and trophies and accomplishments and what's important to you.

ECHOS MYRON

I don't think that was ever about anything specific. It was kind of like a victory song. Like, "Now we're here. And shit yeah it's fucking cool." We were on our way and we kind of knew it. We knew things were happening. I was still kind of boastful, especially at the time. We'd been doing this for a long time, ten years or whatever, and just . . . around town there were a lot of bands that thought something was gonna happen for them. Labels were talking to them or whatever, and we were just not even in the picture. I thought it was pretty funny that we all of a sudden usurped the whole scene. We were invisible.

GOLD STAR FOR ROBOT BOY

At the time, I was still teaching, and I gave gold stars for certain accomplishments in the classroom. One was for a math game called Giant Steps. Kids would line up at the back of the room, four or five kids at a time. I'd show them a flash card; whoever got it right got to take a giant step until they got all the way up to me, and they would get a gold star by their name. We were about to be signed by Matador, and I was gonna be able to quit my job, so now it was time for me to get the gold star. I was the robot boy. Also, there were gold stars that were given for other things in my class, so basically I was thinking about the parallel with my situation. In class it was: if you do what I say, then I'll give you a gold star. And I figured that's what was gonna be happening with me now. I'm gonna be on a record label, and in order to be successful I'm probably going to have to jump through some hoops. It kind of overlapped at the time. I wanted to be careful. I didn't want to come out of the gate and kiss too much ass, doing things I didn't really want to do. And I didn't really know what to expect. The song's tongue-in-cheek, though.

I'm sure there's a little see-I-told-you-so toward my family and other people in Dayton in there as well. It was a source of pride. When you've not been given credit for something that you really enjoy and that is dear to you . . . Not only have you not been given any recognition for it but what feedback there was, was negative, like, "What the fuck's that!" I didn't give a shit: "Maybe you're right". . . . "If I waited for you to tell me the actions I should take"—in other words, I've been on my own. All the decisions were made by me and the people that had been there to support me, the people in my band, and my brother—you know, the handful of people that think it's cool. The thing is, we didn't know what the fuck to do. No one has any musical training, we don't know anything about the industry or anything, we just did it because we had fun. And then to get this negative criticism about what we're doing . . . "We're not trying to do anything! Okay, what would you have me do? What would you have me do to improve my band?" This one guy named Kenny Treadway—right before we broke, too, which made it doubly gratifying—he goes, "I know you're trying to do something with your band; you gotta come up here and see The Dinosaurs at the Little York Tavern. These guys, they're good, they're funny. I know you're trying to do something, I'm just trying to help you out." About a week later we got signed to Matador. But at the time I was like, "Yeah, you're right, I guess I should check out The Dinosaurs." Which, by the way, we're gonna do tomorrow night. Rich Turiel's coming in town and we're gonna go see them. They play every Sunday night. They do these obvious, ridiculous covers, but that's what makes them great. We even entertained the idea at one point, because we're always looking for interesting opening acts—we were gonna take The Dinosaurs out. People'd be going, "What the fuck? Is this a joke or what?" But my thing was, by the time they're almost done and we're ready to go on, people will be dancing.

I AM A SCIENTIST

That's about the study of myself. I'm trying to figure out what's going on—you know, who I am, what I need to do, what I'm doing wrong, what I'm doing right: I'm a scientist. No one else can set you free; everyone's their own scientist. Rock 'n' roll, that's *my* solution—what's yours? It had no particular inspiration. It came from a title. Most of my songs at the time came from titles. Then I just wrote the words. Poems have a better chance at being better, lyrically—of making the song better, lyrically. I used to just go down my notebook page and write a song. Every title gets a song. And then you go back and listen and pick the ones you like. And what I'm finding now, going back to some of those old tapes, is that some of the ones I just shit-canned immediately, now to me are better than the ones that I picked. Which bodes well for my solo stuff. I hope. Another thing about my lyrics is how they sound, how they sing. That's more important than having literal meaning.

A SALTY SALUTE

Based—loosely—on a story about Gibby and the American Legion. They had a fishing trip, they went up to Lake Erie. And one of the guys, Bo Harmon, went overboard into Lake Erie. I guess it was really cold and he was fucking freezing and they fished him out. They sat him down and put blankets on him and gave him a cup of coffee. About a minute later the roof collapsed and the water came down and he got fucking soaked again. I just thought that was hilarious. So I wrote "Salty Salute" as a tribute to that story, to the American Legion, and to Guided by Voices. To drunks everywhere. At the time, too, at this particular American Legion in Northridge, there were some people getting busted for DUIs coming out of there. I thought it was pretty fucked up that our country can be like, "Okay, you did your time serving your country," and they give you this place called the Legion where you can go drown your sorrows, and on top of that they're gonna bust your ass coming out of there drunk.

MOTOR AWAY

Motor away, man. See ya! It's another one of those "fuck-you" songs.

GAME OF PRICKS

It's another one of those "fuck-you" songs. Ha!

"Game of Pricks" is more about deception and lies, and not knowing what's the truth or what's real or if someone's giving you bullshit. People can lie to you so much, it pricks away at you, just life itself, the deception in it. It had to do with the industry again, it had to do with dealing with people who I didn't think were being straight-up with me, and that's . . . that's the game of pricks. Turns out I was totally paranoid—it's not as bad as I thought it was. I think that most of the people I've dealt with—my labels, management, everybody—I think they're all right. I don't think anybody was out to get me. It's just that I was introduced to the industry standard. Some of the industry standard's not right, but that's the way it is. It's still not fucking right. It's complicated; it's one of the things in life you just have to accept. It's like, "If you're gonna fuck me, at least make sure I'm comfortable." And I really don't think anybody's fucking me anymore.

THE OFFICIAL IRONMEN RALLY SONG

That was kind of, to me, about competition of rock bands. Especially males, the male concept of competiton. Kind of like a "We Are the Champions" kind of thing. I don't know. That's our "We Are the Champions."

BRIGHT PAPER WEREWOLVES

Bright paper werewolves are like . . . I was watching Gibby playing these scratch-off things at the Legion, trying to make money, and I saw people buying Lotto tickets, all these really bright, eye-catching things to get people to spend their money, throw it away basically. So that's where I made that up—I called them bright paper werewolves. It's about get-rich-quick schemes. How to make money without using your brain or working for it. The lyrics came first for that, that's why I think it's better lyrically. I like that title.

DON'T STOP NOW

It's "The Ballad of Guided by Voices." The first verse is about Big Daddy, my feud with Big Daddy. And I did see him one day strutting around with a six-pack ring that had somehow gotten stuck around his neck. The second verse is about Big Daddy, too, except Big Daddy becomes the world. Then, you know, we pulled into Economy Island, King Shit and The Golden Boys—that's us on tour. We're out in the world, and that's okay. Then there's the line: "Plenty more where we come from." Not! I would say that at shows sometimes. Not! It's another tongue-in-cheek, boisterous kind of thing. The thing was, when I sang "Plenty more where we come from," I'm just joking when I say "Not!" Dayton at the time, there was a little bit of a spotlight on Dayton, there were some pretty good bands coming out of Dayton at the time. I'm not sure about "plenty," but . . . You know what I really meant when I said that? I meant there's plenty more from us. I think. It had to do with some good local bands, Brainiac and Breeders, uh . . . Brainiac and Breeders. Actually there were good people making music in Dayton. But it was mainly, "Hey, we got more coming, don't worry about it."

DRAG DAYS

Originally called "In a Germantown," and I just tried to fit lyrics to it because "In a Germantown" was ridiculous. I wrote that when I was twenty, twenty-one. Germantown is about ten or fifteen miles to the southwest of Dayton. "Drag Days" is just about being in a lull between things that are exciting—tours, recording projects, or whatever. Plus it was part of the concept record *Power of Suck,* where it was about the band, actually, something to do with the band being bored and getting ready to go on tour. It had something to do with that concept.

REDMEN AND THEIR WIVES

The thing about growing up in Northridge, and probably any blue-collar town, is just what you do is you get married right away. Have kids, have a family, get a job and everything. That's what "Redmen and Their Wives" is about, that concept, that notion. That's what you do. You don't even know what else there is. I was part of that. Redmen are basically rednecks. I escaped it, but it cost me. Your destiny's already laid out for you. So even though I was part of it, eventually I think I educated myself to not totally believe in it.

SAD IF I LOST IT

I think that has something to do with pride or ambition, because I mentioned "I'll wear my maroon blazer all the time." That was what we had to wear when we played basketball for this really disciplinary coach in high school. I played with Gibby and Hamby and Randy and all those guys. We had to wear these maroon blazers on game day, with this striped maroon and silver tie. The thing about it was, that was a source of pride. To be able to wear one, you were part of an elite group of people. You're in Bill Walker's military. You're in Bill Walker's air force. We loved it. We had to wear our hair really short, we ran our asses off and we pressed. We had a good team. He was a good coach. He was kind of like Bobby Knight. He was very successful, and we just did what he said. And we won. He had like ten winning seasons. So "Sad If I Lost It" would be, I don't want to lose that drive.

LEARNING TO HUNT

That was kind of about me again. I was trying to find my identity. I'm both characters in the song. I'm singing to myself. I'm the subject and the object.

THINGS I WILL KEEP

It has to do with gaining secret knowledge through dreams and symbols. "Things that I will keep and hide them in my sleep"; whether you learn from your mistakes or whether you learn from dreams and symbolism, I don't know. They say you should write your dreams down. I read that if you keep a journal of your daily activities, and you're very honest about it, even if you say "I masturbated," or "I fucked a goat," or whatever, and you start to record your dreams also—and they also say you get better with practice; I don't know who "they" is—if you continue, your life becomes one continuous thing through the day and through the night. And pretty soon you have control of your life by doing that. That's a discipline, man. I started doing it and I was having some really weird dreams. I think that would work, and I should do that, and I have a better opportunity to do that than a lot of people because I can set my own hours. But still I'm too lazy to do it. I want to drink coffee, and I want to read the paper; I don't want to try to remember my dreams. It's too much work! It feels like school.

TEENAGE FBI

That was inspired by an event in my class. I got caught picking my nose in class. Some kid busted me going for the one with the golden center. He goes, "Hey, you're picking your nose!" And I go, "Goddamn, I don't need you watching me all the goddamn time and broadcasting it to the whole class." I think that's when I came up with the "Teenage FBI" part. They're out there watching you, all the time. And "cleaning out the hive"—that's when you pull out a nose hair. "When you clean out the hive, does it make you want to cry?" That's a frivolous story based on that kid who busted me in class.

GLAD GIRLS

I don't know. They're all right.

TWILIGHT CAMPFIGHTER

That's just another chest-beater. Just like, "Help me out." "Twilight Campfighter" must be like God or something. "Help us out. Show us the way."

UNSPIRITED

It's about apathy. Everybody gets to the point where they're like, "Fuck you, fuck me, and fuck everything."

HOW'S MY DRINKING?

How's my drinking is "1-800-Kiss My Ass." To hell with my church bells— that's my favorite line in that song. Most people that have a problem with people drinking usually come from some kind of right-wing, church background. In Europe they embrace that shit—it's about brotherhood, and love, and enjoying life together. Drinking's a part of life. And at the time I was getting some pretty rude fucking reviews about my drinking, locally. You just hear for so long about drinking, and I'm sick of it. I'm gonna drink.

FINE TO SEE YOU

That's a relationship song, about when I was in limbo, not knowing where to go, not knowing where home is, before I'd decided what I was gonna do. Not knowing whether the road is home or whether home is home. Kind of like, "I love everybody, why am I being put through this shit?" "I am hypnotizing the highway," that's basically—I was on the road all the time. The highway's not hypnotizing me, I'm hypnotizing the highway.

CHEYENNE

That's not about anything. It's kind of a nod to The Who, lyrically, especially the middle section. All I know about that song is that Doug's lead is fucking great.

PRETTY BOMBS

Totally means nothing. It's about germs.

MY KIND OF SOLDIER

I got the title, I forget where, but I saw a chick bent over with these fucking cutoff army fatigues, and I go, "That's my kind of soldier!" The song itself means nothing.

THE BEST OF JILL HIVES

It's about a fictitious character. I was sitting in one of these Jiffy Lube places waiting for my car to be worked on, and there were a few people sitting there and the television was on, so just to pass time, which I'll do sometimes, I'll start writing down what I think I'm hearing, because I don't hear very well. And the television wasn't very loud. So I started writing down titles, and one of them, I thought they said "The Best of Jill Hives," but they must have said "The Best of Our Lives." It seems like it's a real story about someone but it's totally made up. Like a woman that's kind of fucked around with a lot of guys. Who's important, who's not . . . I don't know. Maybe she's a fucking prostitute. Or a lonely housewife that's fucking around. I like the lyrics, but they really don't mean anything. "Trifle in a crystal bowl." I made a tape one time of just random phrases from the TV to see if I could come up with anything interesting, and I heard some guy go, "Trifle in a crystal bowl." I had to use that.

EVERYBODY THINKS I'M A RAINCLOUD
(WHEN I'M NOT LOOKING)

It has to do with people not calling me back. Seriously, I've had days where I've called every person I know—not a bite. And it pisses me off. "Okay, so it's cool, when it's showtime, and everybody gets to be a big shot back in the rock room, but when I'm home here, and I still want to have a drink, it's like when it's convenient for you, huh?" I think that's the inspiration for that song.

GIRLS OF WILD STRAWBERRIES

Doesn't really mean anything, it was just inspired by . . . I'd seen the Bergman film *Wild Strawberries*, and I thought the females were striking. There's a lot of beautiful women in it, almost to the point of inspiration.

WINDOW OF MY WORLD

Not lyrically important. I like that song because I think it's pretty. Pretty in a more serious way than, and not in such an obvious way as, "Hold on Hope." My problem with "Hold on Hope" was that it was too obvious and cheesy. Whereas "Window of My World," it just had a nice . . . the contrast between the verses and the chorus, or whatever that bridge is, "Give me your number." I think that sounded really good and there were really good changes back and forth, and I thought the structure was really good. And I'm not opposed to writing ballads like that as long as they're interesting, and not obvious. Lyrically, I don't think it's saying anything, it's just like: "Here's what I see. Here's my world, man, and welcome to it."

SING FOR YOUR MEAT

I got the title because I had heard that Kings of Leon weren't doing what they should be doing to become the next Strokes or whatever. They weren't as willing to jump through hoops, and as a result were not selling as many records as expected. But now I think they are. So the original title was "Sing for Your Meat, Leon." You know, "You gotta do it, man." It's like I was told one time by [erstwhile manager] Janet Billig, "Hey, baby, it's about commerce, it ain't about art." So you gotta do it. I think they *are* doing it now. Also, the song is about youth, period. There's the part about twenty-one's the legal age to kill yourself slowly but eighteen's the legal age to die. I've always kind of thought, and I'm sure everybody does, that it's kind of bullshit that you can't drink but you can go fight in a war. And they're drinking over there. I think the legal age over there is eighteen. You can drink at eighteen if you enlist. It's a pretty good way to recruit.

SUBSPACE BIOGRAPHIES

It's a drinking song. I'm determined. I'm determined to get drunk. Check out my subspace biographies, which is totally ridiculous; it doesn't even make sense. Subspace is some kind of in-between dimension.

PEOPLE ARE LEAVING

That had to do with people dying. Because I had a few friends die around that time, like Jack Garnett, and then Jim Shepard died. And then my uncle died. And Timmy Taylor from Brainiac. I just met him. He came over and drank and it looked like we were getting ready to start a friendship for the first time. And he died the next day. So it's like, "Goddamn, everybody's dying, what's going on here?" People are leaving. In total frustration they throw up their hands—they're waved out.

ALONE, STINKING AND UNAFRAID

Another drinking song. "Fuck it, they do it every time to you. Let's go get drunk." I don't know. Maybe it's about getting drunk by yourself, which is something I don't do very well. I'm a social drinker. It's another breast-beater, too. I like writing breast-beating alcohol songs. Chest-beating, I mean. In celebration of it. Is that wrong?

DO SOMETHING REAL

The title says it all. It's about seeing through bullshit, and seeing through things that aren't real, the whole façade of everything: entertainment, and fucking expectations of people and responsibilities, and whether every-thing's moving in the right direction. Like, "Fuck you, do something real." I get sick of looking at TV, I get sick of looking at whatever—music videos, commercials; they treat you like a fucking idiot.

HEY MR. SOUNDMAN

That came out of my paranoia stage. When we played at CBGB the first time Kevin said, "Hey Mr. Soundman, I don't know your name, and you don't know mine either." He wanted more whatever in his monitor. For some reason it made me cringe, just the way he said it. I was like, "Oh, Jesus Christ." And then Horner made up the other part: "You lie to your friends, I lie to mine, let's not lie to each other." That was just something he said. A Hornerism. So basically I didn't even write those lyrics. But it turned out good how the two different statements fit together.

WHY DID YOU LAND?

"You could have stayed in flight forever." That's probably Jesus [laughs]. I don't know. That could be, if we come from a spirit realm, and we incar-nated here in the material realm, why did we do that? And then we're try-ing through meditation and religion and everything to get back to that realm—why did we do that? Why did we land?

MEN MUST WORK AND WOMEN MUST WEEP, NICOTINE INAMORATA (OFF RECORDS 13")

GOT WAR!

Recorded in Portland in '02 and '03, this massive hunk of blood-red vinyl is Bob and Doug's tribute, or antitribute, to the Russo-Portuguese War (1757–59), the "war to end all wars" of its time. In only two short years, more than eleven million combatants died—from weaponry consisting of swords, knives, axes, and clubs. (Amazing but true: no muskets, cannons, machine guns, or napalm appeared in warfare until 1795.)

Standout cuts include: "Porto frio da mola," "Vesnushchatyj baby baby," "O amor é a resposta," "Kazhdyj ohotnik zhelajet gimme gimme," "Por favor não come minha mãe (Bossa Nova Freedom Sing-Along)," and "So the Rooskies Want Onions?" As to the significance of this last title, few today realize that one of the more brutal battles took place in the town we now call Walla Walla. . . . That's the U.S.A., rock fans! (It pays to read a HISTORY BOOK now & then.)

To master the skills required for navigating the Russian and Portuguese lyrics, Bob put in a semester at the Wright-Kowalski Speech Academy. "When you're committed to as weird a fucking project as this one," sez he, "you'll give up nightlife to make it happen. I cut some corners on the Russian material—they're all transliterations. I never learned the Cyrillic alphabet—there are only so many hours in a day."

Work out!

—Richard Meltzer

HOPE

"Bob's one of the best songwriters around. He knows how to do it. And I don't think he even tries. He just has that natural knack. Coming from a person who writes songs, I really consider him one of the better people in the whole business."

—Ric Ocasek, The Cars

Two days after the de facto breakup of the "so-called classic lineup" at EdgeFest in September 1996, ironically, Bob and Toby saw the simultaneous release of their respective solo albums, *Not in My Airforce* and *Carnival Boy,* by Matador. Though understanding of Toby's desire to find an outlet for the songs he'd not been able to place on GBV albums proper, Bob was nonetheless annoyed that Matador chose to release the albums on the same day, in the same way, ensuring that in many magazines the two would be reviewed together, and, even worse from Bob's perspective, compared *against* each other—as if it were a competition.

Bob's competitive spirit was thus roused to a degree by the synchronous release, but he felt that Toby held an unfair advantage, in that *Not in My Airforce* was an outlet for Bob's irrepressible experimental side, which had been somewhat held in abeyance on *UTBUTS,* whereas Toby's album was a full-fledged pop record comprised of songs that he had taken pains to write and record but which had not found their way onto Guided by Voices records—the product, in other words, of a talented guy who had the misfortune, and great good luck, of joining a band with the most prolific songwriter in existence. Bob's fears were not unfounded: Many magazines, most prominently *Entertainment Weekly,* did review the albums in tandem, with *EW* giving a slight edge to *Carnival Boy.* Which annoyed Bob, partly for the reasons already stated, and partly because he simply couldn't believe anyone would like Toby's music better than even a tossed-off Bob effort.

"*Not in My Airforce* is all over the place. It's a lot crazier, and more inventive, I think," says Bob. Emerson's dictum about consistency being the hobgoblin of little minds is Bob's aesthetics of rock.

But there was never any serious tension between Bob and Toby on this or any other score, and as always when Bob speaks ill of the living, he's only half-serious. The serious part is a process of venting frustration, a sort of "kick the dog" syndrome that Bob recognizes and has tried, with some success, to conquer. The half part is his deep loyalty and attachment to anyone, like Toby, who has proved his friendship and support over long years. In order to trigger a permanent rupture with Bob, some more serious breach would be required.

Whatever the trauma caused to hard-core Guided by Voices fans—not to mention the band members themselves—by the breakup of the classic lineup, Bob didn't waste any time moving forward. He'd long been a fan of Cleveland-based band Cobra Verde—a reformulation of one of Bob's early indie-rock faves, Death of Samantha—and especially its lead guitarist, Doug Gillard. He was looking, as always, for a bigger, harder-rocking sound for his new material, and believed that by using Cobra Verde as his backing band—bass player Don Depew conveniently had a sixteen-track recording studio up in Cleveland—he could achieve that goal, economically.

"We had already done the Insects of Rock tour and became friends," recalls then–Cobra Verde/Gem guitarist Doug Gillard, "and when they were in the area we'd go see them. They hadn't been in the area for a while. I found out later that the band had sort of dissolved somehow, and that Bob wanted to use Cobra Verde. I had met Bob a while ago just on my own, in 1992. Robert Griffin had the band in town to master *Bee Thousand*. We were at a party, Bob was there, and I found out that Bob liked my playing from Death of Samantha. He knew all about Homestead Records, and had all our DoS records. He even sang a riff or two that I'd played, riffs that he thought were really melodic and cool. I thought, 'Wow, this guy knows his shit.' I got a call that Bob wants Cobra Verde to make a record with him as Guided by Voices. This was around late summer, early fall of 1996, so I was pretty excited. Because I really liked the band.

"We recorded *Mag Earwhig!*" continues Doug. "Bob and Jimmy came up to Cleveland to make the record. It was really fun, a really positive atmosphere."

True enough, for everyone except, apparently, Mitch Mitchell.

"When we broke up the classic quote-unquote lineup," recalls Bob, "and I started playing with Cobra Verde, Mitch was still in the band. Mitch was gonna be playing bass; he played bass on *Mag Earwhig!* on a couple of songs. But I could tell he wasn't interested, he didn't want to be a bass player anymore. I think he thought of it as a demotion.

"There was no big argument or anything, it was just a feeling I got from him. Or lack of feeling. Mitch wouldn't come around, he wouldn't even call to see how things went. I'd go up to Cleveland to finish some things, and he didn't care. I construed that was because he was playing bass. I wanted Mitch to be in the band. He was with me in the first band I ever played in, Anacrusis. I'd played in rock bands with Mitch for twenty years. Even when we were just fucking around in the basement, it was me, Mitch, and Jimmy. We were the brothers. We became The Needmores. I wanted Mitch to stay in the band.

"You have to do it for the team, man. The thing was, Doug and John [Petkovic] were playing guitar; I don't think John even knew how to play bass. Don Depew was just recording us in his studio—he wasn't even gonna be part of the band. But when Mitch and I had our falling-out, Don said, 'Well, I'll take over.'

"I wrote Mitch a letter and said, 'Let's just part ways now.' There were other minor differences, petty stuff, but the basic problem was that he just wasn't into it.

"Later, I thought about getting Mitch back. I told Jimmy, 'Hey, man, I'm thinking about getting Mitch back in the band.' He goes, 'No.' I said, 'Okay.' End of meeting."

As happy as Bob was with the initial Cleveland recordings, he couldn't help but continue to add some different sounds and moods to the record, which resulted in the inclusion of "Learning to Hunt," "The Finest Joke Is Upon Us," and a couple others. Finally he was happy with the sequence, and the album was released by Matador in May 1997. It was greeted lukewarmly by the press, who weren't sure they liked Bob's harder-edged new direction, although sales remained on par with previous GBV releases. In truth, *Mag Earwig!* was not a bad album, but it was possibly the worst one Bob had released since *Sandbox* a decade earlier. The songwriting remained strong, and showed real progress, but the recording struck an uneasy balance between lo- and mid-fi, and there were careless moments—as in the opening phrase of the leadoff single, "Bulldog Skin," where Bob comes in slightly off-key—that seemed uncharacteristic. It was a transition record, clearly, evidence of Bob's desire to stretch, but as such not entirely successful from an artistic standpoint. Undeniably, there were great songs—the aforementioned "Learning to Hunt," "Sad If I Lost It," "Choking Tara," and "Little Lines"—but there was a certain lack of cohesiveness that may simply have been the result of working with an entirely new group of musicians, with which Bob had little experience.

But the release of the album proved only the start of the real trouble.

"That's when John [Petkovic, leader of Cobra Verde] started looking for ways to—'How can we make the most of this for Cobra Verde?'" says Doug. "It didn't happen until we started talking about touring. Robert Griffin, understandably as Cobra Verde's label head, was also looking for ways to promote Cobra Verde as GBV's backing band. As spring rolled around and we started to play, John was talking about, 'How about if we open some shows as Cobra Verde before we play with Guided by Voices?' I was dead set against it, and so were Don [Depew, CV bass player] and Dave [Swanson, CV drummer]. We talked among ourselves and decided that number one, it wouldn't look good, and number two, we'd be exhausted. We knew we'd be playing at least an hour and a half, maybe two hours as Guided by Voices. John was all for it, and he goes, 'How about just some key cities?' He was pretty insistent, and I said, 'Why not, if they're key cities, two or three, here and there; we'll do something in New York, Los Angeles, what's that gonna hurt?'

"At first it seemed like Bob was into the idea, and then he wasn't, somehow. I don't remember clearly if Bob said yes and then rescinded it, or John had told me that Bob was sort of into it. It could have been either way. I also remember when we were practicing for the tour that Bob said we could put all our stuff on the merch table, if we wanted, and then later he said, 'You know how I feel about that, don't you?' and I said, 'What?' He said, 'I don't want anything on there except for Guided by Voices product.'

"That was my first sort of inkling that things weren't going all that well. The touring went on, and after Bob put the kibosh on Cobra Verde opening any shows—I mean, I wouldn't want my backing band coming out before my band came out either. It's a completely understandable position to take. I don't think it's megalomaniacal or anything for Bob to not want that. But John then purposely did not make Guided by Voices a priority. He didn't want to go back on his word about touring, but he just . . . stopped caring. If he had to work some nights when there was a show, I would just carry the guitar duties. There were two times when that happened. We were still keeping our day jobs, and the touring was a little truncated—we'd do a week here and a week there. John did have to go into work some of those nights.

"I also noticed during the touring and onstage . . . it didn't develop until into the summer, maybe the fall, but John would try to steal Bob's thunder all the time, running around onstage, with the guitar on, not playing all that much—just trying to attract attention. I'd be doing a solo and he'd be over there acting like he was the one playing it. He resented Bob for not drawing attention to Cobra Verde, and it started manifesting itself onstage. I remember in Chicago, we were doing 'I Am a Tree,' and it was right before the middle break where the guitar does that riff by itself. And he runs across the stage and he trips, and he's lying on the ground, and he landed on my pedal. Or he disconnected something. So I started to play and there was just silence. And all you heard was the drum fills. John wasn't even aware that I was there, he was lying on the stage looking at Bob, half-smiling, giving him a dirty look.

"He thought Bob tripped him as he was running across the stage—on purpose, that he'd stuck his leg out and tripped him. Anyone knows that Bob's legs are always doing something when he's onstage; he's doing kicks, whatever. He might have a leg out in front of him or behind him. It certainly wasn't on purpose. But John sprained his wrist that night, his right wrist, and he had to go to the hospital. For the rest of the tour he had to play with a gimp wrist. He was all right, he could still play, for as much as he did play. From then on he was really resentful toward Bob."

It should be noted that Petkovic did not reply to a request for an interview. The tensions surrounding the band drove Bob to drink even more than usual, which, combined with Petkovic's antics, resulted in some of the few truly awful Guided by Voices live shows.

"They played a free show at Central Park," recalls writer Michael Azerrad, "and it was probably the biggest show they played, maybe not in size, but in terms of prestige and it being an event. It was with that Cobra Verde lineup and the crowd was just loving it, they were adoring Bob, and the band really seemed like they were catching fire. He was just commanding, but he was also really full of himself, swinging the mic around, pursing his lips, the whole Roger Daltrey-esque thing. He reaches into the cooler and takes out a full unopened beer and heaves it into the crowd. I remember thinking, 'Oh fuck, someone's going to get hurt, someone's going to get killed.' I thought, 'He's hit this hubris level. Classically enough there is going to be tragedy.' Then he reached back for another, but the bass player held his throwing arm back, and Bob got really mad. He broke his arm free and threw another beer can. I thought, 'What are you doing, you could be sued from kingdom come, your career is over.' I think he threw another beer can after that. And no one got hurt! It wasn't an underhand toss into the ground. If he'd hit someone, they would be dead for sure. That's when I started to lose interest in the band. I thought things were getting out of hand."

"The only time when I was worried about GBV," says Nate Farley, "was before I was in the band, at the El Rey, in Los Angeles, with the Cobra Verde lineup. I remember walking upstairs to the dressing room and no one was drinking and I was like, 'Hey, you guys ready to get a beer?' They were like, 'Maybe after the show.' Bob wasn't even around—he was probably having a beer at the bar or something. I just thought, 'This doesn't even seem like the same band.' And the show: it didn't sound like Guided by Voices to me."

Given the tension level and Bob's evident unhappiness, it was at least in retrospect inevitable that the Guided by Verde lineup was not built to last. But the circumstances of its undoing—in other words, the way the word got handed down to the band members—was handled, entirely by accident, in an inappropriate manner.

"It was in September or October, definitely 1997," says Gillard. "At Bimbo's in San Francisco. Bob got pretty wasted, and Bimbo's has a large back room down behind the stage. We were back there after the show. There was a lot more beer going around than usual. Bob used to love talking to the fans after the shows, he still does, but lately he hasn't been doing it as much, he sort of disappears to the hotel room after the shows to save his voice.

"He was talking to some guy in the corner. It was sort of an interview—the guy had a tape recorder. I don't know if Bob remembers the whole thing either; he was pretty lit up. The guy was from *Addicted to Noise*, which Michael Azerrad had something to do with. This particular reporter was very sneaky, and according to Bob, he told him—and Bob thought it was off the record—he said it in a whisper, something like, 'Personally, I think the lineup's gonna change in the next couple months, I'm gonna get rid of these guys.' Something like that; I don't know what he said exactly. So that guy, being an irresponsible journalist, didn't even tell Bob he was gonna print that—goes home and thinks he has a scoop. Well, I guess he did. But it was a shitty way of going about it. Back in 1997, we didn't know the Internet. We didn't know that *Addicted to Noise* was a primarily Internet magazine—that was a new thing back then. Bob didn't know it would appear three days later. He thought it would be coming out in two months or three months. Or even next year.

"We're home from work and John finds out. I don't know if someone told him or he just found it himself on the Internet. That's when all the angry phone calls started flying back and forth. John was looking for ways to sue Bob; he didn't find any ways. There were shows committed to that the band bowed out of, that we canceled, that the band had to pay for. But there was one in Columbus, at the Newport, that we committed to doing, with Superchunk. That was the last show, in November of '97.

"I went down there with my girlfriend. We just happened to be late, because we got a late start. So did those other guys—it might have been raining. I was the first one there. I was told that we were actually sharing our room with Superchunk. So I was in their room, I set my stuff down, and they said, 'Yeah, Bob's got the whole room upstairs.' All his friends and family were up there. Wife, kids, all the Monument guys, other relatives. I think he wanted that support; I think he was bracing for a fight. Truth be told, from what I've heard, I think John, Dave, and Don just wanted to get onstage, play the show, and leave. They didn't want any trouble—but they weren't very happy with what was going on. They didn't think it had been handled very fairly.

"But I did go up and say Hi. For some reason Bob wasn't as mad at me, through all that, as he was at the other guys. But he must have perceived something different that night, just because I was late getting there. I was a little confused, but I wasn't angry. I just wanted to get through the show and see what would happen afterward, not make any rash decisions.

"We're onstage tuning up, right? Bob doesn't have to be onstage yet. The whole audience is there at Newport, watching; I think they were playing some music over the speakers. He first comes up to, I think it was John—I don't recall exactly what he was saying, I think he called him a pussy. He went up to every one of them—Don, and Dave, and each one of those guys. They didn't want it to escalate, they just wanted to play the show, so they didn't say anything back. They say he was trying to start a fight. Which he probably was. And then he comes over to me, and he was kind of angry and pumped up, and he goes, 'Hey, Doug, if you fuck with me onstage tonight, then you're fired.' I said to myself, 'Why did he say that? Why's he angry at me?'"

Bob's version of events differs somewhat in the details. According to him, the members of Cobra Verde froze him out, refused to even hang with him before the show, so that by the time he went onstage it was the first time he'd seen or spoken to any of them all night. So he proceeded to go up to each member, including Doug, and say very simply, "You're a cunt. You want to do something about it?" And no one, by his account, did.

Gillard continues: "I proceeded to fuck with him onstage that night, sonically. I just played leads everywhere, I didn't care how I played. I didn't play sloppy, I just—I wanked all night, on purpose, just to see if it would piss him off. He didn't notice. A lot of our fans, since then, have told me, 'Yeah, I was at that show, I didn't notice anything, I thought it was a good show.' Many people couldn't tell there was tension, and they couldn't tell I was overplaying. And truth be told, back in '97, that whole tour I was overplaying. After that year, I started to be a lot truer to the older songs. On purpose—it was self-imposed restraint. I was like, 'What am I doing—this is Guided by Voices, I can't play like that anymore.' Bob didn't care, he liked when I played leads, or embellished, like when we made 'Hot Freaks' more of a heavy metal song.

"Even before breaking up the Cobra Verde lineup, he gave me mixed signals. I think he wanted to not have especially John and Don in the band anymore. And he wanted to keep me. I think that's how he felt at the time. I kind of got that vibe at the time."

"He's probably right about that," agrees Bob.

"He recognized that I was excited about the new demos that he gave us, which ended up, after a lot of permutations, as *Do the Collapse*. There was a batch of demos, and none of the other guys had spent any time with it, or commented on it; I think they were just kind of . . . I don't know. I don't think those guys wanted to stay in the band. Don was leaving anyway—he was leaving both Guided by Voices and Cobra Verde—because his wife was having a baby. We even got Matt Sweeney to play with us in Europe and some other dates because Don was with his wife. Dave and I were going to quit Cobra Verde no matter what. Not Guided by Voices, but Cobra Verde. I thought John was being a bit ridiculous that year and we just didn't want to put up with that crap anymore.

"In the end," he continues, "the personalities didn't mesh. Instead of guys that came up with him in Dayton, this time Bob got a band with more seasoned guys that had been in bands for years. With a little bit of a chip on their collective shoulders. I'm not saying that's a bad thing, it's just—that was the mixture."

Once again, Bob didn't waste any time dwelling over miscues, and quickly moved on. He released his second solo album, *Waved Out*, on Matador in June 1998. Significantly, he recruited ex-Breeder Jim Macpherson for drum duties on a number of the songs, and soon thereafter he asked Jim to join the band permanently.

"I think Bob wanted Doug Gillard to see me play," recalls Jim Macpherson, "so he had Real Lulu, the local Dayton band I played for on and off, open up for Guided by Voices in Indianapolis. I think that was my audition. Then he asked me to play on *Waved Out*, which was a lot of fun, and then when he asked me to join full-time . . . let's see, I'd just gotten out of that mental ward band [The Breeders/Amps, during a period when Kim was rumored to be having substance abuse problems], but I was a big fan. I'd seen them when we played Lollapalooza together, and I'd gotten to know Bob, and I liked him a lot and I liked his music a lot. So it wasn't a difficult decision, really. GBV didn't tour for a year like The Breeders had done, so I wouldn't be away from my family all that much."

"I think it was after January, or even late December," says Doug, "I got a phone call from Bob. He was real polite and sort of formal about it.

He said, 'Well, I called to invite you, if you would like, to stay with me in Guided by Voices, and work on this new record,' or words to that effect. I think he even gave me time to think about it, but that is what I wanted to do.

"Bob had mentioned this time he wanted to work with bigger producers—I think he'd been talking with his management about that—and Ric Ocasek's name was brought up. I said, 'Yeah!' I mean, when I was a kid I had a wall in my bedroom that was kind of dedicated to The Cars, sort of a Cars shrine. That wasn't what made me want to stay, but it was a factor."

With both Macpherson and Gillard on board, Bob set about writing and recording demos for the next record. As Gillard says, Bob was exploring the notion of taking the band into a big studio—a real big studio—and hiring a producer—a real producer—to make the next record.

The Matador people were supportive, to a point. Reports from the last tour had them worried—that Bob was drinking more than ever, that he was out of control, that some of the shows had been disastrous as a direct result of said drinking—and before deciding to bankroll a big-time move like the one Bob proposed, they wanted to make sure that he was, well, good to go. So they called a meeting at their offices in New York. The topic of discussion was alcohol.

"The thing with Matador," says Bob, "I think that came from John Petkovic telling on me to Gerard [Cosloy]. Because my drinking—'How's my drinking?'—my drinking was pretty good on that tour. I conked him in the neck with the mic one time. Not intentionally, but his goofy ass was out front acting like he's playing lead. But that's speculation on my part, I don't have any proof.

"It pissed me off a little bit at the time 'cause I felt like I was being ganged up on. What they don't understand is the drinking, that's part of the appeal. That's why people like to come and see our shows. And it did get better in recent years, where we learned how to gauge our drinking. And the shows were just about consistently always good. . . . At one point they weren't, but still it was fascinating for people to see. 'Who are they gonna see here, what's gonna happen?' That element of unpredictability.

"Without having a really fucked-up gig, how do you measure what's a really great show? If you didn't go too far, then it would just be an act. You would be professionals. We're certainly not choreographing what we do. We never claimed to be professionals. We play until we fall down—

whether it takes alcohol to do it, or whether it's from fatigue. But we play for three fucking hours, and you get your money's worth, and so does the club. Instead of the band playing for an hour and they sell beer for an hour, they get to sell beer for three hours. And not only do they get to sell beer for three hours, they get to do it with us up there being role models, showing 'em how to do it, and making 'em thirsty. You watch Guided by Voices, you gotta have beer, man. If you come to a Guided by Voices show and you've never gotten drunk before, you will."

"I honestly don't remember that meeting," says Cosloy, Matador's co-owner. "It's a thin line, because on the one hand I don't like to be preachy. I don't think it's fair to apply my own standards to that stuff, because I've had my own problems that I haven't handled too well. And I didn't have someone like an employer or manager telling me, 'You gotta clean up.' It's hypocritical for me to wag a finger and tell Bob how to live his life. At the same time, I'd like to see him live a long time. I'd like to see him put on a show that people can really enjoy. My feeling about a lot of gigs is that they are usually really, really good, but there have been times over the last six or seven years that have suffered because of heavy drinking—not all the time, but on occasion they've veered toward self-parody.

"I'm not the only one who feels that way. There are people who buy the records, people who are not getting paid for exploiting him and putting him on the road, who love those songs and love him to death, that cringe when they see him getting overly drunk. By the same token, you have the people who are just getting a vicarious charge out of 'Hey, look at this guy getting fucking wasted.' It's like he's doing it so they don't have to. He's living the rock and roll dream/nightmare, and they're going to work tomorrow."

Whatever damage was done to Bob's relationship with Matador by the warning about his drinking, it did not affect his plans to go forward with the Big Studio Album. Ric Ocasek agreed to produce the album for free, which helped hold down the recording costs, and after a period of writing and recording demos and writing and recording more demos until Ric felt confident he had the right songs and had worked enough with the band on arrangements, Guided by Voices—including, once again, Greg Demos on bass—made the trip to Electric Ladyland in New York to start recording.

"Ric was great," remembers Jim Macpherson. "Bob asked me to go up with Pete Jamison, go over to Ric Ocasek's house; he played us Weezer, which he had produced and sounded great.

"We did a pre-pro [preproduction rehearsal] and he did give great advice on songs like 'Liquid Indian.' 'Wrecking Now,' too—I have to admit that was Ric Ocasek coming up with the feel. I thought his stuff was great. I had a real good natural drum sound in the studio. I did all my basics in four or five days, then I left; we had to watch the money. Which is one of the things I always admired about Bob—he was always real conscious of that stuff. Sometimes maybe to the extreme."

"For the song 'Wrecking Now,' Ric brought out his whole guitar arsenal for us to use," says Doug Gillard. "These Travis Bean guitars that Elliot Easton gave him as a present, these fancy, weird-shaped things where the dots would light up on the fretboard. On that song, it was a B.C. Rich Warlock–shaped thing that was a ten-string, where the low A and E didn't have the companion strings but all the others did. But it was designed to be electric; it had all these switches on it. I think I played with a capo. It's just an inherently beautiful song."

One of the problems for Bob and some of the other members of the band was that, because Ocasek had produced Weezer, they expected that he would make them sound like Weezer, without understanding that by major league standards the $90,000 allocated for recording and mixing *Do the Collapse* was not near enough to allow the time necessary to manufacture something as powerful-sounding as they would have liked. In addition, that had never been Ocasek's intent.

"It does suffer from the production," opines Gillard. "The whole time doing that record, I had problems with the way Ric was approaching the production. Especially mix-down time. We were locked out of the studio the whole day, and Ric would say, 'Come back around six, we'll probably have a mix for you.' So he and his engineer would work all day. We weren't allowed to see it through. One time Bob and I went to a Mets game and came back. It was just me. Bob was rolling with everything that was happening. He was just kind of 'Ric's the producer, let him produce. I'm kind of excited to see what he'll come up with.' And I'd be saying, 'Man, what about that reverb? There's too much.' And he'd say, 'No.' Or 'What about the drum sound, it's so wimpy. It sounds like he's tapping the snare, but you were there when we did the basic tracks—he was

Meet the Pollards: clockwise from left, Debbie, Bob Jr., Lisa, Judy, Jimmy, 1964. Courtesy Robert Pollard.

Up on the roof, 1991. Courtesy Robert Pollard

Early band photo. Peyton Eric, Toby, Bob, and Mitch, 1984. Photo by Todd Robinson. Courtesy Robert Pollard.

One of these people is not in the band. The Needmores, 1985. From left: Bob, Mitch, Jimmy, Father Time, Kevin. Photo by Todd Robinson. Courtesy Robert Pollard.

Insects of Rock tour, April 1994. Courtesy Matt Davis.

Sweaty Bob, 1997. Courtesy Robert Pollard.

Jimmy Pollard, rock star, 1994. Courtesy Robert Pollard.

Cut-Out Truck, 1999. Photo by Matt Davis. Courtesy Robert Pollard.

Happy band, circa 1995. Courtesy Robert Pollard.

Bob at Electric Ladyland, sadly sober. Courtesy Doug Gillard.

Jimmy, Greg Demos, Ric Ocasek, Bob, Doug Gillard backstage at Tramps in NYC. 1998. Photo by Caroline Zobeck. Courtesy Doug Gillard.

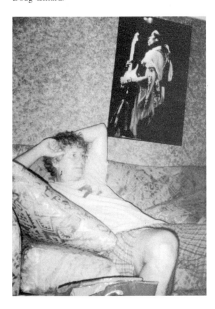

Four man band: Jim Macpherson, Bob, Doug Gillard, Greg Demos, 2001. Courtesy Robert Pollard.

Nate Farley and Kevin March during Earthquake Glue session, December 2002. Photo by Matt Davis.

Jimmy Mac on drums, circa 2001. Courtesy Robert Pollard.

Bob on guitar during Earthquake Glue session, December 2002. Photo by Matt Davis.

Seventy-four bottles of beer on the bill. First half of wing committee's tab, Boxing Day, 2004. Courtesy the author.

Last set list ever, in Bob's own handwriting, Dec. 31, 2004, Chicago. Courtesy Jimmy Pollard.

GBV in Rome, 2003: Doug Gillard, Kevin March, Bob, Nate Farley, Sam Powers. Photo by Ana Luisa Morales. Courtesy Doug Gillard.

```
      BW-3/BUFFALO WILD WINGS
        HUBER HEIGHTS,OH
           (937) 237-7771

GCK# 22                    IN
           BAR/CTR      SRVR 20
 74 LITE BTL      185.00
    ONE SHOT
  5 CUERVO         20.00
    ONE SHOT
    CR ROYAL        4.50
    ONE SHOT
  5 CUERVO         20.00
    ONE SHOT
    CR ROYAL        4.50

    MOZZ   STICKS    4.29
    ONE SHOT
  6 CUERVO         24.00
    ONE SHOT
    CR ROYAL        4.50
    ONE SHOT
  2 CUERVO          8.00
    --------------------------
       TAX         .33
     TOTL      275.12
==================================
 CSHR BAR 2
 0181 16:30 #04 DEC.26'04  REG0004
```

Doug Gillard in full New Year's regalia, last show, Chicago, Dec. 31, 2004. Courtesy Percy Kew.

Bob high-fives his own foot, crowd stunned, Irving Plaza, NYC, 1996. Courtesy Robert Pollard.

Invisible Train to Earth, an original collage by Robert Pollard. Courtesy the author.

He's the uncle: Mitch Mitchell tries to ignore Bob's feet, Urban Art Bar, Houston, TX, 1994. Courtesy Robert Pollard.

Takes a lot of guts to hang with GBV. Jimmy's gut with Rockathon sign at Monument Club, 1999. Photo courtesy Matt Davis.

Converse. Photo-realistic painting by Tobin Sprout. Courtesy Tobin Sprout.

From left: Charlie Balderson, Billy Dixon, and Mark Gibbs at the Public Hi-Fi Balloon, 1999. Courtesy Robert Pollard.

Rallying the troops, from left, standing: Mark Kinsella, Mike Lipps, Bob, Doug Gillard. Front row, from left: Ed Kinsella, Jimmy, Mike Camer, 2000. Photo by Matt Davis. Courtesy Robert Pollard.

Crazy Kevin face (with hair), circa 1995. Courtesy Robert Pollard.

Check local listings: promo for *Austin City Limits.* November 9, 2004. Courtesy Robert Pollard.

Simon and Garfunkel at Cro-Mag. Courtesy Robert Pollard.

Last band practice, Historic Oregon District. Dec. 28, 2004. Courtesy the author.

Bob hearts Billy Dixon at Marion's Piazza, Dec. 27, 2004. Courtesy the author.

Father and son backstage, last show, Chicago, Dec. 31, 2004. Courtesy the author.

Bob and Jimmy, Monument Club, September 1999. Photo by Matt Davis.

The classic lineup: back row from left: Dean Crabtree, Mark Dempsey, Jim Hamby, some guy. Front row: Jimmy and Bob, 1995. Courtesy Robert Pollard.

First NYC show ever, July 20, 1993.

attendance required:

new bomb turks
gorilla
zipgun
prisonshake
guided by voices
gaunt
soul vandals

cbgb in beautiful nyc
tues jul 20 8:30
presented by scat,
thrill jockey,
empty, and crypt

Passing on wisdom to the children of Titus, circa 1999. Courtesy Robert Pollard.

pounding the thing.' And Bob goes, 'I kind of like it.' In the end I didn't care what Ric or his engineer thought of me, I wanted the record to sound like something I'd be completely proud of. I was kind of expecting something more.

"I would layer about six rhythm guitar parts on a song like 'Teenage FBI,' and I'd be like, 'Another one?' and Ric would say, 'Yeah, give it a different color.' 'But it's the same chord pattern.' 'Yeah, it'll be a pad. A pad of guitars.' And I'm like, 'Oh. All right.'

"We came back from the vacation between recording and mixing and it'd be like, 'What's that keyboard there?' Ric would go, 'Oh, I added a keyboard there. And I threw in a rhythm guitar there on Mr. Buckles.'

"But in the end, it's a pretty good record," concludes Gillard.

"It was a small budget," confirms Ocasek. "I knew that Bob liked to do things fast, and I thought that was part of the charm of all the Guided by Voices records . . . you know, letting what's there be *it*, trying to do it with that in mind, but also trying to get it a little bit more concise, recording-wise. I'd say to Bob I didn't want it to be too slick, and he'd go, 'No, this one's going to be like my first real record.' I was trying to push the other way, I was trying to get it to be like a slick demo or something."

"We tried to maintain what we're about," says Bob. "To make a big record but not to sacrifice the Guided by Voices idiosyncrasies. When you work with a producer it's kind of their baby, it's like they're the director of a movie."

"I imagine it would make him uncomfortable handing the reins over to a producer," says Ocasek. "I definitely understand that—maybe because I've made my own records, or whatever; and at the beginning I was probably as concerned with every little thing, too. But you know, we had a really good time, and there was absolutely zero tension. He was extremely cooperative. I was probably thinking, 'I can't say no to him.' I was probably intimidated by his art, you know. It seemed to me he was a seasoned veteran, it really did. When he got behind the mic, he was perfect, he was confident, he just did it right.

"He's a phenomenal singer. His performances are I'd say always consistently good. It wouldn't be a matter of 'Oh, is that line better than this one?' He might have done two vocals for each song. And he sang really well. Also, I didn't want to get into that kind of real record-making thing where I would do six tracks of vocals."

The only really controversial aspect of the session itself was Ocasek's no-alcohol policy, which as you can imagine did not sit well with Bob—though to his credit he agreed to abide by it. But not being able to drink made the actual, physical task of recording less fun for Bob, and that, coupled with some later record company struggles over the song "Hold on Hope" and the fact that many longtime fans of the band considered *Do the Collapse* a sellout, colored his perspective for many years. In the fullness of time, however, it has become one of the best-received Guided by Voices records ever made.

"Bob did not really drink while he was recording," says Ocasek. "That was a thing I just naively said, because I didn't really know much about that aspect of him. It was just one of my general policies when I go in the studio, you know. With alcohol it just takes a lot longer, and . . . it just kind of takes you out of the realm of it. Maybe that was a little bit difficult for him, but it didn't seem like it was. I just thought we had a really good . . . We changed a couple little things here and there, arrangement-wise and stuff. We might have made a couple songs a little longer. But it was done pretty quickly, without any fanfare. I have to say it was really a pretty smooth experience. I loved his lyrics. Told him he should write a book. He sent me one recently, called *Eat*, which I thought was phenomenal.

"I didn't think it was a sellout. I thought it had a good quality of a demo-y kind of thing, for a slick record. Maybe it seemed overproduced to some people just because for the first time the music was recorded properly. That made it sound better than usual. But it's not like we did ten takes to get the right take, any of that stuff. It was pretty much on the fly.

"I do think it was a good document of Bob's ability to do a great pop record—a nice twisted pop record. Not blatantly commercial, or any attempt to be—but just hearing the songs recorded in a proper way, and consistently, made it sound like a more finished record. But I was definitely trying to stay away from it being too slick or anything. I love the songs. And I still think it's pretty stellar when it comes to that. But his songs are always stellar.

"I knew going in that it might be difficult for fans of his home tapes—that's what I was a fan of, too. Obviously for someone to take a chance and just throw stuff out as it is, is a great artistic statement. I was hoping that I wouldn't lose that. But I think *Do the Collapse* holds up really well, and I think in the long run it will hold up, as a record in his repertoire. People change over time anyway. [The older fans] might accept it years later when they're not so finicky about issues of fidelity."

"For me it wasn't really until the Ric Ocasek record that you started hearing that Bob's songwriting wasn't musical shorthand anymore," says R.E.M.'s Peter Buck. "I think that the big production on that record allowed people to hear where Bob was coming from in a more specific way. Which is probably why a lot of people who didn't know the band all that well understood that record better. It wasn't all minute-and-a-half songs, you know; there were some four-minute songs on there."

"There's a cycle that happens with our fans, or nonfans," says Gillard, "people that're familiar with the band. I'm going from what I'll hear, the scuttlebutt I'll hear on the Postal Blowfish lists. Sometimes it takes five years for people to warm up to an album that was absolutely hated at the time. That happened with *Mag Earwhig!* and I think it's starting to happen with *Do the Collapse.*"

Having completed the record, Bob had every intention of putting it out with Matador, but Matador, which at the time was in the waning months of a P&D deal with Capitol Records, was not fully confident that the results would be worth the expense.

"I really felt management—not so much Bob, but management, people whom I did not have a lot of respect for, Janet Billig and the guy who came after, Aaron Blitzstein—was breathing down our necks to sell more records," says Gerard Cosloy. "And then they began making *Do the Collapse* and they wanted to make the record with Ric Ocasek, and they wanted to do it a different way, and make a more professional, commercial record. We encouraged them to do it. We fronted the money to make the record. When the record was finally finished, with the exception of 'Hold on Hope,' I thought it was a great album. I personally thought 'Hold on Hope' was embarrassing. But I think there were some people in management in particular who thought it represented a potential crossover for the band. And I thought,

'Cross over to who?' The era of the power ballad had passed, and I just don't think that 'Hold on Hope' was a great calling card for the band."

"You know, there *was* something funny about that one, looking back," says Ocasek. "I agree with him on that. There was something about 'Hold on Hope.' It was such a simple song, and it should have been, like, John Lennon or something. But because it was so simple, and so kind of accessible, it ended up being a track that we overworked, in retrospect. Maybe it was one of the magic songs that didn't get recorded as magically as it should have been. It didn't come out as kind of demo-y as it should have. Bob's demo was better. The studio version was too done-up; I still think that to this day. That was the only one that was a little, just, weird."

"So the record was done," continues Cosloy, "and management was like, 'We need to get the record on the radio,' and you know, at the time, Matador—our deal with Capitol ended shortly after that particular period. But we brought Bob out to L.A., where we had a couple of meetings with Capitol, but our feeling was, they were not going to be into the record. Although they were paying lip service to the notion that Bob's a genius, Guided by Voices is a great band—they'd already been through a number of financial disappointments with other Matador bands like Pavement, the Blues Explosion, and they were on their way to some not-so-great numbers with Liz Phair, and I think our feeling was that *Do the Collapse* was not going to be a priority record for them with radio.

"We wanted keenly to put the record out independently, but management was telling us that the record had to come out through a major because there was a clause in the publishing deal with MCA that the publishing advance for the record would go up exponentially if it were to go through major distribution. And we respected that, but we knew if we put the record out through EMI, then we would lose money; the bare-minimum marketing costs associated with doing a record through EMI were prohibitive. We had talked with management about what type of campaign they were looking for to work a commercial record on the radio. We were looking at a minimum of a quarter of a million dollars for any promo. Between that and all the other associated costs, we would have to sell in the two-to-two-hundred-fifty-thousand range just to break even—not to break even for the band, to break even for us. As much as we loved that record, and thought that it did represent a big leap forward for them, we were not confident that we could sell that many records."

Once it became clear that Matador was not going to take *Do the Collapse* through its major label route, Bob began the process of looking for someone who would. "That thing fell through with Capitol or we would have probably stayed on Matador," says Bob.

Not surprisingly, there weren't a whole lot of major label suitors willing to take a flier on an aging indie-rock band, even one that had taken a giant step in terms of sonic accessibility. But there was some interest, and some of that interest was keen. In particular, a New York–based label called TVT, which had started by selling compilations of television theme songs and had since diversified into rock, hip-hop, and whatever you want to call bands like Nine Inch Nails, pursued Guided by Voices with a fervor bordering on mania. Its A&R man, Adam Shore, was a longtime fan, and thought with *Do the Collapse* and the resources of TVT he had the tools necessary to break the band into the mainstream. He visited Dayton, always a risky proposition, but necessary for any true acolyte, which resulted in a trip to the fabled Pine Club, which resulted in Bob and some of his Monument Club friends being banned for life from the Pine Club.

"That was embarrassing, man," says Bob. "Some of my friends were just being drunk and loud and shit. I thought, 'This guy from TVT is gonna think we're trouble. He's not gonna want to sign us.'"

Not only did Shore persuade the head of TVT, Steve Gottlieb, to sign the band, but eventually the lifetime ban from the Pine Club was lifted (though not before "Goddamn the Pine Club!" was added to the liner notes of *Do the Collapse,* retracting *Alien Lanes*'s encomium "God Bless the Pine Club"). So pretty much everything worked out great for everyone.

Except Matador, of course. Losing GBV to TVT was a hard blow. "There was the kind of feeling—much the same way that they were able to forget about Robert Griffin so easily, they could forget about us just as easily," says Gerard Cosloy. "In some ways that was our karmic payback. I do understand when somebody comes along and says, 'We can sell your records and take you to the next level.' So that was our payback, but the thing was, and I'll be frank, the thing that was frustrating for me is that it wasn't a cheap deal when we signed Guided by Voices originally. It was like the biggest deal we'd done, and I always felt a tremendous pressure from the band's management to sell records and make the band commercially successful. But at the same time, the band is continuing to put out records outside the Matador deal—as many as they want. The sheer glut of the product made it difficult, and still makes it difficult. . . . I don't really think it makes it difficult for the fans—I give the fans a lot of credit. Guided by Voices fans are extremely loyal and inquisitive. But just for the guy running a record shop, it was impossible. It automatically put a ceiling on how high the band could go commercially."

As for Bob, he quickly realized that the drawbacks in dealing with even a semimajor label like TVT could outweigh the benefits. The first real contretemps was over "Hold on Hope," which the label seized on as a potential radio hit. The problem with radio hits is that they have to sound a certain homogeneous way or else radio won't play your jams. And so an album cut has to be remixed by scientists in lab coats who specialize in extracting the faintest hint of personality from a potential hit song. The process was repeated with varying degrees of success by a series of remixers, but each time a horrified Bob would veto in the strongest possible way the results of the remix. Shore even flew over to Europe while the band was on tour, latest remix in hand, to try to sway Bob's opinion, but to no avail.

"I told him, 'You can't do that, because it's gonna screw up my career,'" says Bob.

Eventually a compromise was reached: "We finally agreed to send radio stations an EP with four mixes, including the original album version, with the rejected remix as the fourth track, giving the station the option as to which one they wanted to play."

"If you take 'Hold on Hope' off *Do the Collapse* that's probably my favorite [Guided by Voices] record," maintains Cosloy. "And we didn't even put it out."

"I didn't know that Gerard liked that album, man," responds Bob. "That's funny. I was really embarrassed by 'Hold on Hope.' Just all the hoopla over that song kind of left a bad taste in my mouth about the album in general. But I listened to *Do the Collapse* not too long ago and I thought it sounded fucking great. I think it's a good record; I think it's a weird record, even. I have fond memories of the entire experience, especially working with Ric."

* * *

Do the Collapse sold somewhat better than previous GBV releases, but Pollard's gold record dreams were still well out of reach, despite a major promotional push and an extensive bout of touring. The cost of the promotional push meant that despite the minor bump in sales, the band stood no chance of "recouping," meaning GBV would be in debt no matter how many records it sold. The way this works is: everything the company spends to manufacture and promote an album, from studio costs to packaging and poster costs to radio promotion to remixing a song for radio to making a video to tour support, on down to buying dinner, gets counted against sales, so that it often happens that a band doesn't "recoup" even if it goes gold, because the record company has posted so much money against the band's account that the band is still technically in debt, and the record company doesn't have to pay royalties until the record has recouped its costs. To be fair, taking a band from one level to the next, as Gerard Cosloy explained earlier, is a costly process. Which is why, once a band understands the economics of recouping, the phrase "nonrecoupable expense" becomes one of the sweetest in its vocabulary. Not to mention the fact that management takes 15 percent of a band's gross income, meaning, for instance, that if a band gets an advance to make a record, management gets paid 15 percent of that advance whether the band makes money or not.

Very few major label bands recoup, ever, which is one way the big record companies have managed to stay in business despite the general slump in sales (often blamed on piracy and illegal downloading, which, while certainly a factor, have much less to do with the problem than the industry-wide insistence on putting out really terrible music from bands that maybe have the right look and can be chummed to the sea of fans for one or two big hits, then cut loose). In fact, the tiny minority of acts that, mirabile dictu, consistently sell millions of records subsidize their lesser-selling colleagues.

Bob's ambivalence toward the idea of success did not help Guided by Voices' chances of breaking into that tiny minority. While fully capable of writing a hit song, the artist in him bucked against the idea—lyrically, he could only serve his muse, and even a blatant attempt like "Hold on Hope," with the exception of the chorus, could not help but befuddle mainstream listeners, who by and large respond to songs that respond to them.

Lyrics like "Animal mother / she opens up for free," and "At the station / there hides the cowboy / his campfire flickering / on the landscape" are not the sort of easily digestible pap likely to connect with fans of anyone except, well, Guided by Voices—not to mention that the song, while espousing a universal message, is suffused with typical Pollard melancholy, referencing "this life of misery," and centered on a chorus which explains that hope is "the last thing that's holding me." It sounds more like the grasping effort of a near-suicide to come to grips with his "mute frustration" than an uplifting song of triumph over the slings and arrows of outrageous fortune.

There has always existed in Bob a dichotomy between the committed eccentric, happy to share his self-expression with a small but steady group of supporters, and the would-be rock star who grew up worshiping Pete Townshend and whose ego could not be contained within the world of indie rock—a world he felt uncomfortable inhabiting, and came to despise. Because he had trouble reconciling these two sides of his personality—a restless experimental side, unsatisfied with simple song structures and easy melodies, and an uncontrollable tendency to write poetry rather than lyrics, poetry with a very often indecipherable meaning, or rewritten to obscure the literal meaning, because Bob has a metaphorical hatred of the literal—one might argue that Guided by Voices was able to progress without destroying its essential qualities.

In the end, though, Bob was simply unwilling—even constitutionally unable—to jump though some of the hoops necessary to achieve success on the level he thought he deserved. He despised doing radio promotion; he hated playing acoustic sets; and doing in-store record signings was simply a *Spinal Tap*-esque embarrassment. For him, the rock show was promotion enough, and the one thing Bob was willing to do more of, because by now he was beginning to enjoy touring a lot more than he had in earlier years. He had a band he liked, both musically and on a personal level; and though record sales might not have increased as much as he would have appreciated, Guided by Voices' reputation as an exceptional live act had created a substantial following in most cities across the country, and many in Europe as well.

The one problem with the current lineup was that it was only a fourpiece—Bob, Doug Gillard, Greg Demos, and Jim Macpherson. And while Doug was certainly capable of carrying double duty on guitar, the songs from *Do the Collapse,* Bob felt, needed the added heft another guitarist would bring to do them justice. To solve the problem, he turned to an obvious choice—someone who'd been there before and proved himself under the most trying conditions.

"After The Amps/Breeders debacle," recalls Nate Farley, "I decided to come home. *The New Yorker* said I was severely depressed. Their fact-checker called me, 'cause I did an interview with them about The Amps and The Breeders and working with Kim [Deal]. In the interview I said I just got bummed out 'cause nothing was happening, so I just went home.

"So the fact-checker calls me later on, she goes, 'Okay, let me get this straight, you were severely depressed, blah blah blah.' I go, 'Wait. I never said I was severely depressed. I might have said I was bummed out.' And she goes, '*The New Yorker* doesn't write *bummed out.*' And I'm like, 'All right, whatever.' At that point I was feeling like, 'You know what, I think I'm done playing music for a while, maybe forever.'

"I started waiting tables. That was the first real job I'd had in a long time. I was a server in a café at the Dayton Art Institute. I found this girl Heather who had an incredible voice but knew nothing about punk rock, so I made a tape that had X, X-Ray Spex, The Avengers—pretty much everything you need to know about girls singing in punk rock. I started a band called The Indicators with Mitch [Mitchell], where I played bass, and Mitch played guitar, and Craig-o played drums, and Heather sang. We were a super-local band, played a few shows around town. That turned into the band Robthebank. That was my old bass player C.J. on bass, and I went back to playing guitar, and Heather.

"A little while later I was at Canal Street at a show, and Jimmy came up to me, and he was like, 'You might be getting a tap pretty soon.' I had already been to see GBV where it was just Demos and Jimmy Mac and Doug and Bob in Cincinnati.

"I knew they needed another rhythm guitar, and I think they knew that too. I forget how it happened, I think Bobby just called me up and asked me if I wanted to do it, and I was like, 'Hell yes!' I went over to the Monument Club, and he gave me a cassette [of *Do the Collapse*], and a list of old songs to learn, so I would sit there with the cassette and just play along with the cassette. A week goes by, and Bobby calls me up and says, "I'm gonna come over there, and me and you will go through the songs." Bob's a morning guy, and I'm a noon guy, and he comes over at like nine A.M., and he was surprised that I didn't have coffee made. We sat there and went through the songs for about two weeks, just me and him playing guitar.

"Bob—I tell people all the time, and I'll never quit saying it—he's an incredible guitar player. He downplays it sometimes, how good he is, with his timing and his feel. He's not gonna smoke an Eddie Van Halen lead, but he has incredible feel."

With Nate on board, GBV embarked on an ambitious and extended touring schedule, during the course of which, as often happens during ambitious and extended tours, two or three of the band members experienced serious relationship problems. The most serious of these—for the purposes of this book, not to slight anyone else's troubles—resulted in the dissolution of Bob's marriage to his wife Kim, after twenty-two years.

The first sign that changes were brewing was when Bob bought a black Mustang and drove it around on tour; as incredible as it might seem for a guy who obviously had never settled down, at least in the conventional sense, it soon became clear that Bob was going through a fairly typical midlife crisis, at age forty-four. His kids were out of high school, or close to it, he was away from home most of the time, and almost as if a switch had been thrown, he shed his previously steadfast, road-tested fidelity to Kim like snakeskin, which is perhaps an unfortunate simile, but we'll leave it.

Because the details of Bob's fall will be treated in a later chapter, we will pass over them for now, and mention only that the period before and during the recording of the band's second album for TVT, *Isolation Drills*, was a very difficult one for Bob. Though many claim they can detect in the music and lyrics of *Isolation Drills* the effect of Bob's personal turmoil, and even though he admitted at the time that some of the songs on the album reflected his situation, it would be a disservice to a great record to say that the content was mostly autobiographical. That's simply not the way Bob writes—and it would be difficult to point to songs like "Glad Girls," "Run Wild," "Chasing Heather Crazy" and draw any kind of personal inferences, unless you were hell-bound on doing so, in which case you would simply end up both wrong and in hell.

Once again Bob opted to work with a producer, this time Rob Schnapf, an easygoing guy who'd worked with Beck and the Foo Fighters and Elliott Smith and a bunch of other mediocre artists. Schnapf promised to deliver the bigger sound Bob had failed to achieve on *Do the Collapse*. Perhaps more important, he had no policy against drinking in the studio.

"I really didn't discover how Bob likes to work until after the first three records, including *Mag Earwhig!*" recalls Doug Gillard, "because on *Isolation Drills* that was Rob Schnapf producing. So it was another producer situation; although it was a little more conducive to creativity, and a little more spontaneous, it was still Rob producing. And I think after that, Bob discovered that he'd rather not work with a known producer. Even though Rob's a great guy—he didn't order us around, he just made suggestions. But he was still a producer."

"*Isolation Drills* was the best experience in a studio I've ever had," says Jim Macpherson, who was tickled red by the drum sounds Schnapf coaxed from him. "I'd told Bob before we started that I was quitting the band, so I was mostly just trying to do a good job, because I think he was mad at me."

Once again, Bob had lost another key player to the siren call of family and security. "For me it was a matter of just being away too much. I was just wanting to be at home, quite honestly. My daughter Caitlyn was ten, and I felt like I'd missed so much of her growing up, both from The Breeders and Guided by Voices. My son JJ was born and I had to go straight off to Lollapalooza. . . . I wanted to be more a part of their lives."

The loss of Macpherson, coupled with Bob's unsuccessful efforts to keep Greg Demos in the band, initiated a revolving door of bass players and drummers over the course of the last three Guided by Voices albums, but by that point the band had become established to the point where Bob never had any trouble finding good musicians to fill spots at a moment's notice. The myth that Bob's some kind of hard-ass taskmaster who can't keep a band together is just that—myth. He's rarely had to fire anyone, and most have left of their own accord for, as noted, reasons of financial security and family that had nothing to do with Bob's personality or management style.

But at the same time, his refusal to suck up to the industry may have prevented his rise to a level that might have provided financial security for band members who instead decided to leave. It's a two-edged thingy, a whatchamacallit with a double blade.

"During *Isolation Drills,* we went up to [TVT label head] Steve Gottlieb's office," recalls Bob. "He swung out from under his desk and I swear he had a hard-on. I'm not kidding. He says, 'So is this album gonna sell a million copies?' And we're like, 'Uh, yeah! We appreciate your enthusiasm, Steve.'

"It's not long after that I decided we didn't really want to be on TVT anymore. Gottlieb kept saying, 'I know you got a hit! You guys are holding out on me! Give me the hits!'

"Our A&R guy, Adam Shore, is a nice guy with a true passion for music. He signed us and Brian Jonestown Massacre. He started his own label and I believe his heart is in the right place as far as trying to discover and bring to people the best contemporary music.

"But it wasn't enough for us to stay. It just didn't feel right. We had a two-album contract and we decided to leave. There were people going around saying we'd been dropped. Bullshit!

"You don't drop Guided by Voices."

BRYAN POLLARD—#3 IN A SERIES OF THREE VIGNETTES

"No, no, no. Like the thing is . . . David Bowie and my economics professor chose the Arcade Fire's *Funeral* for the best album of 2004 and I have a suspicion that next year everyone will agree that the new Bright Eyes album is the best. It's so . . . so . . . so . . . sad and brilliant. What do you think?" the dark-haired guy beside me asked, twirling a greasy lock of hair.

"I'm sorry. Could you repeat the question?"

"What do you think?"

"Not that part . . . I meant repeat the statement that came before. I really wasn't paying any attention. The last thing I heard was something about Stephen Malkmus living in Portland and how you have made it your life's goal to track him down. So I was kind of wondering . . . what would you say if you found him? How could you overcome a clear case of an awkward fan/celebrity encounter?" I said, trying my best to avoid answering his question.

"I mean, dude, the guy like created an album as great as *Crooked Rain, Crooked Rain,*" the darker-haired guy across from me said, batting his eyes confusedly.

I exhaled, ordered a Scotch and water, and resumed watching the Division I-AA college basketball game on the television above me. It's the only sporting event on television at 2 A.M. in the West. The two guys glanced at one another, adjusted their crooked, Buddy Holly glasses, and ordered another IPA.

"So . . . it's Bryan, right?" the dark-haired one began. I nodded as I bit into an unsalted peanut.

"So, Bryan, what do you think of the Arcade Fire; you know they have just agreed to play this summer in the Gorge with the Pixies,

Modest Mouse, and Wilco. . . . What's that outdoor concert called? They have it every year," he said, snapping his fingers at the darker-haired guy.

"Sasquatch," the darker-haired guy quipped, and turned toward me. It was clear from his cocksure glances that he was blessed with indie-rock omnipotence.

"I didn't know that. Um . . . I don't know what I think about the Arcade Fire or if I have ever thought about them at all. . . . Um . . . I guess they remind me of Sonic Youth without the New York hipster attitude or that smug edge," I said, shaking the ice cubes in my almost empty glass of scotch.

"You're just saying that because they both have a girl in their band," the dark-haired guy hissed, causing the rancid white film that for the past few hours had slowly spread across the entire inside of his mouth to shoot between his teeth and end up dangling an inch below my left eye. I realized that he was definitely right, so I didn't take offense.

Awkward silence ensued. The bartender yelled last call, flipped off the television, and slung a beer-soaked rag over his shoulder. The two offered each other a frantic, final glance and hurriedly said, almost in unison, "Hey, is your dad Robert Pollard of Guided by Voices?" Suddenly I understood why these two strangers had sat down at my table and had proceeded to ramble about every *Pitchfork* article available.

It is a question that, outside of Guided by Voices concerts, I get maybe five times a year. Every time that I hear it my initial response is "Goddamn it is a small world," as if I had just run into an ex–college roommate's ex-girlfriend on the streets of Hong Kong. I think, "I am three thousand miles from home, sitting all alone in a darkened bar with two strangers, and they know who my father is. I wonder if they know Aunt Lisa or mom's hairstylist Bernadette." It takes a few seconds before I remind myself that my dad is the lead singer of Guided by Voices. In fact to even write that statement is for some reason kind of embarrassing. Not in the sense that I'm ashamed to have a father who is in a rock 'n' roll band; nothing could be further from the truth.

For some reason such an admission feels a little vain, a young male's natural inclination to delusions of paternal grandeur, especially when the discussion depreciates into a "my father vs. your father pissing contest" between peers. It's like when you are ten you warn your peers about how "my dad can kick your dad's ass." Only I know my dad can kick your dad's ass (metaphorically of course) and so to brag about it, or even to admit it, is superfluous and hence discomforting. I kind of pity those guys whose fathers wouldn't drink a dozen beers, drink tequila directly from the bottle, and say something ridiculous like, "My brother can play guitar better than Joan Jett."

Both guys stared at me, eagerly awaiting my response to their question. "Yeah, he is," I said, trying to appear both humble and proud. I motioned for the bartender and ordered all three of us one more round of drinks. The mood of the conversation changed. Their last question brought frat boy camaraderie and loquaciousness where before there had only been awkwardness and annoyance. Over these final drinks we made plans to go to a few record stores the next afternoon and to afterward listen to any of the dozen or so GBV/Robert Pollard solo albums that they had never heard. Sometime during the finishing of our drinks and amidst the "what Guided by Voices means to me" conversation I gave them my address.

Early the next morning while I sat drinking coffee and writing a vignette from childhood for this biography, I heard a knock at the door. I walked over and suspiciously glanced through the peephole. The guys from the night before stood at my door, wearing the same outfits and the same silly grins. I quickly dropped to my knees and crawled behind the couch, hiding in a scythe of shadow that cut across the corner of my living room. After a few more knocks I heard silence and then the unmistakable coughing of a decade-old Cavalier's engine. Even when I heard the car pull away I tiptoed to the window, gently pulled down a section of blind, and stared out with two parts relief, one part guilt at an empty parking lot. That sense of pride and connection had faded overnight and all that was left was the memory of the dark-haired guy's voice saying, "Dude, *Built to Spill* is like if John Lennon and Paul McCartney had gotten really drunk in the eighties and just wrote an album overnight."

BICENTENNIAL

The rhythm of our industry
in these beautiful rolling hills
proudly serving briars
fireworks and grills

R. Pollard

LOVE

Pentagon reveals rejected chemical weapons
15 January 2005

The Pentagon considered developing a host of non-lethal chemical weapons that would disrupt discipline and morale among enemy troops, newly declassified documents reveal.

Most bizarre among the plans was one for the development of an "aphrodisiac" chemical weapon that would make enemy soldiers sexually irresistible to each other.

The proposals, from the U.S. Air Force Wright Laboratory in Dayton, Ohio, date from 1994.

NewScientist.com

One of the more important contributing factors to the longevity and success of Guided by Voices has been the devotion of its fans. That might sound obvious; every musician or band depends on the devotion of their fans, or else why, when the People's Choice Awards are handed out to artists who completely suck, do those artists, after thanking God, who presumably voted, thank "the fans, without whose support we wouldn't be here"? (Sure, that and a boatload of payola you'll never recoup, buster.)

But very few bands have enjoyed the near-umbilical connection to their fans that Guided by Voices has fostered. There are a few reasons why. First, there's Bob's accessibility, especially in the first few years after the band signed with Matador and began touring. He would sometimes spend hours after the show hanging out with fans, never condescending, always appreciative, and possessed of unbelievable stamina.

Much more stamina than the rest of the band, it should be noted, and especially than the tour manager (though not Pete, who was always busy in some back room drunkenly totaling up the night's receipts, and who never drove the van anyway), who wanted nothing more than to get back to the hotel and sleep the few hours remaining before getting back in the van and driving to the next city for the next night's show.

Writer Byron Coley has attributed part of Guided by Voices' initial appeal to the fact that "they kind of came on the scene just as The Replacements were ending. So people looking for that kind of drunken, sloppy rock experience, where you never knew what you were going to see from night to night, Guided by Voices were a good substitute for that. From the records, you maybe thought you were going to see R.E.M., and the Sun City Girls were there instead. Plus the band—it was still guys who had jobs. They all looked like they never came out of their room." In essence, in Coley's view, Guided by Voices replaced The Replacements.

In part due to his training as a teacher, and in part to his official iron-man constitution, Bob can subsist on very few hours' sleep, and generally wakes up, whether on tour or at home, around 6:30 A.M. His ability to stay up until all hours and wake up early (albeit in an often terrible mood for the first few hours) has led to a few minor incidents, and one major rule: You do not honk the horn of the van or (in European instances) tour bus at Bob in an effort to get him to wrap things up. If you do, he will first ignore you, and second, when he is, at length, ready to leave, he will board the van or bus and light into you like Bobby Knight at halftime (see, or rather hear, the intro to the *Some Drinking Implied* video for an example of the latter). This is a lesson quickly learned, and a rule now so established that new tour managers are warned by the band first thing.

Additionally, Bob is a tireless letter-writer, and has from the beginning made an effort to respond to anyone who takes the time or figures out how to write to him. Early on, it was easy: His address on Titus was listed on the back of at least one album, and he was similarly available in the phone book or via directory assistance. It's more difficult to get to Bob now, since he moved to XXX E. XXXXXXX St., and changed his now-unlisted phone number to XXX-XXXX, but a letter to Rockathon's present HQ in Madison, Wisconsin, will eventually make its way to Bob, and Bob still makes an effort.

Another reason the band's fans have remained loyal is that they have themselves—inspired by the community of close friends with which Bob surrounds himself, and the myth surrounding those friends—created a self-contained community, which exists mostly on the Internet, but which occasionally spills over into what MTV likes to call the Real World. These are the hard-core fans, the most supportive but also the most judgmental, whose longevity and loyalty has earned them, in their eyes, a right to bury as well as praise. Without them, Bob could not have sustained his series of side projects. The Postal Blowfishers, as these GBV junkies call themselves (we would have preferred the cuter Postal Blowfishies), are named after the GBV song "Postal Blowfish," mainly because, we suspect, it has the words "postal" (because it's to do with correspondence) and "blow" involved. There is no context in which the word "blow" is not funny. Splinter groups have also established themselves, sleeper cells of fans who for one reason or another prefer to cluster in their own close circles: Girl Called Captain, for instance, caters to the distaff diehards. Worshipful Web sites unrelated to the official Guided by Voices site have sprung up as well: Guided by Robert Pollard, run by a superfan who calls himself King Shit, and GBVDB, shorthand for the Guided by Voices Database, an inhumanly thorough resource that seems to contain each individual grain in R. Pollard's sandbox, run by Jeff Warren, upon whom we have relied for the discography at the back of *Hunting Accidents*, as well as a number of other facts and favors too numerous to mention.

The present manager of Rockathon World HQ, webmaster of the GBV (and now Robert Pollard) sites, and occasional tour manager, Rich Turiel, recalls the genesis of Postal Blowfish.

"In '94, I had read a couple articles that Greg Kot [Chicago-based rock critic] had written when they played Thurston's [in Chicago] and Dan Toohey was with them," says Rich. "I was living [in Chicago] then. Before they played, he wrote a big article and talked about *Propeller* and *Vampire*. In late '94 I had seen Bob Mould and he was saying in between songs, 'What are you guys listening to, you gotta get *Bee Thousand*, that's one of the best albums I've ever heard,' so I bought it soon after that and kind of flipped right away.

"It was the first bloom of the Internet, and I started searching for GBV stuff and came across Brian Mikesell's GBV website, which he had just started, and then this guy Bruce Melandy out in California had started Postal Blowfish on April 1, 1995.

"Mikesell lived in Dayton, in the Oregon district. He started it as a work project; he was doing Web work at Lexus/Nexus. They told him to pick something he would enjoy and do a Web site on it. Pete Jamison was involved with registering the GBV.com name. I was one of the first people to join Postal Blowfish. Over the years there's been consistently around four-hundred-plus members. It's like an e-mail chat group. One person starts by e-mailing an item of interest to the rest of the list, then people respond, and so on. When it started the only topic was Guided by Voices, but by now everybody knows each other so well, it's like, 'So I just bought the new Modest Mouse, what does everybody think?' Nowadays, it's about everything *but* GBV."

That's not entirely true—the list also spends lots of time critiquing live shows (who got drunker than whom, who made an ass of himself onstage, how great the show was, how awful the show was, debates about the merits of any new GBV album or FCS release).

Newly hooked on Guided by Voices, and trained in information technologies, Rich naturally began searching the nascent Internet for traces of the band.

"I got in touch with Brian Mikesell," he recalls, "and we struck up an e-mail correspondence. Then in '95 the band played at the Patio in Indianapolis and before or after that did an in-store at Todd Robinson's record store, Luna. It was the very first time I saw GBV live. Brian and I made a plan to meet at Luna; that was when I met Brian and GBV all in one day. The bootleg *For All Good Kids* [GBV live at Maxwell's] had come out, and I got the whole band to sign a copy.

"All the indie-rock bands I had known before had big mailing lists and Web sites. I felt like GBV had none of that so I dropped everything, every other band that I liked at the time. I decided, 'This is it, this is what I've been looking for.'

"I started helping out Brian; in a period of a couple years it went from just him doing it to both of us to just me. It happened really, really fast.

"About a year later, Rockathon started, and around that time [Indianapolis-based] Luna Records owner Todd Robinson [a former

Daytonian Bob had met when Todd managed Gem City Records in Dayton's Oregon District back in the mid-'80s] started putting out stuff, too. I think the first thing was the *Jellyfish Reflector* bootleg [another 'official' bootleg that included live tracks, including a rare-at-the-time live version of 'Redmen and Their Wives' and some outtakes from the Albini session, including 'Pantherz'].

"During that time, for work I was doing computer networking for a brokerage firm," says Rich, "then later for Easter Seals, so I've always been basically an IT guy. Doing computer work makes it easy to work on GBV stuff at the same time as doing my regular job."

Rich's eager participation helped give Guided by Voices a national presence. At the time, Rich lived in Chicago, but he has since moved to Madison, Wisconsin, where he continues his Webmaster role and has added oversight of Rockathon and frequent tour manager assignments to his GBV-related duties. Over time, Bob has come to rely on Rich more and more, in part because Rich is amazingly reliable.

"I live in Madison reluctantly. I'd much rather be in Chicago, or better yet in Dayton with those guys. The clubs suck, the bands suck, the people kind of suck. Which isn't that different from Dayton, I guess, except for the people.

"I pretty persistently kept coming to shows and kept coming to shows and I was doing the Web site. I became better and better friends with Bob every year; I think he realized at some point he could trust me, that I wasn't somebody who was trying to make money off my relationship with him.

"After the classic-lineup breakup, I still went to shows. That's what made it possible to hang out more with them, and talk to Bob more. . . . At that point I was going to shows all the time, and Bob would just start riding with me in the car and then I'd go to Dayton and hang out. At one point, I said that I would tour-manage for free. Bob took me up on that. I'm obsessive about the money. Every morning on tour I wake up and recount all the cash and go through all the paperwork, even though I know it's all there. The only drag is, I maybe get to drink half as much as I used to."

His offer to tour-manage for free—despite Bob's insistence on paying Rich, always refused—stands in stark contrast to the vaguely bitter remonstrations of ex–Manager for Life Pete Jamison, a contrast we will examine in some depth in the next chapter. For Rich, though, he was living the rock life in the only way an IT guy from Madison, Wisconsin, could. "Way back when," he says, "I was kind of thinking that if I could pick a dream job, it would be tour-managing for GBV. And now it's cool, because I'm doing Rockathon and the Web site as well."

The story of Rich's nonhostile takeover of Rockathon, which started as the merchandise arm of GBV and morphed into a record company, requires that we bring in another GBV über-fan, Matt Davis, who for a while worked with Pete Jamison as Rockathon's unpaid assistant.

"I've lived in Dayton my whole life, but I'd never heard of Guided by Voices," recalls Matt. "I was going to school in Cincinnati, and we went over to see Pavement at Southgate House, probably right after *Crooked Rain*, I would think. They were fucking terrible, boring as hell. But Guided by Voices—I was like, 'You've got to be kidding me.' At first I didn't even know what to think, because it was so different from anything else. It was entertaining just from the standpoint of 'I can't believe I'm seeing this.' If you're used to regular indie rock, or being a Rush fan, that's like Mars. The first ten times I listened to a tape of the music, I didn't like it. It was a compilation tape of some of the stuff off of *Bee Thousand* and *Vampire On Titus* and some of the EPs. I was like, 'What is this?' My mind was just completely not in the right place, because of being more of a metal fan, and a Rush fan, and Yes, that kind of stuff. Then we went camping and got hammered and listened to the tape again and 'Gold Star for Robot Boy' got stuck in my head, I just pressed repeat, repeat, repeat, repeat. From the next day . . . I remember driving back home, and I was completely hooked. I started going to shows—there was a show at a place, I think it's called Celebrity's now, up on Main Street. That was the first show where I'd decided to go see them.

"The most important show I saw, from a future perspective, had to be the one at Tipp City [a suburb north and west of Dayton which served as the title of a song by The Amps, on their lone LP, released in 1995]. There was nowhere really to play in town, so they played the old post office there, with The Amps. That show was actually the first time I met Pete. I'd gone to New York to see the band, been to Monument Club a few times.

"On the day of the show Pete called and said, 'Hey, do you wanna come pick me up and go to the show?' and I was like, 'Yeah, sure.' When I picked him up he said, 'We're gonna go get Bob and Jimmy.' At this time

I was still just a fan, and I was like, 'Holy shit, you gotta be kidding me!' So we go over to Bob's house, and Jimmy was there, and it was Bob and Jimmy and me and Pete, and Bob had a tape of what was called *Office of Hearts* at the time, which became *UTBUTS*, and he's like, 'Let's listen to this,' and it was like, 'Oh my God!'

"We go to the Tipp City show, which was great, and on the way back, we go to the Waffle House. There's a bunch of people at the Waffle House at three A.M., a lot more than usual. I was like, 'What's going on?' And Nate, who was in The Amps at the time, goes, 'Dude, Michael Jordan's sitting right there.' I was like, 'What? No way.' I looked over, and you could just see three tall black guys sitting there, just the tops of their heads. I thought about it, and I knew the Bulls were playing either that night or the next night in Dayton against the Pacers in a preseason game. So I kind of looked around the corner and I'm ... 'There's Michael Jordan.'

"I go home to my roommates and I say, 'Guys, you won't believe this, I drove Bob and Jimmy to the show. And I met Michael Jordan, shook his hand.'

"I became friends with Pete and started going to the Monument Club," continues Matt, "playing basketball and shit, and showing up to shows more often. I forget the date, but whenever the Hershel Savage and the American Flag record was done, we were at the Monument Club and Bob put it in. I loved it, I thought it was great. Really different—poppy and sugary, but I loved it. Pete was sitting there, and basically said, 'Would you want to help me put this out? Bob wants to put this out, and we're getting ready to, and I need help.' I was like, 'Yeah, sure, I'll help you out.' Then he says, 'Maybe you can be my Rockathon assistant.' I was like, 'Hell yeah.' I went down to Rockathon HQ; it was in the same place as Cro-Mag, down right off of West Third. It was a nice space, pretty big, with twenty-foot ceilings, huge windows.

"I showed up, and I swear, he had shit stacked up like ten feet high starting from halfway back. The place was totally disorganized. He'd given up. Not given up, per se, but just—making homemade T-shirts had turned into something that he needed help with. First thing I did was go through and clean it up and reorganize everything. We actually got a telephone line installed, so Rockathon had a telephone number.

"Pete's ability to have fun at shows sometimes affected his ability to keep track of merch. I think Pete had a sense of 'I paid for it, I made it, and if I want to give some away, I will.' But Bob had a sense of 'I haven't seen a check in a while.' I became the intermediary between Pete and Bob. Trying to get stuff so that it was organized, to make some money so that Bob could get paid and get a statement. That was when it went from being an assistant to being a little more active in the actual operation.

"Typically we didn't do anything that wasn't going to make money. *Tonics and Twisted Chasers* [a fan club album featuring unreleased Bob/ Toby four-track collaborations] made money. Hershel Savage made money. And then it got to Thomas Jefferson Slave Apartments [featuring Columbus-based Ron House, whom the attentive reader will recall as the guy who had Bob send *Propeller* to Robert Griffin at Scat], and we were totally fired up about putting that one out. After we got the record done, they proceeded to tell us that they were breaking up. Then there was The Tasties [a local band, who also served as the backing group for the Fading Captain release *Lexo and the Leapers,* later on, as mentioned earlier], and we put that one out, and they were supposed to open up for GBV at the Southgate House, and either nobody told them, or they forgot, but in any case they never showed up. They got in a big fight and basically broke up, too. So the Rockathon roster just evaporated. We had nothing. But our intentions were good.

"The GBV merch always did well. I came up with the hats; they did well. We did numbered shirts; they sold out. It wasn't like we were just coming up with gimmicks, but we couldn't just keep doing homemade shirts. Everybody already had a homemade shirt."

Problems soon started to crop up on the merchandise side of Rockathon. "Pete was delusional about what he thought people were gonna buy," says Matt. "Bob said, 'Pete thought that if you put GBV in white block letters on anything, on curtains, it doesn't matter, people are gonna buy it.' Pete would be very conservative about what he would spend, and he'd get the cheapest thing he could find, instead of stepping up and getting something that was good. For instance, the beer cooler was a great idea. But the beer cooler itself was . . . not so good.

"The change in Rockathon was Pete realizing that he was never gonna make enough money to have his own place, to retire on. I think he hit an age where he was like, 'What am I gonna do?' Because he was teaching part-time, which would give him some money, but which also allowed him to go on tour. I think he felt he wasn't making enough money tour-managing, and so he just decided to go in another direction. I'd stayed as the middle-man between Bob and Pete for a while, because there is such a love affair there, and a history, between Pete and Bob, but they've got that brother thing going on at times, too, where there's an issue but neither one of them wants to talk about. Bob will tell me something, and Pete will tell me some-thing, and that's where my value started. 'How much do you think you need to make you happy, Bob, from a check you haven't seen in a while?' and then 'Pete, how can we get some money in, to get him a check to make him happy?' That stayed as my sort of unspoken job responsibility. I never got paid a dollar.

"For a while Pete tried to just oversee Rockathon without showing up to the office. He took a teaching job in Columbus. He hired this guy Mike Justice [a longtime local musician] to help out. Mike liked the band but he wasn't a true fan. Pete started coming back less and less and less and less. It got to the point where he didn't want to pay for the space any-more. All the stuff got moved over to Mike Justice's place. That's when I think Bob got upset about it—no offense to Mike Justice, but all of a sud-den Rockathon is in the hands of somebody he barely even knows?

"I was like, 'Pete, we gotta do something.' I talked to Bob and said, 'What about maybe giving Rockathon to Rich, I just can't do it. I got a job, and a family.' I talked to Rich and he was like, 'Let me think about it, let me see if there's a way I can make it work.' One day I said to Pete, 'What about giving Rockathon to Rich? He's always been there, doing the Web site and everything else, and I think he'd do a good job.' That was kind of the end for Pete. He didn't want Rockathon, but he also didn't want to give it up. That was it. Rich bought out or took all the stock, and he came out and took it back to Wisconsin.

"Right around then, Bob called me up one day," continues Matt, "and he said, 'Hey, I'm in between labels.' It was after *Mag Earwhig!* but before going to TVT. 'I want to put something out.' He gets antsy and wants to do something. 'I got this idea for *Kid Marine*—why don't we do a thousand vinyl?' I was like, 'Great.' He was happy with what I'd done with Rockathon; he knew I'd busted my ass for no money. To a certain extent he was doing me a favor, helping me make some money too. He calls back later and goes, 'I've been thinking about it. Why don't we do CD *and* vinyl, and just make it a regular release.' It got to the point where I started to get worried about being able to handle the job, so that's when I felt like I needed some help. I asked Bob, what if I got Todd Robinson to help, as half of my fifty-fifty. He said, 'Whatever you want to do.' I asked Todd Robinson to do Fading Captain with me. That's when Pete really felt left out—why wouldn't Bob give Pete the record to put out on Rockathon?

"*Kid Marine* came out in 1999; I think there was some overlap there with Pete's involvement. But as I remember it, Pete had already decided, 'I need to do something else,' and then this happened and he felt cut out, and that really sealed the deal. I gave Pete some checks for Fading Captain. I gave him five percent of the overall—which is still a pretty good portion—for a while, to try to keep him involved. But it got to a point where the whole thing didn't taste right to him anymore. He was gone. He was in Columbus, and he stopped coming around. Then he'd complain that no one would come to visit him in Columbus. But that's not how the rules work.

"What happened was, it changed," sums up Matt. "It used to be a party, and that's all it ever was. If all the merch got stolen—so what, they were homemade T-shirts. There was a point in time when *Bee Thousand* came out, there's all this excitement, the clubs get bigger, now you're selling out, in '96, two nights at Irving Plaza. All of a sudden it started to shift where it was like, 'We can make some pretty good money off merch, let's keep better track of this. We're actually doing this the right way, we're making money.' It turned into a business, and it wasn't as fun anymore for Pete. The responsibility level increased, but his pay level didn't, and the love of Bob and the band and the music wasn't enough to keep him going."

"Pete just totally gave up Rockathon," says Rich Turiel, "when they were recording *Earthquake Glue*. That's when Matt talked to me about it. Because I've only had Rockathon for about a year and a half now [2004]. Matt Davis said, 'Either you can have it or Bob would just rather kill it, but only take it if you want it.' I was so psyched.

"They had a Web site, Pete had a garageful of product, but there was never any system for e-mail payment—it was all done by check. Because I ran the Web site, people would e-mail me and say, 'Is anyone still there?

I sent a check in but didn't get anything.' I took what we had and designed a whole online store. One of the best things was coming up with ideas. Bob started getting really involved coming up with ideas—just like he is with the music. For instance, it was his sticker design and his key chain.

"The merch sales are pretty steady. For the past six months Bob's been doing a lot of eBay stuff, selling old autographed posters or extra copies of rare albums, always hand-signed, and those do really well. I handle that for him. We also did Bob's poetry/art magazine *Eat,* which sold six or seven hundred copies.

"As far as tour managing goes, the very first show I tour-managed was Bloomington, Indiana, and there was a huge snowstorm. Nobody showed up at the club. I remember thinking, 'This is easy.' Then there was a power outage at the hotel, and it wound up that there was no room after all, and finally they said, 'Well, we have a suite.' It was like six of us in one room that first night. I went from thinking this is the easiest thing in the world to—'Oh no!' "

With the demise of Rockathon—at least the Pete Jamison version—a clear division was made between Rockathon version 2.0, which would focus exclusively on Guided by Voices merch, in tandem with the Web site, under Rich's purview, and the Fading Captain Series, which would serve as an outlet for Bob's many side projects. His management had negotiated a deal with TVT whereby Bob was allowed to release as much side product as he wished, as long as he first gave TVT the opportunity to put it out if they wished, which they never did.

"Essentially Fading Captain was an extension of *Tonics and Twisted Chasers,*" explains Todd Robinson, who now handles production and distribution for Fading Captain. As of the moment this book is being written, there are an almost unfathomable thirty-one Fading Captain releases, including probably the most high-profile release, *Suitcase,* which included selections from what at the time (although no more, as we explained earlier) was presumed to be an actual suitcase of cassettes full of Bob's odds and sods.

"I made a bet with Bob and Jimmy," recalls Matt Davis. "I didn't know anything about their past; I didn't know how good they were at basketball. So I made a bet—I had a couple of friends who played. I said,

'We'll go three-on-three with you guys. If we win, I get the suitcase, and if I lose I'll get the Monument Club a popcorn machine or whatever.' First of all it was a stupid bet, because there was no way we were gonna win. At the Monument Club court? Against Bob and Jimmy? Bryan was gonna be their third. Lucky for us, the game never took place. I ended up buying a couch and a love seat for the Monument Club, 'cause it needed it, and I would have lost the bet anyway. The irony is, of course, that since we put out *Suitcase* on Fading Captain, I sort of got the suitcase anyway. You give and you get."

Bob had threatened for years to put out the contents of his basement tapes, but in the end it took an act of God to turn threat into action. Davis recalls, "What happened is—and again, the timeline's kind of mushy— but either there was a leak in his basement and he thought he lost the suitcase, or it happened while we were doing it, but there was point in time where he said, 'Listen, let's at least digitize it, get it off of the tapes.' I had a laptop and a tape deck. He brought over a shitload of tapes, and he said, 'Let's just go.' It was him and Jimmy sitting there, and me and my buddy, and we started going through the tapes. We did that for three or four straight nights, three hours at a time, and we had two hundred fifty songs, which I had never heard. That represented—just of what he brought out— maybe fifteen to twenty percent of the tapes. So there was enough there, obviously, and I think he used about seventy-five of those, and then he found twenty-five more that I believe he did with Todd Robinson, and that became *Suitcase*. I think Bob's favorite part was coming up with the band names for the different tracks. That was probably our biggest Fading Captain release, our biggest seller."

"There's definitely a core," adds Todd Robinson regarding the steady sales of Fading Captain. "Anything that has Guided by Voices on it, and then Bob secondly, are always clear-cut safer bets. I'm in the unique position of being on the retail side of things, and looking at Matador's one sheets and catalog—one of my vendors is Revolver, and that's who takes care of our distribution—maybe every weekend there may be a twenty-page fax, and I can kind of see scans of separate releases versus other things." We would like to state for the record that if the reader is confused by the above business terminology, he is not alone. But we assume it means something to someone, and certainly must have meant something to Todd; otherwise he wouldn't have said it.

"When we weren't getting along so well I heard the main albums but I missed some of the early Fading Captain stuff," remembers Robert Griffin. "And then years later I caught up and I've got everything again. And the thing that amazed me was just how far he would stretch himself in all these directions. I'm not talking so much about the more-for-fun experimental records, like Acid Ranch or Circus Devils, but all the side stuff. He manages to go to new places, but it's still instantly recognizable as his work. And it seems to me he can keep doing that."

The profusion of side projects did not seem to bother TVT, to whom Guided by Voices had become less of a priority after *Do the Collapse*'s failure to sell an amount of records that could be measured in tons, rather than pounds; but when the band eventually re-signed with Matador in 2000, carrying with it the same side-project proviso included in the TVT deal, Gerard Cosloy took a different, somewhat dimmer view. "Sales have been in a downward spiral for us since *UTBUTS*," says Cosloy, "and part of that is due to the volume of Guided by Voices–related product—just the difficulty that creates for you at the individual record shop and with music journalists. We had an experience in the UK this year where we serviced the new album to magazines—and it's a record we were really proud of, and we feel it being the farewell record, it deserves a certain amount of coverage. Although the record, again, was well-reviewed, we had a lot of people saying, 'We just wrote about the band eleven months ago.' We had other people saying to us, 'We just received a Robert Pollard record in the mail; we're going to review the two records together and we like the solo record better.' They're welcome to make that judgment, they're free to make that call, but we're the ones that spent all this money to put this record out. So that's not necessarily what we want to hear.

"The point I'm making is, we are in a world where people have so much stuff competing for their attention, that for anyone beyond the super-committed following to keep track of this embarrassment of riches that Bob keeps flooding the universe with—he's making great records, but it presents a challenge to anyone putting those records out."

R.E.M.'s Peter Buck sees both sides of the Bob coin. "If all the work he does is good, that makes it harder for a company that invests a lot of money in it," he says. "I mean I don't know how much in advances he gets or whatever, but when you're talking about taking out advertising for a guy who's had three records out that year, yeah, that must be hard.

"On the other hand, it's stupid to do less work than you want to do just for marketing purposes. I've always felt that if you've got songs and you want to record them and you feel like doing something, then you should just do it.

"I know that the marketing thing is hard, but, I don't know. You invent the business that you want to be in."

A PERFECT THIRST

Buzzing people
buzzing outside
buzzing raindrops
inside the egg
of citizenships

Do you hear them?
Smooth and moving?
Singing in our sleep?
Our God
and domestication
our need

I do indeed
seek qualification
in my search
for a perfect thirst

R. Pollard

LOSS

"Action is consolatory. It is the enemy of thought and the friend of flattering illusions."

—Joseph Conrad

The poet John Keats once famously defined "negative capability" as "when a man is capable of being in uncertainties, mysteries, doubts, without any irritable reaching after fact and reason." F. Scott Fitzgerald similarly wrote: "The test of a first-rate intelligence is the ability to hold two opposed ideas in the mind at the same time, and still retain the ability to function." By these and many other platitudinous standards (Fitzgerald's axiom in particular smacks more of truism than truth), Bob Pollard is—to overuse an overused word—a genius. In the original Latin meaning of the word, a genius is simply a guardian spirit that watches over a person or place, meaning that everyone has a genius, the nature of which it is our task to understand and to develop. Even in that literal sense, Pollard has done well by his genius.

The qualities of genius are by definition selfish, insofar as they are governed by or emanate from the ego, and self-deprecating asides aside, Bob's monument-sized ego has been well-established, both by word and deed, and verified by supporting statements heretofore presented. If that's not enough: once, while on tour nearly a decade ago, Bob carried with him a microcassette recorder that had been given to him as a birthday present. His roommate woke at four in the morning—this was the night after a show, remember—to the sound of Bob softly singing into the recorder in the bathroom. He explained that he had dreamed a melody and wanted to record it before he forgot. "At four in the morning?" asked his incredulous roommate. "That's why they slap that 'genius' tag on me, son," replied Bob, climbing back into bed. It was a joke, but it was not a joke.

The original version of Brian Wilson's "I Know There's an Answer" from the Beach Boys' album *Pet Sounds* was titled "Hang on to Your Ego"— but Wilson was nuts, and stoned, and the true artist works to expand or explode the ego to universal proportions, progressing by (spiritual) declension from "I" to envelop every pronoun, including heteroclites (more common in this ungrammatical era). For Bob, especially in his songwriting, Martin Buber's I/Thou formulation is misleading, because very often Bob is both I and Thou, and neither I nor Thou, and you, or we, are invited to substitute or extrapolate meanings and subtext of our own design. In this context, selfishness is just another way of giving yourself away.

You give yourself away too much, though, and bad things happen. Guided by Voices had by 2001 achieved a measure of renown unthinkable by its leader, Bob Pollard, for the first thirty-six years of his life. Success, however, inevitably exacts a price, and Bob's achievements were accompanied by an accumulation of loss—defined in many ways, but as a catchall accurate enough. Every loss is accompanied by a gain, however difficult that gain may be to see, measure, or even accept.

Bob's relationship with his wife, Kim, while superficially a lazy river, could from time to time turn into a raging torrent. Bob's temper was usually the cause, though Kim certainly gave as well as she got, and it's fair to say she was more accepting of Bob's eccentricities, both artistic and temperamental, than she was supportive. There was never any physical abuse, but as with many couples who've been together for many years, the way Bob could suddenly snap at Kim, and her equally heated response, could shock visitors unused to the dynamics of their domestic interaction. What seemed like a serious argument would often evaporate in a moment, and an onlooker might be left confused as to whether there had been any real anger behind the angry words.

Sometime just before the recording of *Isolation Drills,* the river flooded the banks of their marriage (to stretch a metaphor to its breaking point), and though the problems that overflowed then were not the first, they were the first that involved infidelity.

In fact, Kim had gone so far as to serve Bob with divorce papers ten years earlier, before Guided by Voices had achieved any real recognition. The inciting incident is illustrative not only of Bob's relationship with his wife but, again, of his deep frustration with his family's failure, in his eyes, to recognize or in any sense honor his musical efforts.

"One day we were just kind of ribbing Bryan," says Bob, "me and my friend Bruce Greenwald, about like, 'Are you working? You're not gonna get any better playing video games all day.' I'd been doing cocaine all day—something I rarely did then and certainly never do now. I wasn't violent or anything—in fact, we were just drinking and having a good time—but Kim called my mom and dad, and they came over, and my dad was a little drunk, and he was like, 'What's the problem?' And I said, 'What do you mean what's the problem? Nothing!' And then my dad said, 'I'll tell you what the fucking problem is, it's him,' and pointed at Bruce Greenwald. Greenwald was like, 'Hey, pal, don't go pointing your finger at me.'

"So finally I said, 'I'll tell you what the fucking problem is. It's that I'm a fucking genius and nobody gives me any fucking credit for it.' Which is—forgive me for that fucking egotistical statement. And my mom goes, 'At what?'

"I told them to get the fuck out of my house, and that was the end of it, I thought, but two days later, on Monday at school, it was the end of the day and school was letting out, and some lady came and knocked on the door of my classroom. And she goes, 'These are your papers—I'm sorry to have to give them to you—divorce papers.' I go, 'Divorce from what?' I didn't know what she was talking about. I couldn't even contemplate that I would be given divorce papers.

"Anyway, Kim and I talked it over and worked it out. This was in about '92, just before we broke. Then we signed to Matador, and things were good—for her and for my family—financially. When we had to start touring and I was gone all the time, obviously that takes a toll, and I think that's what eventually . . . We started moving in different directions. I'm gone all the time and then I come home and it's like, 'There's that guy again.' Obviously other factors on the road came into play a little later than that. But I only broke down, let my guard down on the road, because I just didn't feel things were going very well at home. Not to say it was right, to fuck around, but I could tell it wasn't happening on the home front.

"I started thinking about it: 'What am I, Grandpa now?' The kids were grown-up. 'What am I gonna do, sit on the porch with the fucking cat?' There's nothing wrong with that, but it's not me; I'm not that patriarchal type. We never ate together at the family table. I wanted to—my kids didn't want to. I was never one to enforce or demand that: 'We will sit at the table, like a family.' You know what that is, that's an excuse for the old man of the house to take his shit out on people. I never went for that kind of thing. I coached, I did things with my kids, we did stuff, went on vacations and that kind of thing, but other than that I gave them freedom. They weren't allowed to stay out late doing drugs and drinking, they had to be home by a certain time, but ... It was fairly traditional, but not heavy-handed."

His relationship with Kim had weighed on his mind for some time. Once, late in 1996, he sat at a table in Marion's, and after a few beers started thinking out loud that it might be time for him to have an affair on the road. Though he did not act on this impulse for several more years, clearly the seed had taken root, prompted in part by his exposure to the wider world through constant touring, which had the double effect of broadening Bob's horizons and taking him away from the constancy and consistency of his marriage, giving him both perspective and doubts.

Another time, freedom cruising on the streets of Northridge, he complained, "We have nothing in common, except for our children. Nothing: music, film, literature. How long can that ... I should have figured that out a long time ago, before we even got married and had kids. But you don't know when you're that young."

And so, somewhat inevitably, during the *Do the Collapse* tour "I started having a relationship with someone on the sly," says Bob. "And I was trying to figure out how to handle it. I was gonna tell Kim and somehow straighten things out. Either we'd break up or stay together; I hadn't decided what to do yet. I did decide to stay, at one point, but after a while I realized—the damage is done, it can't be worked out."

Before he could discuss the matter with his wife, "Somebody ratted me out. I don't know who—I can't get it out of her. But I shouldn't have been doing that anyway. I'm not defending my actions. I don't like rats, though. People should mind their own fucking business. I was getting ready to try to make a decision and talk to her about it, but I didn't get the chance to do that. It's just a situation that I wish could have been handled a little bit better."

Eventually, after giving the marriage another try, Bob decided to end things with Kim. "It was pretty rough at first," says Bob. "She didn't take it very well. But someone had told me, 'You know, she's never gonna trust you again.' I thought about that, coupled with the fact that the person I was with had no one. That was my reasoning, that I'd kind of made my bed. . . . 'This person, I don't want to fuck her life up either.' It was a terrible position to be in. I'm not blaming Kim or anyone but myself for our divorce. I have no regrets, but I do think that touring all the time is what ultimately contributed to my letting my guard down. If I'm gonna go out and do this and no one gives a shit when I come home, then I'm gonna have a good time on the road.

"In the end, Kim got a deal where she was well taken care of. We talk, when it has to do with our kids. It's reasonably amicable. But it's sad. It's always gonna be there, like a scar. I fucked up. I couldn't believe I fucked up. I didn't think I was *capable* of fucking up. And I did. So I guess I deserve whatever criticism I get. I don't like doing that. I like having a girl. I don't like fucking around—to me that's not fun. I've never been what I call a 'groover,' going out to bars and try to be all 'Hey, baby'; I can't do that shit. That was the thing—rock makes it a little bit easier. When you're the center of attraction at a show, it's a little bit easier."

Bob's newfound bachelorhood did provide him with some comic relief, at least—or what Bob might consider karmic payback. On tour in Australia, after a show in Sydney, a carful of fans drove up to the venue and invited Bob to a party, an invitation which in the past (and certainly today) he would have declined. But on impulse he said yes, and got in, and "we must have driven like a hundred miles, way outside of the city, like into the outback or whatever," Bob recalls.

"We're sitting around, and I will admit that the reason I'd decided to go was because there was a young lady who I thought might be interested in me. But nothing happened, and eventually everyone went off to bed, and I fell asleep on the couch. A couple of hours later, I woke up in complete darkness and someone—or something—was licking my face. At first I thought . . . But it turned out to be this huge fucking black dog. I just froze. I couldn't move, I was scared shitless. I thought the dog was like the devil or something, I didn't know."

Eventually daylight came to Bob's rescue, and the dog evaporated or went outside to chase kangaroos or returned to hell. "I called my manager back in New York. I told him I had no idea where I was, somewhere in the outback—the Outback Steakhouse, maybe. A couple of hours later the van pulled up at the house. I have no idea how they found me."

But despite what Bob was going through, there were moments of alcohol-inspired levity on tour with a band that included drummer Jim Macpherson, whose history Down Under, both with Guided by Voices and before that The Amps, for some reason tended to involve the abuse of tequila. One of the world's genuinely nicest guys, for some reason tequila had a psychoactive effect on Jimmy Mac, turning him into "Tequila Man," capable of almost single-handedly tipping over the band's trailer at an outdoor festival, tying a cape around his neck and launching himself through the trailer door like Superman, throwing a chair at Nate Farley. . . . But all this was mere prelude to an incident on the Tour of the Black Dog.

"It was in New Zealand," remembers Jim, sort of, "and I actually got a cartoon drawn of me [by famed New Zealand musician Chris Knox] because of this. The drum rental place didn't give me a piece of carpet, and I was up on a real high riser, and my whole kit just started flying forward, but I was bangin' super hard because I was kind of, uh, hammered, and I flipped all my drums and these microphones into this big beer pile. I ruined like five thousand dollars' worth of mics. The whole kit fell off-stage, then I got all the drums back on and continued to play.

"At least I didn't have to pay for the mics. I probably do, but I don't know it."

Things got worse back in the States. "I took my own drum kit out at the San Diego show, started doing a couple too many shots. And I can remember looking at some people at the side of the stage and I was getting ready to take another shot and they were all going, 'No, no.'

"I should've taken their advice, because then I think I was so drunk I couldn't finish, so I just stood up and started tearing my kit up. It was late in the show, but by Bob's standards I still had another forty-five minutes. So Bob said, 'I guess Jim just finished the show.'"

"There were some people saying you could hear what was going on in my personal life in *Isolation Drills*," says Bob, "which is mostly not accurate. On the other hand, the songs on the B-side of the EP *Dayton, Ohio—19*

Something and 5 [number five in the Fading Captain Series, for those interested] were all about that. It's really sad."

But although rumors of Bob's domestic disturbance accompanied the release of *Isolation Drills*—fueled in part by cryptic comments he made in some of the interviews concerning the album, and in part by rock world gossip—and while the album was undeniably of a somewhat melancholic cast, it was no more literal or autobiographical than any of Bob's previous records, which have always been suffused with a core sadness that's difficult to source.

"There were some really insensitive criticisms of *Isolation Drills* at the time," says Bob. "People saying, 'Fuck the skeletons in the closet, we don't want to hear that, get back to the crazy shit.' Fuck you. All the albums have a crazy side; even *Isolation Drills* has that. People called that album turgid trash. I don't get quite where it's turgid. It has some power, it has some feeling. How's it turgid?"

Around the same time, things started to sour in another important relationship, with GBV's Manager for Life, Pete Jamison. As noted earlier, Pete made the decision to leave Dayton, which resulted in his de facto abdication of Rockathon and of his position as Manager for Life.

"A lot of the reason [I left] was because I couldn't make a living," says Pete. "And I saw how the band was not really growing anymore. There were a lot of things I felt Bob should be doing as far as making it grow. And it just seemed like it would get to a certain number and stop. People were putting money into the records, but he wouldn't do any radio promotion, things like that."

"What was he, my label?" responds Bob. "I just did as much as I was willing to do, you know, what the fuck? Did he understand that he wasn't really our manager, that that was a fictitious thing? Manager for Life—that's a joke."

"I was making three hundred dollars a week as tour manager," says Pete. "So I ask for a raise, and he gives me a fifty-a-week raise, and then he would take two hundred a week back in merch. I can understand his thoughts, but there was no regard for how I was doing. When they got the money from *Alien Lanes* from Matador, and everyone went on salary, I didn't. He wasn't taking care of me like I thought he should. I was an afterthought."

"Pete, you weren't in the band," says Bob. "Does he think he was in the band? I compensated him for ten years from Scat. I gave him the same percentage I gave Toby and my brother—eleven percent, I think. And it was out of appreciation for the fact that for our first six albums we financed them, and Pete probably put in more money than anyone else. But I thought after ten years, especially after Pete had stopped coming around, how long do I have to keep paying him? So I quit paying him. But he got I *know* well over than what he had put in.

"He completely had no organization with Rockathon. He would give me, maybe once a year, three or four hundred dollars. Since Rich [Turiel] has taken over Rockathon, I get a check for a thousand dollars a month. The thing about the money for tour managing, about paying him three-fifty or whatever, that's what he asked for. He could've come to me and asked for more if he wanted. No one knows where the money from the merchandise came from or went. Pete handled whatever merchandise we had, which was all his generic shit, and he could've taken as much money as he wanted. Like I said, once a year he handed me a check for three or four hundred dollars. I don't even recall making money on merch at shows. That was up to him, what was paid out. I didn't even keep track of that shit."

"He's a tightwad, like his dad," counters Pete. "If you look at Bob's ego—as far as money and GBV goes, he doesn't have enough compassion to take care of or worry about others. He's so consumed by himself, there's no room for anybody else, even his brother. That's why Jimmy never wanted to be in the band. When Jimmy blew out his knee, you never saw the remorse from Bob. And I think he maybe was relieved that Jimmy never made it. Unless Bob's the center of attention and getting everything he wants, he's the biggest baby in the world."

"I once saw Pete at a bar during happy hour and he put chicken wings in his coat pocket to take with him and eat later," recalls Bob. "How could anyone that would steal chicken wings call anybody a tightwad?"

These are harsh charges, and deserving of a considered reply. For that we turn to the reclusive Jimmy Pollard.

"That's bullshit! You're kidding me!" Jimmy calmly replies. "Bob was my biggest fucking fan, man. Goddamn. What's wrong with that fucker? How long did he think he was gonna get a fucking free ride for doing nothing? Sure, at the beginning, he went in with me and Bob and we got the loan. He never did anything musically. All he did was contribute financially. So he's Manager for Life, which means nothing. And then he becomes tour manager, which, really, he never did anything but handle merch. So when's his free ride over?

"Put this in the book: 'Bob was a jealous motherfucker of me, and he was so glad that I blew my knee out. . . .' God. That's funny. Bob was at every one of my fucking games, he bragged about me to everybody and shit. . . . That's crazy! He's the guy who made me what I was, you know, as far as athletically, pushing me when I was a kid, kicking my fucking ass, so why wouldn't he want me to succeed? He was tougher on me than my dad, by far.

"If Bob had such a huge ego, then he wouldn't have wanted me in the band with him in the first place. If he's so jealous of me, then why would he want me by him in the band? Pete would be someone I wouldn't think would be bitter. Because he had a fucking fun trip on something he didn't really have anything to do with. Pete's push was before I got home, and got a guitar, and got in the basement, and bought a tape recorder. We would've started doing that anyway."

For his part, Bob responds to Pete with equal equanimity. "That is complete insanity! I wasn't the one who said, 'You blew it.' I'm the one that said, 'Congratulations, you're in Guided by Voices now.' What are you supposed to do? He wasn't injured to the point where he couldn't do anything. He couldn't play basketball anymore. As far as showing remorse— sure I did. My thing was to take his mind off it and say, 'Well, let's fucking play music now.' He wasn't sulking around or anything anyway. His attitude was 'Good. Fuck that shit anyway.'

"The thing is, Pete is underestimating our love. You cannot find a pair of brothers that's closer than me and Jimmy. You can't. For him to try to say that . . . We've had fights, and we come from a competitive-minded family, but we've never held grudges against each other, and we've always been very, very close and we still are. And he's full of shit.

"In my opinion, for something to be good you have to have a leader. I've chosen the role to lead. It's not that I don't give a fuck about anyone else around me. Without Pete, there *is* no Guided by Voices, and I'm always going to be indebted to him for that. He's the first person to have confidence in me. I gave Pete a mythological status with people, by calling him Manager for Life and pumping him up to be the shit. He's like our in-house manager/mascot. Matador ran a full-page profile in *Spin* or *Rolling Stone* or whatever on Pete. They did Charlie Ondras from Unsane, and they did Johan Kugelberg, who worked at Matador at the time. They only did three people, and he was one of them."

Which, it should be noted, Pete believes made Bob jealous, and resulted in his eventual demotion by neglect.

"That's insane!" exclaims Bob. "I've never, ever been jealous of anyone in my band, or around my band. When we broke, magazines wanted me in front. I used to say, 'Put Mitch in front, he looks cooler. Put him out there. He *is* Guided by Voices."

Thus endeth the strange, sad saga of Manager for Life Pete Jamison, who made feeble noises about attending the Last Show Ever, but did not, and who will not return Bob's calls, or anyone from Dayton's calls, not even when Gibby died, not even when simple human kindness would dictate that he, of all people, would want to bear witness to the end of the thing that he, of all people, was there to witness the beginning. Of. Although we should note that he was quick enough to return a call requesting an interview for *Hunting Accidents*.

Postscript:

"Pete showed up to the Columbus show on the farewell tour," recalls Matt Davis. "He was already in Hammered Pete mode, and in a good mood, and telling stories, and proceeded to . . . not really drink heavy, but drink—and then all of a sudden he was just really trashed. And I think after about five or ten songs he left. And Bob was calling for him, 'Where's Pete? Where's Pete?' But he wasn't there."

For every loss, a gain. After deciding to leave TVT, Bob found to his surprise and delight that Matador was more than happy to have him back. And he was more than happy to return. He'd made what he considered a good-faith effort to bring his band to the next level of mainstream recognition, and while he'd managed a couple of stellar records, the expected result had not been achieved. Nothing could be more agreeable to Bob at this point than to remove the pressure to succeed, other than artistically, and no label was more congenial to that attitude than Matador.

"That was one of the fastest negotiations we've ever had," says Gerard Cosloy. "I seem to remember that it happened over a matter of days. That might be an exaggeration, but it's just—from the time that overture was made to getting the deal done . . . it was almost overnight. There was never any animosity between us and the band, although I don't have a lot of respect for TVT. But that predates their association with GBV. I just think they're a label that puts out a lot of bad records. GBV was a rare exception. The bottom line for us was music, and not so much about petty personal grievances. We were thrilled to get the call."

For his part, Bob was quoted in a press release at the time as saying, "It's great to be reunited with our good friends at Matador, fellow rock geeks with the same basic philosophy on record artistry. We are very happy getting back to autonomously making records ourselves and have the ball back in our court."

"The problem with late-period Guided by Voices," comments Cosloy, "was that the fact they were the hot story of the mid-1990s, which helped get the band a lot of attention, in some ways turned into their albatross. It's like, 'It's a band that makes all their records on four-track, and doesn't know anything about quality control.' That's the myth, and that's all people want to know, because it's kind of a charming story about a quirky little band. It's difficult to transcend that, which is unfortunate, because if you just sit down and listen to the [later] records from start to finish—that shit is irrelevant. The records are fantastic! But we're in a marketplace where content is not the only way things get bought and sold; depending on where you are in your career trajectory, it might be the least significant factor. Each generation wants its own band, and Guided by Voices are seen as this archetype of the mid-'90s.

"It's like if The Grifters got back together—how many records would they sell? Those guys were a great band, really talented. And so with Guided by Voices, they're always going to be seen as being part of a particular era, remembered romantically. I think even if Pavement got back together . . . I don't know how successful that would be. In the eyes of the people who control public access to this stuff, whether it's radio or press— Guided by Voices has had their day. They had their chance in the mid-

1990s, and after they didn't have a big breakthrough it was like, 'Here's the annual Guided by Voices record.' Although I think there is a general level of respect for what Bob and the band do, there's just so much emphasis placed on what's new.

"And I have to say this for the record—although I respect the right of the artist to have management in place, and I understand why it's useful in some cases—the biggest disappointment to me about the ongoing relationship with Guided by Voices and Bob is that, for me at least, there hasn't been much of a relationship with Bob. All communication has gone through management for a long time, and when we did this we weren't doing it to sign Janet Billig and we weren't doing it to sign [current manager] David Newgarden. I would never tell somebody to change management, I would never tell somebody you can't have a manager. Everyone has a right to those things.

"For my purposes I just wish there was more direct communication with Bob. If there's something we are doing badly I would like to hear it from him. It would matter more coming from him. Sometimes I think the ideas we have get to him thirdhand. They come across in a very different way than we intend. Which can be frustrating."

Universal Truths and Cycles, Earthquake Glue, and *Half-Smiles of the Decomposed,* the three albums recorded and released by Matador in the years leading up to the breakup of the band, taken as a whole or separately, as you wish, are quite likely the best records of the band's career. Not that you'd know it by the collective yawn with which each release was greeted by what Cosloy calls "the people who control public access to this stuff," but if you are a member of the listening public, and you are reading this, you are advised to put this book down and a) go listen to those records right now before reading further, or b) go buy those records and listen to them before reading further. You might even be better served by selling this book on one of the Internet sites devoted to selling things of transient value, like *Hunting Accidents,* and buying something of permanent value, like any one of those three albums.

The quality of this last salvo from the GBV cannon was partly the result of a genuine, and general, improvement in Bob's songwriting, and partly the result of the band's having learned, at long last, how to negotiate on its own the special requirements of the recording studio.

"We did take what we learned from [working with producers Ric

Ocasek and Rob Schnapf], I think," says Bob, "and then once we started working on our own again or with producer Todd Tobias, we were able to be really creative in a big studio. That was always my fear from the beginning with Guided by Voices; that's one reason why I didn't promote ourselves at all and kept it to ourselves, because I was scared to death of going to a big city like Cleveland or New York. Because we can do this on our own with just our friends, but can you imagine like going into a big studio and working with a big producer? That was terrifying. So we were able to go in there and kind of successfully pull it off, and I think we came out of it with something to go with.

"We reached a halfway point with how we wanted to sound. It's not necessarily lo-fi, but it's not made for radio. It still kicks. One of the problems with lo-fi for me was that it just didn't kick ass enough. I liked the way it sounded, but I wanted it to have more balls. So that's why we wanted to go in the studio.

"You have people who say that *Bee Thousand* was better," he continues, "and that I was a better songwriter back then. But what they don't understand is that at that point all of my efforts went into a Guided by Voices record; there weren't all these side projects. So now, the serious shit goes on a Guided by Voices record. The crazy shit might go on a Circus Devils record or a Robert Pollard record. It's splintered into different projects now, because we got to the point where we could afford to do that. Back then, all we got was one Guided by Voices record, and some offshoot EPs and stuff.

"I still think we do a good job keeping things diversified; there was a lot of variation on the later records. There wasn't quite as much as there was back in the early days, because first of all we had the ability back then to go down into a basement anytime I had an idea and bang it out right away, and just do as many ideas as we could. People say I don't edit myself very well. Back then I didn't edit myself at all. Everything we fucking did we recorded. Every time I had a thought we recorded. We recorded skits and all kinds of stupid shit. Because it was on a four-track, and you can do that. It doesn't cost any money, and it doesn't take any time. A lot of people, they call that the classic lineup, and those were the classic days, the four-track days. But I *know* I'm a better songwriter than I was then. My songs are structurally more complicated, more interesting. I forced myself to do that. I knew I needed to become a better songwriter instead of just banging shit out. I still bang shit out, and I'm still not as disciplined as

I'd like to be, because I still can't see spending days and days and days writing a song.

"People who are stuck on the lo-fi shit, and the so-called classic lineup: whatever. Go listen to that forever. I can't keep doing that. You have to challenge yourself and try to grow as a songwriter. That's how you keep yourself entertained. You don't want to write the same song over and over and you don't want to use the same formula over and over."

By the time his band returned to Matador, Bob was used to doing things a certain way. He's always been a creature of habit, and drawing him out of his patterns of action requires a great deal of effort. One of the reasons Bob prefers to deal with Matador through the buffer of his management is that when asked to do something directly, he'll almost always say yes. But with Bob, "yes" very often means "no." Because he has trouble saying no to people, he hires a manager to say no for him.

Other people continued having little problem saying no to Bob, however. Jim Macpherson announced he was quitting the band, and Bob was unable to convince Greg Demos to join full-time, which forced him to rely on a revolving set of drummers and bass players through the final three GBV albums, despite which each is a gem, though in general an overlooked gem. The decline in sales that Cosloy earlier referenced with regard to album sales was not a precipitous one, certainly; there's a steady core of fans who will buy a Guided by Voices record, and an even steadier, though smaller, core who will buy anything Bob releases under whatever pseudonym.

Of which there's an overwhelming lot, frankly. The new millennium has seen a ceaseless issue of Bob-related product: two box sets; thirty-plus Fading Captain Series releases (including *Suitcase,* which counts as one of the box sets; the other was Matador's Greatest Hits Plus box, which included a DVD reissue of Banks Tarver's excellent documentary of mid-'90s GBV, called *Watch Me Jumpstart*); an entire rerecording of the vocals by Bob—with new lyrics and melodies—on an album by Phantom Tollbooth, a 1980s personal fave; plus contributions here and there to compilation albums and such.

One of which led to an important new ally in the rock trenches: the O.C., by which we do not mean a popular television show featuring the antics of nubile teens, but Original Critic, as in Original Rock Critic Richard Meltzer, whose book *The Aesthetics of Rock* was written between 1965 and 1968 but was not published until 1970, by which time the subject of his labors (rock) was dead, and who thus unfortunately invented the genre of rock criticism that has plagued the corpse of whatever you want to call pop music from then until now.

Meltzer met Bob through the agency of Portland, Oregon–based videostore owner and musician (and eventually, the very last bass player for GBV) Chris Slusarenko, who in 2000 put together a concept record called *Colonel Jeffrey Pumpernickel* for which he solicited a song from Bob, and then asked Meltzer to write the liner notes (Chris had struck up a friendship with Meltzer because his video store was the closest to Richard's house).

"Chris asked me one time if I'd like to read some stuff, opening for Guided by Voices," says Meltzer, "and I said, 'Sure, what the hell.' I had listened to the *Pumpernickel* record, but I hadn't really paid attention to the Guided by Voices song. You have to understand, I don't hear much current rock music, and I don't like much of what I hear—I listen to more jazz than rock and roll now.

"To put that in context, in 1965 and '66 there were no more than twenty or thirty bands that were worth listening to—there weren't even that many being released. By 1970 all the record companies decided that they had to sign everything, because even if you weren't going to release a band you'd have to sign them so somebody else couldn't have them, and so from a certain point on, every band that existed was signed. I wrote reviews for a while, but managed to either quit or get fired from most of the places I wrote, and as soon as I stopped receiving free promo copies, I stopped buying records. That was a long time ago. So the only stuff I knew, the only new stuff I got to know, was stuff that friends played for me.

"Anyway—this was I think in 2001, and the time comes and I go to the show, and I was supposed to meet up with everybody like an hour or two before showtime. I get there and Bob wasn't there yet, and I didn't even know what he looked like anyway. So I go over to the backstage, you know—where the food is. I sort of remember American cheese. Drank a lot of beer and ate some chips. Finally Bob is there and we hit it off pretty good. I mean, he was just a prince of a guy, and we're getting along, just talking, and I still haven't heard them, so by the time they went on I've had a few beers. Finally I hear them, and it's like maybe three or four songs into it and, uh, I just fell in love.

"You know: British Invasion garage band—what more could you want? My favorite thing, way back when, was the British Invasion, and to do the lo-tech version of it, to do the nonprog version of it, to really be doing it— as innocently delivered real music—it was just so touching to me.

"When the British Invasion itself happened it was like—you know, people talk about the fifties, but the fifties really only lasted about two years: from 1956 when Elvis was on Ed Sullivan till about '58 when it completely petered out. And then rock and roll didn't exist. I mean, yes, they played stuff on the radio and people still bought records, but nobody talked about it as something current; rock and roll was the past. So when The Beatles happened in late '63, and Kennedy got shot around that time, it was quite amazing, astounding, that rock and roll again existed. You don't get too many second comings of anything. It was amazing to get a second helping of rock and roll; it was not something anybody ever expected to happen again. I still feel the big bang from that today. And I felt almost the same way, seeing the first show I ever saw of Guided by Voices. It was like, 'Here it is again'—you know, our birthright.

"It was just this communal feeling of something so generous, and so, you know—where's the word? Without fangs. I mean, yes there's danger and all that stuff, but in the same way there is to any art that matters. But it wasn't Mick Jagger announcing that that 'Oh, I'm the devil' and 'Oh, I'm Jack The Ripper'—you know, 'Any version of evil you want, it's me.' With Guided by Voices it's the opposite of, you know, 'I own your soul,' which lately I feel is where, chronologically, rock and roll literally went to hell. The post–Brian Jones Stones. I actually never listened to them after *Exile on Main Street*. I don't own any records by them.

"But still, there are musical things that they did that are there in Guided by Voices. The sense that—having seen them now about five, six times and it just keeps expanding—my sense of what . . . of how generous they are. All of them, Bob and the whole crew.

"I love Doug and I just got his CD—he had these songs about his mother. It's called *Salamander*. It's very sweet. There's something just very sweet about it. The other thing, you know, little by little I acquired all the CDs. After seeing them the first time I just went and got them all. Seeing them play for an audience maybe the last three times and seeing the kids who park themselves right at the stage and sing along with everything and my sense is that they don't even know what half the lyrics mean because it's impossible! It doesn't mean anything. Anything more than anything else.

"And that's what to me is so amazing: that Bob, this poet, actually gets people to sit and dance to poetry. You know, when it's not even metaphoric of anything—it's just poetry. There's something very terrific about it. The last show was two nights ago and it was, like, very religious. It was just . . . the connection between him and them, and he didn't waste a word, he talked a lot but everything he said was just so full of poignancy and oompah.

"The first night that they played here, I had a doctor's appointment in the morning and it was an appointment I really couldn't miss, so I said 'I'm not gonna get as drunk tonight as I will tomorrow night,' and Bob kept offering me tequila. I told him this story once about getting this near-death experience from drinking mescal in South Texas and eating the worm and he just sort of, he almost got sick listening to that story and he told me afterward, 'Ah, you don't have to drink tequila.'

"It's funny, you know—there are people, friends of mine, that have never heard of them. When I mention the band by name they'll say, more than once, 'What's that, a white gospel group?'

"Once upon a time, the concept of 'the score' was always a part of it—if you're kids, and you started a band, you can be as big as Elvis maybe. But it got to where, since MTV at least, it isn't as if there's a kind of, like, dichotomy or polarity between art and commerce. They are very much the same thing."

There's an audible sigh before Meltzer continues. "I don't exactly know what it means for the real world to contain good music anymore," he says. "I don't know that it matters that what's being made continues to be viable in the hands of today's kids. It's just a rite of passage."

For every loss, a gain.

Bun E. Carlos, as the reader may be aware, is the drummer for Cheap Trick, a band Bob Pollard has often cited as a Primary Influence. Beginning in the mid-'90s, Bob had the opportunity to tour with his early heroes. Carlos writes here about touring with Guided by Voices, and his love of the band's music.

BUN E. CARLOS, CHEAP TRICK

TOURING

The first time we worked together, GBV opened for us in Cincinnati at some downtown street fest gig in the mid-'90s and I watched their show from stage left. Excellent, by the way. As their set time ran out, our stage manager came over to me and asked, "Shall I pull the plug or what?" I said, "Tell 'em five extra minutes and you gotta go." Stagehand overtime and other issues would come into play if they ran any later. They finished five minutes late, and two songs shy of the end of their set list. I thought it was great that they tried to cram as many songs into their forty-five minutes as possible.

I heard we had a chance to do some shows with GBV. Management was concerned with GBV's rep as boozing troublemakers. I said, "We'll deal with that if it happens." I'm a big GBV fan and I was aware of their rep as onstage party dogs.

We did four shows with GBV: Philly, NYC, Boston, and D.C. Every night during GBV, I'd go up and play cowbell with 'em for a song or two. All of us got a kick out of it, and I was thrilled to be onstage with GBV!

Roseland in NYC was the second gig, I think, and Bob ran up to sing on "Surrender" and he knocked over one of Tom's [Petersson, bass player] basses from its stand when he ran out. Maybe our stage manager at the time, or Tom's tech, got steamed about it after, I don't remember; Tom didn't freak out, as I recall. After the show, one of our staff was bent out of shape. I got on his case about it. I said something to the effect of "Big deal! Get over it! If you can't deal with it, go fuck yourself." I got pissed about it being a big deal. In my opinion, it was some roadie's tempest in a teapot. Not Cheap Trick's, the band.

In fact, the last gig two days later in Philly, we invited the whole band up to sing "Surrender" with us. Nate and the bass player—I forget his name—jumped up and pogoed all over the stage and we had a blast. After the show I asked backstage, "Where was Bob?" Someone said, "When 'Surrender' started, he ran out his dressing room door, tripped, and knocked himself out, so that's why he wasn't there!"

A couple of years ago, we did another short run with GBV. In Rockford, our hometown, after the show I was told that GBV had wrecked their dressing room and trashed the furnishings, and they should be thrown off the tour, etc., etc. It turned out to be a busted beer bottle and a couple of cigarette burns on an old carpet! Again, I had to tell our stage manager to "go fuck himself" if he couldn't handle it.

GBV's reputation seemed to cause them a lot of grief they didn't deserve. Sometimes they didn't help the situation, either. But, if I had to do it all over again, I wouldn't change a thing. What a great band!

RECORDINGS, ETC.

I first heard GBV in the early '90s. Some Cheap Trick fans, especially Mike Acquisto and Bob Ott, started sending me albums and bootlegs. I became an instant fan. We knew "right where" they were coming from musically. Live, they were excellent. The recordings were cooler, though. Lo-fi or hi-fi, it was always great production. I didn't hear a CT influence on them, but I don't listen for that kind of stuff. My favorite GBV song was one I really got into when we toured together, "Do Something Real." Another had the chorus "Someone tell me why"; I forget the title ("Teenage FBI"?).

As for a fave album? I only have a half dozen of their albums but I also have a couple dozen compilations from friends and collectors. So, I don't know. The Ric Ocasek album was a real strong one, as I recall. Another special GBV track is a version of our song "Downed," which GBV tracked when there was talk of us doing a two-sided single. It didn't happen because the four of us couldn't agree on a GBV tune for us to record for our half of the single.

I deejayed a couple of GBV after-show parties at the Smart Bar when GBV would play the Metro. It was a treat for me to play my fave tracks for those guys at the party. Plus, I got to see them play; plus, I got paid for it. I would have done it for free!

Every GBV gig I ever saw was excellent. Every one.

ROADS BY THE RIVERS

Gathering roads by the sides of the rivers
we choose to run
anywhere I choose or you
it is begun
starting to run
A to Z all the way
from stars high and blue pools

Boy do I like you to be with me
on practically every small journey

R. Pollard

WHAT I'VE LEARNED

ROBERT POLLARD, MUSICIAN, 47, DAYTON, OHIO

Robert Pollard announced last call on Guided by Voices in 2004, ending his band's two-decade-plus run. MAGNET *asked him to look back at some universal truths.*

Touring is something you get used to. It can be difficult and grueling, especially for a band like us that drank a lot and played three-hour shows, but I learned to enjoy it. I learned to relax during the long drives and make better use of the hurry-up-and-wait aspect of load-ins and sound checks (like, not attend them). By the end of the tour, I'm more than ready to go home. After a couple of weeks at home, I'm anxious to go back on tour.

Writing is easy. It's an ongoing process, like eating, breathing, or sleeping. It shouldn't be painful or difficult. It's a report on the state of the soul and, like the soul, should be continuously evolving. It does so through inspiration, from people, books, film, music. When inspiration is lacking, you get writer's block.

Three-way phone conversations can blow me.

Real friends come to see you play even if they don't like your music anymore.

Everything seeks perfection but never achieves it. Imperfection is better. Try it. It's easier to attain.

Anger is a twisted form of courage. It wishes to obliterate fear.

In the early days of Guided by Voices, when no one was listening, I was impatient. I used to tire of people in the band very quickly. I had physical altercations with them. I even resorted to bullshit tactics, like telling the band I was quitting and we were breaking up, then re-forming a month later with new members. I have learned to allow people to exist, grow, and find out who they are in the band. Give them all the time they need. As long as they are enthusiastic about the music, they can do whatever they want.

Lo-fi is like any genre. If you have the songs, the attitude, and the vision, it's going to be inspiring. If you don't, it's going to be lifeless. Lo-fi was the last truly charming and inspirational movement, the perfect extension of punk. Not only did you not have to know how to play, you didn't even have to worry whether it sounded good by contemporary production standards.

Sing, scream, whistle, drink, and have a good time every night.

True culture and the enhancement of life is being devoured by technological progress.

We are all gods. You can never underestimate the creative potential of a human being. Nor the destructive potential.

Traveling allows you to see people living in comfortable habitats, existing as if their small circle of movement is the only one that matters. You return to these places, including your own, and you see that nothing has changed. Time moves in a predictable pattern for them because of routine. When you're touring, there's a time warp. One week seems like a month. It's always good to go home, where time decelerates back to the point of predictability.

When you're depressed, hard work is the cure. The next time you get depressed, go out in the backyard and dig a six-foot hole. But don't jump in it just yet.

Life is a series of mistakes. You have to learn from them, and you can't dwell on them or condemn yourself. The biggest mistake I made was cheating on my wife while on the road. I didn't do that for six years but finally succumbed, and it cost me everything, including my happiness. But you have to pick up the pieces and move on. A person gets more than one chance in life, but you have to learn from your mistakes.

If you write a song and your mom thinks it's good, shit-can it immediately.

The goal of competition—be it in war, sports, education, politics, etc.—is energy theft. The winner feels elevation, having stolen his opponent's energy, and the loser feels empty and dejected, having lost it. We are born into a hierarchy of energy theft.

After a while, marriage becomes almost like a brother/sister/son/mother relationship, and if your interests in life don't converge, there are conflicts and a growing apart—even animosity. You still love each other and have the mutual bond of your children, but there's no shared spark or passion for other things. It becomes very frustrating.

Cheap coffeepots piss me off.

I've never considered myself to be a runaway success at anything I've done, including parenthood. But I've at least allowed my children to pursue their own interests without too much vicarious interference, and I think they both turned out pretty good.

Of all members in a rock band, the drummer succumbs most frequently to the urge of removing his shirt.

You can take ten people from various ethnicities, backgrounds, professions, whatever, who can't give a single shit about one another, put them together, get them drunk, and by the end of the night, they're all either hugging or punching each other. What else does that besides religion?

My good friend Billy Dixon was my center in football from seventh through twelfth grade. One day during practice, our head coach yelled, "If anybody sees anybody standing around with his thumb up his ass doing nothing, run over and knock him on his ass." Five minutes later, Coach was standing on the sidelines drinking a cup of coffee. Billy ran over and knocked him on his ass. I learned that day that, for the most part, we're all just standing around with our thumbs up our asses.

REPRINTED BY KIND PERMISSION OF *MAGNET* MAGAZINE. THANKS!

AGAIN

"All in all, and in spite . . . of inept assertions, and of confusions of names, dates, and events which can be instanced there, it is less in the statement of facts than in the interpretation made of the facts that error and mendacity often flourish in the Historia Augusta.*"*

—Marguerite Yourcenar, *The Dark Brain of Piranesi and Other Essays*

"Writer's block is for pussies": Bob's message on our voice mail just yesterday, in book time, although many months from now (or even years; we are not soothsayers) by the time you are reading this sentence. The context of his message—it should be noted that we received the voice mail on a Monument Sunday; in other words, that he had come to his revelation while in an altered state of consciousness—was meant to apply not to us, because although we are a pussy we do not suffer from writer's block, but to songwriters whose muse dries up like rainwater on summer streets.

Bob has (obviously) never suffered from writer's block, and despite his belligerent assertion we think we know why: because R. Pollard is afraid of time. Or more precisely, of death: intimations of mortality have always been plain in his songwriting, and you could make the case that his body of work in general is one long screed against the dying of the light, although we are neither so ambitious nor so fond of generalities. Having said that, his rejection of ordinary religious formulations has given him at least an outwardly jaundiced eye toward the rituals of death. "When I die, stick a bone up my ass and let the dogs drag me away," he's said, on more than one occasion, and whenever he says it, you feel somehow comforted

yourself at the prospect of dying—because it's a joke, because Bob turns it
into a joke, and laughing at the Reaper is either an effective defense or the
plain truth. However Bob feels about religion, he clearly believes in some
idea of the soul, and thus his contempt for funerary rites is just an extension of his certainty that the soul, or spirit, of a person is more important
than the transient vessel it inhabits.

"Please, God, just let me live until *From a Compound Eye* comes out,"
he said, months earlier, driving the snow-shawled byroads of Dayton,
Ohio. *From a Compound Eye* is the present name of Bob's first post-GBV
solo album, which, factoring music industry vagaries, will come out either shortly before or shortly after *Hunting Accidents* hits the streets with
an inaudible thump. It is unequivocally one of Bob's Best Records Ever,
a sprawling double-album masterpiece recorded with producer Todd
Tobias, with whom Bob has forged a symbiotic relationship. ("I'm having difficulty imagining not working with Todd," Bob says. "It'll probably be a partnership for the rest of my life, unless something happens.
But it's like now I'm spoiled. He just does so many cool things to songs.")
Whether *F.A.C.E.*—lookie-loo, an acronym!—receives its due plaudits
depends on so many variables that it is impossible to predict, but we hope
it does. The record's been finished for quite some time, and advance
copies have been circulated to a select few in the hard-core fan community, to a near unanimously ecstatic response. It's within the realm of
the possible that by the time of its release the record will have under-
gone a complete *F.A.C.E.*-lift (joke!), as is often Bob's wont, but we think
probably not, because at least for now he seems, and has increasingly
seemed with recent Guided by Voices records, satisfied with the results.
His drive to create more, and more, and more, which in earlier days
would have prompted a restless reworking of any given album, has instead found outlets in side projects, like the twisted postpunkery of the
Moping Swans, a temp band assembled from pieces of Bob's past—
including Greg Demos, Jim Macpherson, and Tony Conley, originally
of Anacrusis—tying a neat knot from the long rope of Bob's musical time
line. "Just because Macpherson and Greg weren't in the band, they still
came back and played shows from time to time, and I still did things with
them, like the [Fading Captain Series release] *Soft Rock Renegades*. And
now they're in the Moping Swans," says Bob. "I have trouble letting
people go."

You'll have had ample opportunity to listen to *Lightninghead to Coffee-pot,* the title of the Moping Swans' EP, which was released in May 2005, and you will notice that in addition to the usual collection of pithy gems, the title track is a nearly nine-minute-long, mostly instrumental song, un-thinkable in the *Bee Thousand* era, but very thinkable now that Bob has removed all restraints on the doability of what is no longer, if it ever was, a classifiable sub-sub-genre of what we once called rock. Listen to Circus Devils' next album, *Five* (they skipped "Four," for inscrutable reasons), for further evidence. Those who would straitjacket Bob as a throwback or rock Luddite would do well to spend some time with this long player, which comes as close as anything probably can to providing an aural equivalent of Bob's celebrated collages, a recent example of which adorns the cover of this book, for instance—but if you've ever seen a Guided by Voices album cover, with a few minor exceptions (*cough* TVT *cough*), you've seen his visual art, and if you haven't seen his short collection of poetry and collages, *Eat,* you should track down a copy, or wait until *Eat 2* comes out later this year. Bob's collages are as carefully constructed as his songs, though he relies on happy accidents in art as much as he does in music. Circus Devils, though: sure, you can hear traces of what people now call postrock as performed by those guys The Turtle, from Chicago, for ex-ample, but we hear influences ranging from late-period Talk Talk to Eno to Beefheart to maybe The Godz, and there's enough keyboards and samples and loops and goofy vocals to keep the most inert stoner occu-pied for days.

In other words, unique, and please keep in mind that every aspect of Bob informs and influences every other aspect, and that these aspects are now deliberately compartmentalized, whereas in earlier eras the whole jew-elry box would have been dumped onto one glittery pile. It is our opinion that the opportunity to fraction his musical personalities thusly has im-proved each of them, which in turn has improved the overall cast, so that when Bob comes to make a "proper" record, which in this case would mean something like *F.A.C.E.,* the results are consistently inconsistent, whereas a record like *Alien Lanes* was inconsistently consistent. The important dif-ferences are intent, and skill, and confidence.

As for the "what" of his later records—that is, speaking to content—Bob's always relied on the same few themes for lyrical gist, and you can't tell us that the "50-Year-Old Baby" (a title from *F.A.C.E.*) who wrote "Love

Is Stronger Than Witchcraft" (a title from *F.A.C.E.*) isn't a better songwriter than the thirty-five-year-old schoolteacher who wrote "Metal Mothers," as great as that song was/is. Smart people interpret these themes in different ways, but their reducible core, according to (again, for example) Richard Meltzer, "you could call boy/girl songs. I mean they're like The Beatles were, the first moment that rock bands—I mean the white people who weren't just stealing from R&B—were all good love songs. And Bob's stuff feels like that. You know, just primordial boy/girl."

"I like the lyrics to be kind of otherworldly and open to interpretation for the listener," says Bob. "I've always said that songs are better than poetry, because it gives them another dimension, it puts them out in the ether, floating around now, because it's been given melody, which allows it easier access to the human consciousness. It makes it more eternal, even. It appeals to an additional sense, which has to make it more meaningful in the long run."

"We used to be way cooler before it mattered," says Bob, and part of the reason for breaking up the band has to do with the desire to get back to the basement, to the old days, when there wasn't any pressure because there wasn't any future. With the crucial difference, this time, of a certain degree of security.

"I feel like I'm a little too old to do rock," says Bob. "I don't consider myself to be a rock musician anymore, I'm not in a band—that's one of the reasons I broke up the band. I'm me. That's what I do. It's established; people have been buying my records for twelve years around the world. It's kind of like my thing. There's a certain amount of people who like what I do. There don't have to be any pretensions. We're not Guided by Voices anymore, it's Robert Pollard. I can still play shows if I want to, I can make as many records as I want, or I can write a book if I want. I've kind of settled into it. I guess I deserve it. And I don't have to jump through hoops anymore. That's kind of my point with the record label and management: I told them, 'I'm laying back, I'm laying low now. I don't have to do the same thing.' We sell the same amount of records no matter what we do. Because there's a certain amount of people that buy our records, that are fans of my music. So it feels good to be forty-seven, and be settled in with something that you think there is a small amount of security in."

R.E.M.'s Peter Buck can relate: "The way it works is that—and I think Bob feels the same way—whether you like it or not, the name of the band is a brand, like Coca-Cola. And the audience expects certain things from that brand. One of the things they expect from R.E.M. is for Michael [Stipe] to sing the songs. Whenever I do an instrumental record with [side project] Tuatara, that would just be pointless to put out under the name R.E.M. I've got a lot of Bob's stuff, and even though he's the singer I can see why he has kept the Guided by Voices name as a place for stuff that people will expect him to do, and then the real fans will go and get all the other stuff."

"As much as I don't think people consider Guided by Voices a huge band, there are a fair amount of expectations about who they are and what they are and what you're going to see when you go see them play. I will say this: The older you get, the harder it is to make compromises between yourself and your bandmates. Sometimes you just want to do exactly what you want to do without talking, and other people around, too.

"But I respect whatever Bob does, and I'll be looking forward to see- ing whatever records he puts out under whatever name."

Bob first announced the decision to break up Guided by Voices to his bandmates about three months after *Half Smiles of the Decomposed* was finished.

"For some reason I wasn't surprised," says Nate Farley. "It made sense to me. *Half Smiles* did sound like a perfect wrap-up to everything, and Bob's at the perfect age—I'm not calling him old by any means—it's his time to do his songwriting thing, he needs to get in sound tracks, and this and that. He's got so much talent to spread around."

The effect on the rest of the band was much the same: The rest of the band decided to have fun. Chris Slusarenko, who joined the band for the final album and the Electrifying Conclusion, acquired the nickname "Blad- der Boy" for his frequent—and, it should be noted, medically excused— bathroom breaks. "One time at a show in D.C. I had to take a break," Chris recalls, "and Rich Turiel led me offstage and through this set of double doors to the piss bucket [a three-hour set has necessitated easy access to such a thing]; I couldn't hear anything that was going on onstage. So I'm heading back to the stage, and all the houselights are on, and Bob's leading the crowd in a chant: 'Bladder Boy's got to piss!' I crawled the rest of the way back."

There were, somewhat remarkably, no hard feelings, and even more remarkably, only a sense of gratefulness on the band members' part for being chosen to participate in something special. "I was just about to give up drumming for good," says Kevin March, the final occupant of the revolving drummer's seat. "Then I got a call from [manager] David Newgarden asking me to call Bob, who had known me from [post-Grifters outfit] Those Bastard Souls and [Boston noisemakers] The Dambuilders. He asked if I wanted to join the band. I called my wife at work and told her—'You're not going to believe this; I was just asked to join Guided by Voices. What should I do?' And she said, 'That's a no-brainer.' So in fact Bob saved me from giving up music, and made me realize that I must continue to play; it's a part of me that I cannot deny. GBV was also one of the most exciting and educational band experiences I've ever had. Bob is a true genius with a great sense of humor. One of his most charming aspects is his loyalty and love of his friends." [Editor's note: Kevin is one of the best, most solid drummers we have ever had the pleasure of seeing/hearing. If you are a rich rock musician looking for a drummer, please consider Kevin.]

We could go on all book telling tour stories, like the time Bob's Jack Daniel's–drinking friend Buffalo showed up at a gig in Denver and proceeded to get hammered, to the point where he decided to pick up one of Nate's unplugged guitars and wander onto the stage, the guitar strap crisscross around his neck, playing air guitar for what Bob thought would be one, maybe two songs; but instead Buffalo plowed through seven songs before falling headfirst off the stage and onto the unforgiving floor of the club. "Man down," Nate Farley remembers yelling into the microphone. He and Bob walked to the edge of the stage to see Buffalo, bloodied but unbowed, lying on the ground. The security guys who carted him off to the hospital told Nate, "I hope you got another guitar player, because this guy's done." Somehow the band managed to finish without him.

Or we could tell the story known as Ted Leo Sucker Punch. There is apparently a band called Ted Leo and the Pharmacists, who apparently opened for GBV at a show somewhere, and according to Nate: "Ted Leo's version is that we just kicked their asses because they drank some of our beer. But the fact of the matter is, they played too long, and so our set got cut short, and so Bob said, 'I'd like to thank the opening band for playing too long.' And then I walk outside, and all I see is Bob and Ted getting into each other's faces, and then Ted just clobbers Bob in the nose out of nowhere, total sucker punch, and then I look over and see Ted's brother standing there, and I go, 'Well, it's on, I might as well kick his brother's ass.' Which I did. And then the cops came and I took my girl and ran around the building and sat on the bench and started making out with her like we weren't even part of the show—I watch a lot of gangster movies.

"It's funny, because they think the whole thing is over them drinking our beer. And anyone that knows us well, knows that our beer is their beer. Beer's like Doritos—they'll keep making it. We're not a hard band to get along with if you're opening for us. You're welcome to come into the dressing room, we love hanging out with other people, and drinking and bullshit and stuff like that. And actually, we didn't even know they took any of our beer. And really wouldn't have given a shit anyway. We were mad because we didn't get to play our whole set, and felt like we were ripping off our fans."

All of which begs the question, who the fuck is Ted Leo?

"I don't know," shrugs Nate in reply. "Ted Leo and the Pharmacists. I think he's from Jersey, or Canada. Some foreign land."

Mark Spitz spent a few weeks covering the Electrifying Conclusion for *Spin* magazine, the biggest piece ever accorded the band, as well as the last (obviously). He has graciously sent us this communiqué from an undisclosed rehab facility:

It's been sixty-six days since I got off tour with Guided by Voices and I'm still hungover. I remember asking Bob what he was going to do immediately after getting off tour and he told me he was going to start running again, getting in shape. I pictured him getting up the next morning, pulling on some sneakers and jogging through the streets of Dayton. [Editors' note: He's correct.] That's the kind of constitution I imagine the guy has. I was quitting smoking . . . badly, while traveling with GBV, and I kept looking at Bob. He was giving them up too and I remember studying how he was dealing with not having a cig ready to punctuate every thought or action. [Editor's note: Bob still smokes, though not as much.] I noticed a lot of people looking at Bob while I was looking at Bob or . . . to Bob. For different reasons. He probably didn't know he was setting examples left and right. But he was. GBV set an example to other bands . . . including the Rolling Stones (who 'suck,' I'm told) and Bob's beloved Who about how to end these things with grace. I don't expect there'll ever be a reunion. Forget about the fact that Bob basically *is* GBV so there's nobody really to reunite—this said with total respect to all the other guys, who play like motherfuckers and treated me really warmly on tour. Even if he wasn't, I bet he'd find it vulgar and fake. If he needed the money, I could see him working in a record store instead . . . or maybe that's me.

That's my point, I guess. If I ever found myself in a similar position, I would ask, "What would Bob Pollard do?" Maybe I'd fuck up and do the opposite. Maybe I'd get it right. Basically he's the wisest trash talker we've ever had. I've been lied to by rock stars. Lots of rock stars. I get paid to be lied to by rock stars. I don't think Bob's ever lied to me [Editor's note: only if he told you he liked you]. The end—in Chicago—felt like an end . . . because it was. I didn't see any back door. Didn't smell any bullshit either. And because of that, I can say I was there. Think of how the people at the "last" Who show in 1982 feel now. Shitty. Right? I feel great. Except for the hangover.

We read Mark's piece to The Who's Pete Townshend, currently learning scrimshaw in his dotage from Inuit natives in Greenland, and he replied, "I listened to [Guided by Voices], and to be honest I couldn't really connect. Obviously the connection is there for others, but not for me."

You'd expect Bob to be deflated by such a flat response from one of his idols, and he probably was, but as we've noted before, he hides it well.

"That's good," he shoots back without hesitation. "It means that we're obviously not overly influenced by The Who. If he can't tell, then we must be doing something right."

(beat)

"I haven't been able to connect with much of his music lately, either. Like for twenty-five years."

(beat)

"People like Pete Townshend, or Keith Richards, or whoever, have become so high and mighty, like they're gods. They don't listen to anything but their own shit. I'm almost becoming one of them. But not quite. I still dig. I still go down and smell around."

The last sentence of Bob's quote is a line from "Blatant Doom Trip," a song off *Same Place the Fly Got Smashed,* and evidence, if any more were needed, of Bob's total recall with regard to his lyrics. Or you could look at it this way: The world that Bob created, sprung fully formed from his head like Athena from Zeus, or whichever Greek god from whichever Greek god (see: *Bullfinch's Mythology;* we're busy), is the world he inhabits. Nabokov defined genius as "an African who dreams of snow," the novelist apparently being unaware of the existence of Mount Kilimanjaro, but you get the idea—and what you experience as the real world, he sees through a set of filters, whether of his own design or by virtue of a higher will. You would no sooner forget the names of your children than Bob would the names of any of his metaphoric offspring, although when asked how old his actual children are, Bob had to puzzle out the numbers with help from his girlfriend, Sarah. (Bryan's twenty-three, Erika's nineteen. He's pretty sure.)

"It's my world," confirms Bob. "It's my schizophrenic world that I created. It's not so much breaking up the band as freeing me from my own self-constraints.

"Now when I make a record, I choose some people to play with me, and it's 'Thank you very much, good-bye.' You get stuck with a band. If it's not their decision to leave, they've been fired. So it's a no-win situation. I've been through forty or fifty people in that band. There's some bitterness, but there's nothing I can do about that. I made a decision a long time ago that I would make any necessary changes to keep the band progressing, to keep growing."

The promise of a new day, to crib from Paula Abdul. That's the correct answer to what drives Bob, keeps him going, keeps him writing songs and poems and making collages. The promise of a new day. We remember dropping Bob off at his house on Titus many years ago, after a night of drinking, when by chance his wife and kids were out of town. "I don't want to go in," Bob mock-whined. "Please don't make me. I don't want to be alone."

"It's not like I'm afraid of the dark," explains Bob. "I like to be around people, especially at night. Every day's symbolic of an entire life, and nighttime's death and morning's life again. I don't so much anymore, but I used to get bummed out at night. I thought I was gonna die.

"When I'm alone, I work, and I don't typically like to work at night. So basically, going home means I don't work—it's bedtime. I think people have an aversion to bedtime, that we're forced to go to bed at a certain hour growing up. We had to be in bed at nine o'clock, at a certain age. That's brutal! You don't make people go to bed when they're not tired. Maybe I carried that with me for a while.

"It's not so bad anymore. I know pretty much what I want to do throughout the day, and then maybe go out and drink—I drink a lot. I don't know if people know that.

"That's another thing: I get to bed at a reasonable hour, even on tour, unless the show goes really late. Listen: I go to the hotel after the show and go to sleep. I don't stay out all night long doing drugs and shit. It's not as bad as you think. You *see* what I do. That's the extent of it.

"At home, a typical night for me is, I drink from six o'clock to ten o'clock at night, and then I go to bed. And then I get up in the morning and work. And that's probably partially habit from all those years of getting up early as a teacher. It's better to work in the morning. You're fresh, you get up, it's a new day. For me, anyway."

Life for Robert Pollard is better now than probably at any time in the past several years. "Things are good: I got a house, and Sarah," he says.

Sarah Zade met Bob at a show on April 25, 2003. Guided by Voices was playing in Columbia, Missouri, at a venue called Mississippi Nights. Sarah was not in any way a fan of the band, but was dragged to the show by a friend who was. Sarah loved the show, and uncharacteristically got carried away, to the point where "I got down in front and was dancing around and jumping up and down," says Sarah.

"There was some typical GBV guy doing the same thing down there," she continues, "and we ran into each other really hard and my lip split open and there was blood running down my chin. This was right at the end of the show. After the last song my friend took me over to Bobby and said something like, 'Do you see what happened to her because of you?' In actuality she just wanted an excuse to talk to him. He responded by getting

Rich—or somebody; I don't even remember who—to get some towels so I could clean up. Then he coyly suggested he could 'make it feel better,' you know, because he's smooth like that [Editor's note: Sarah is joking]. That was the winning line right there, can you believe it? How ridiculous!"

Sarah and Bob kept in touch after that incident, and it wasn't long before they started dating and eventually moved in together. Sarah exerts a calming influence on Bob, and on tour has taken charge of ensuring that Bob gets back to the hotel safely and early. It's endearing to see Bob meekly submit to Sarah's ministrations, and further to see the obvious affection they have for each other, publicly—a thing you rarely saw with his ex-wife, Kim, mainly because she rarely came out with him, either on tour or in Dayton, whereas by contrast Sarah is either there, or will be there, often serving as designated driver for her blotto boyfriend. (In fairness to Kim, she was tasked with raising two kids, but even if not, she didn't *want* to go out drinking with Bob, and if she had they would not have had much to talk about besides domestic matters.)

"The only thing I feel bad about in my relationship with Sarah," says Bob, "is that I'm so much older than her, and I'm gonna be a crusty old fucker when she's still young and good-looking. It's approaching a little quicker than I hoped for. And ultimately I'm gonna be dead, while she's still relatively young."

The couple's new house, in Northridge, was not an easy acquisition, considering Bob's uncertain income stream ("self-employed" is not something banks like to see on a mortgage application), so to help finance the house, as well as the work that needed to be done on it, Bob started, with Rich Turiel's help, a "Fuck the Bank" auction on eBay, where he would sell autographed copies of extra and often highly prized GBV-related collectibles. This proved remarkably successful, and is currently in round sevenish. It was during one of these auctions that an original copy of *Propeller* sold for $6,200, which has to be some kind of record for a record.

The house has been bought, the work is under way, a new version of the Monument Club has been installed, and Bob's latest home improvement project is a kind of Guided by Voices museum. He bought some display cases of the kind you find in record stores, and a poster rack, and plans to carefully winnow from his cache of everything the most important specimens, to exhibit for friends and family, and we suspect most of all for himself, to remind himself of all that he has accomplished, and to spur himself to accomplish more.

Bob turned down an invitation to join the Dayton Hall of Fame a few years earlier, on the grounds that his career was not nearly over and that his best stuff was still to come. The band is featured in the Rock 'n' Roll Hall of Fame in Cleveland, however, in a special Ohio exhibit, which includes the broken ballpoint pen with which Bob wrote the lyrics to "I Am a Scientist"; a gilt-framed full-sized photorealist painting of Bob as Julius Caesar by Toby; the secret 501st copy of *Propeller*, officially numbered 000, whose cover art spells "Guided by Voices" in the commingled blood of brothers Bob and Jimmy; Mitch Mitchell's original touring van: complete, still runs, still leaks gas; a paper bag full of crumpled napkins covered in song titles; a list of every GBV song anagrammed into incomprehensibility, but which, *rumor volat,* if rubbed lightly with a blue cloth after first solving every anagram in order, reveals in golden letters the Secret Of Life; a coffeepot melted by a direct lightning hit. Among other things.

So go, don't delay, right now to the Rock 'n' Roll Hall of Fame, because this collection is due to be replaced by The Wax Trax Story in a few months, and you will never see these things again, they will be returned to their owners, or buried in a time capsule in Trotwood, Ohio, on the off chance that human beings still exist one hundred, two hundred or more days from now.

Question: You don't really write about personal subjects, do you?

Answer: No. My ex-wife, and Sarah, they think that . . . Don't fucking think that I'm writing about you, just because it has a girl's name in it or it says "she." Don't even flatter yourself. And I have written songs for girls, for my . . . *mate.* "Tour Guide at the Winston Churchill Memorial" is about Sarah because that's what she was; that's what she did at one time. There've been other ones that I don't want to mention because Sarah will get pissed. But there's a lot of times where I have had to apologize to people in advance. I have to go, "Listen, I'm writing a song here but it doesn't really mean fucking anything." Don't get pissed off at shit I write. I don't write songs about people in particular for the most part.

Question: Do you think the band will endure? In other words, do you think in twenty years' time people will still revere Guided by Voices?

Answer: Let's let Esteemed Rock Critic Michael Azerrad handle this one: "What they have in their favor, when I think about bands who are remembered twenty years hence, is that they have great songs. Not just a sound, although they did have a sound. But it's not a texture or superb rhythm section or something like that. That can get you over temporarily. It is actually the lasting quality of the songs. Those songs can be covered by people till doomsday. That's something that . . . Even Kraftwerk had really great songs, and they lasted. That's the kind of thing that GBV does have. There is definitely that potential there."

We should let people know that the universe is dissolving. Or, more accurately—merging. We should let people know that. But maybe it's better if they find out from Bob, if they listen to his music, really listen, and understand that whatever R. Pollard's feats and foibles as a person, there's another P-O-L-L-A-R-D that exists in the dimension of song, unrelated to Robert, Bob, Bobby. That has always existed and always will. Happy Birthday.

"Did I tell you about the time I was extremely stoned and the answer to everything came to me and I couldn't grasp it?" recalls Bob, apropos of everything. "I was like, 'Oh God!' And I couldn't hang on to it, man. It was something that would really fucking help out, somehow. And it probably goes to people, every once in a while. And it's probably really difficult to comprehend and remember. I think part of it is to alter your consciousness just slightly, your assemblage point, to where you come into contact with other realms of thought. It was a revelation. And as quickly as it entered my head it just left. But I knew it was something."

Which, Bob would like at this time to reveal, is the definition of Guided by Voices. That experience. That ungraspable answer. The truth.

APPENDIX I

GUIDED BY VOICES
SELECTED DISCOGRAPHY
1983–2004

This discography includes selected recordings from the Guided by Voices catalog. Most promo items, non-U.S. releases, or compilations without exclusive tracks are not included.

Guided by Voices

Lineup: Robert Pollard and various members (see GbV family tree for details)

ALBUMS

Devil Between My Toes
Label/Catalog #: Y (Schwa) GBV0001
Released: 2/15/1987
Format: LP *(Also available on CD and LP as part of Box box set.)*
Country: U.S.

Label/Catalog #: Get Happy!!! BIG 02
Released: 1993
Format: LP
Country: Germany

1. Old Battery
2. Discussing Wallace Chambers
3. Cyclops
4. Crux
5. A Portrait Destroyed by Fire
6. 3 Year Old Man
7. Dog's Out
8. A Proud and Booming Industry
9. Hank's Little Fingers
10. Artboat
11. Hey Hey, Spaceman
12. The Tumblers
13. Bread Alone
14. Captain's Dead

Sandbox
Label/Catalog #: Halo 1
Released: 1987
Format: LP *(Also available on CD and LP as part of Box box set.)*

1. Lips of Steel
2. A Visit to the Creep Doctor
3. Everyday
4. Barricade
5. Get to Know the Ropes
6. Can't Stop
7. The Drinking Jim Crow
8. Trap Soul Door
9. Common Rebels
10. Long Distance Man
11. I Certainly Hope Not
12. Adverse Wind

Self-Inflicted Aerial Nostalgia
Label/Catalog #: Halo 2
Released: 1989
Format: LP *(Also available on CD and LP as part of Box box set.)*

1. The Future Is in Eggs
2. The Great Blake Street
   Canoe Race
3. Slopes of Big Ugly
4. Paper Girl
5. Navigating Flood Regions
6. An Earful o' Wax
7. White Whale
8. Trampoline
9. Short on Posters
10. Chief Barrel Belly
11. Dying to Try This
12. The Qualifying Remainder
13. Liar's Tale
14. Radio Show (Trust the
    Wizard)

Same Place the Fly Got Smashed
Label/Catalog #: Rocket #9 OX846
Released: 1990
Format: LP *(Also available on CD and LP as part of Box box set.)*

1. Airshow '88
2. Order for the New Slave
   Trade
3. The Hard Way
4. Drinker's Peace
5. Mammoth Cave
6. When She Turns 50
7. Club Molluska
8. Pendulum
9. Ambergris
10. Local Mix-Up
11. Murder Charge
12. Starboy
13. Blatant Doom Trip
14. How Loft I Am?

Propeller
Label: Rockathon 001
Released: 1992
Format: LP *(Also available on LP as part of Box box set.)*

LP covers and back covers were hand decorated by the band.

Label/Catalog #: Scat 49
Released: 1996
Format: CD

1. Over the Neptune/Mesh Gear Fox
2. Weed King
3. Particular Damaged
4. Quality of Armor
5. Metal Mothers
6. Lethargy
7. Unleashed! The Large-Hearted Boy
8. Red Gas Circle
9. Exit Flagger
10. 14 Cheerleader Coldfront
11. Back to Saturn X Radio Report
12. Ergo Space Pig
13. Circus World
14. Some Drilling Implied
15. On the Tundra

Vampire On Titus
Label/Catalog #: Scat 31
Released: 1993
Format: LP

Label/Catalog #: Scat 50
Released: 11/15/1996
Format: CD, LP

1. "Wished I Was a Giant"
2. #2 in the Model Home Series
3. Expecting Brainchild
4. Superior Sector Janitor X
5. Donkey School
6. Dusted
7. Marchers in Orange
8. Sot
9. World of Fun
10. Jar of Cardinals
11. Unstable Journey
12. E-5
13. Cool Off Kid Kilowatt
14. Gleemer (The Deeds of Fertile Jim)
15. Wondering Boy Poet
16. What About It?
17. Perhaps Now the Vultures
18. Non-Absorbing

Bee Thousand
Label/Catalog #: Scat 35
Released: 6/21/1994
Format: CD, LP, Cassette

1. Hardcore UFO's
2. Buzzards and Dreadful Crows
3. Tractor Rape Chain
4. The Goldheart Mountaintop Queen Directory
5. Hot Freaks
6. Smothered in Hugs
7. Yours to Keep
8. Echos Myron
9. Gold Star for Robot Boy
10. Awful Bliss
11. Mincer Ray
12. A Big Fan of the Pigpen
13. Queen of Cans and Jars
14. Her Psychology Today
15. Kicker of Elves
16. Ester's Day
17. Demons are Real
18. I Am a Scientist
19. Peep-Hole
20. You're Not an Airplane

Bee Thousand: The Director's Cut
Label/Catalog #: Scat 65
Released: 9/20/2004
Format: 3 LP

Instructions To The Rusty Time Machine (Disc 1)
Side A

1. Demons Are Real
2. Deathtrot and Warlock Riding a Rooster
3. Postal Blowfish
4. The Goldheart Mountaintop Queen Directory
5. At Odds With Dr. Genesis
6. Hot Freaks
7. Queen of Cans and Jars
8. Bite
9. It's Like Soul Man [4 Track Version]

Side B

1. Supermarket the Moon
2. Stabbing a Star
3. Ester's Day
4. Her Psychology Today
5. Good for a Few Laughs
6. Smothered in Hugs
7. What Are We Coming Up To?
8. Peep-Hole

Instructions To The Rusty Time Machine (Disc 2)
Side C

1. Revolution Boy
2. Indian Was an Angel
3. Zoning the Planet
4. Scissors
5. Crayola
6. Kicker of Elves
7. 2nd Moves to Twin
8. I'll Buy You a Bird

Side D

1. Awful Bliss
2. Echos Myron
3. Why Did You Land? [Slow Version]
4. You're Not an Airplane
5. Crunch Pillow
6. Rainbow Billy
7. Tractor Rape Chain
8. Crocker's Favorite Song

Misc & EP Tracks (Disc 3)
Side E

1. I Am a Scientist
2. Buzzards and Dreadful Crows
3. A Big Fan of the Pigpen
4. Mincer Ray
5. Way to a Man's Heart
6. Twig
7. Gold Star for Robot Boy
8. Hardcore UFO's
9. Yours to Keep
10. Shocker in Gloomtown [Early Version]
11. Break Even [Early Version]

Side F

1. I'll Get Over It
2. Shocker in Gloomtown
3. Alien Lanes
4. Off the Floor
5. Break Even
6. Bee Thousand
7. I Am a Scientist [7" Version]
8. Curse of the Black Ass Buffalo
9. Do the Earth
10. Planet's Own Brand
11. My Valuable Hunting Knife [Andy Shernoff Version]

Bee Thousand: The Director's Cut (Abridged)
Label/Catalog #: Scat 65
Released: 9/20/2004
Format: CD

1. Demons Are Real
2. Deathtrot and Warlock Riding a Rooster
3. Postal Blowfish
4. The Goldheart Mountaintop Queen Directory
5. At Odds with Dr. Genesis
6. Hot Freaks
7. Queen of Cans and Jars
8. Bite
9. It's Like Soul Man [4 Track Version]
10. Supermarket the Moon
11. Stabbing a Star
12. Ester's Day
13. Her Psychology Today
14. Good for a Few Laughs
15. Smothered in Hugs
16. What Are We Coming Up To?
17. Peep-Hole
18. Revolution Boy
19. Indian Was An Angel
20. Zoning the Planet
21. Scissors
22. Crayola
23. Kicker of Elves
24. 2nd Moves to Twin
25. I'll Buy You a Bird
26. Awful Bliss
27. Echos Myron

28. Why Did You Land? [Slow Version]
29. You're Not an Airplane
30. Crunch Pillow
31. Rainbow Billy
32. Tractor Rape Chain
33. Crocker's Favorite Song
34. Way to a Man's Heart
35. Twig
36. Shocker in Gloomtown [Early Version]
37. Break Even [Early Version]
38. My Valuable Hunting Knife [Andy Shernoff Version]

Alien Lanes
Label/Catalog #: Matador OLE 123
Released: 4/4/1995
Format: CD, LP, Cassette

1. A Salty Salute
2. Evil Speakers
3. Watch Me Jumpstart
4. They're Not Witches
5. As We Go Up, We Go Down
6. (I Wanna Be a) Dumbcharger
7. Game of Pricks
8. The Ugly Vision
9. A Good Flying Bird
10. Cigarette Tricks
11. Pimple Zoo
12. Big Chief Chinese Restaurant
13. Closer You Are
14. Auditorium
15. Motor Away
16. Hit
17. My Valuable Hunting Knife
18. Gold Hick
19. King and Caroline
20. Striped White Jets
21. Ex-Supermodel
22. Blimps Go 90
23. Strawdogs
24. Chicken Blows
25. Little Whirl
26. My Son Cool
27. Always Crush Me
28. Alright

Under the Bushes Under the Stars
Label/Catalog #: Matador OLE 161
Released: 3/26/1996
Format: CD, LP + 12", Cassette
Country: U.S.

1. Man Called Aerodynamics
2. Rhine Jive Click
3. Cut-Out Witch
4. Burning Flag Birthday Suit
5. The Official Ironmen Rally Song
6. To Remake the Young Flyer
7. No Sky
8. Bright Paper Werewolves
9. Lord of Overstock
10. Your Name Is Wild
11. Ghosts of a Different Dream
12. Acorns & Orioles
13. Look at Them
14. The Perfect Life
15. Underwater Explosions
16. Atom Eyes
17. Don't Stop Now
18. Office of Hearts

The following tracks were included as a bonus 12" EP for the vinyl version and as extra tracks for the CD version:

19. Big Boring Wedding
20. It's Like Soul Man
21. Drag Days
22. Sheetkickers
23. Redmen and Their Wives
24. Take to the Sky

Label/Catalog # Matador OLE 161
Released 3/26/1996
Format: 2 CD
Country: United Kingdom

Includes the tracks on the U.S. CD on the first disc plus the following bonus tracks from Tigerbomb and the Guided by Voices/Superchunk split single on the second CD:

1. My Valuable Hunting Knife
   [7" Version]
2. Game of Pricks [7" Version]
3. Mice Feel Nice (In My Room)
4. Not Good for the
   Mechanism
5. Kiss Only the Important
   Ones
6. Dodging Invisible Rays
7. Delayed Reaction Brats
8. He's the Uncle
9. The Key Losers

Label/Catalog # P-Vine/Blues Interactions PCD-24005
Released 12/16/1998
Format: CD
Country: Japan

Includes the tracks from the U.S. version on the first disc along with the following bonus tracks:

25. Finks
26. The Finest Joke Is Upon Us

Mag Earwhig!
Label/Catalog #: Matador OLE 241
Released: 5/20/1997
Format: CD, LP, Cassette
Country: U.S.

1. Can't Hear the Revolution
2. Sad If I Lost It
3. I Am a Tree
4. The Old Grunt
5. Bulldog Skin
6. Are You Faster?
7. I Am Produced
8. Knock 'Em Flyin'
9. Not Behind the Fighter Jet
10. Choking Tara
11. Hollow Cheek
12. Portable Men's Society
13. Little Lines
14. Learning to Hunt
15. The Finest Joke Is Upon Us
16. Mag Earwhig!
17. Now to War
18. Jane of the Waking Universe
19. The Colossus Crawls West
20. Mute Superstar
21. Bomb in the Bee-Hive

Label/Catalog #: P-Vine/Blues Interactions PCD-24006
Released: 2/10/2000
Format: CD
Country: Japan

Same tracks as U.S. version but with the following bonus tracks:
22. Running Off With the Fun   23. None of Them Any Good
    City Girls

Guided By Voices
Do The Collapse

Do The Collapse
Label/Catalog #: TVT 1980
Released: 8/3/1999
Format: CD, LP, Cassette
Country: U.S.

1. Teenage FBI	9. Mushroom Art
2. Zoo Pie	10. Much Better Mr. Buckles
3. Things I Will Keep	11. Wormhole
4. Hold on Hope	12. Strumpet Eye
5. In Stitches	13. Liquid Indian
6. Dragons Awake!	14. Wrecking Now
7. Surgical Focus	15. Picture Me Big Time
8. Optical Hopscotch	16. An Unmarketed Product

Label/Catalog #: Creation CRECD 251
Released: 8/3/1999
Format: CD
Country: United Kingdom
Label: TVT
Released: 8/3/1999
Format: CD
Country: Japan

Same tracks as U.S. version but with the following bonus track:
17. Avalanche Aminos

Isolation Drills
Label/Catalog #: TVT 2160
Released: 4/10/2001
Format: CD, LP
Country: U.S.

1. Fair Touching	6. Sister I Need Wine
2. Skills Like This	7. Want One?
3. Chasing Heather Crazy	8. The Enemy
4. Frostman	9. Unspirited
5. Twilight Campfighter	10. Glad Girls

11. Run Wild
12. Pivotal Film
13. How's My Drinking?
14. The Brides Have Hit Glass
15. Fine to See You
16. Privately

Label/Catalog #: P-Vine/Blues Interactions PCD-24080
Released: 6/10/2001
Format: CD
Country: Japan

Same tracks as U.S. version but with the following bonus track:
17. Isolation Drills

Universal Truths and Cycles
Label/Catalog #: Matador OLE 547
Released: 6/18/2002
Format: CD, LP
Country: U.S.

1. Wire Greyhounds
2. Skin Parade
3. Zap
4. Christian Animation Torch Carriers
5. Cheyenne
6. The Weeping Bogeyman
7. Back to the Lake
8. Love 1
9. Storm Vibrations
10. Factory of Raw Essentials
11. Everywhere With Helicopter
12. Pretty Bombs
13. Eureka Signs
14. Wings of Thorn
15. Car Language
16. From a Voice Plantation
17. The Ids Are Alright
18. Universal Truths and Cycles
19. Father Sgt. Christmas Card

Label/Catalog #: P-Vine/Blues Interactions PCD-23256
Released: 6/10/2002
Format: CD
Country: Japan

Same tracks as U.S. version but with the following bonus track:
20. The Pipe Dreams of Instant Prince Whippet

Earthquake Glue
Label/Catalog #: Matador OLE 574
Released: 8/19/2003
Format: CD, LP
Country: U.S.

1. My Kind of Soldier
2. My Son, My Secretary, My Country
3. I'll Replace You With Machines
4. She Goes Off at Night
5. Beat Your Wings
6. Useless Inventions
7. Dirty Water
8. The Best of Jill Hives

9. Dead Cloud
10. Mix Up the Satellite
11. Main Street Wizards
12. A Trophy Mule in Particular

13. Apology in Advance
14. Secret Star
15. Of Mites and Men

Label/Catalog #: P-Vine/Blues Interactions PCD-23422
Released: 8/10/2003
Format: CD
Country: Japan

Same tracks as U.S. version but with the following bonus track:
16. Broken Brothers

Half Smiles of the Decomposed
Label/Catalog #: Matador OLE 612
Released: 8/24/2004
Format: CD, LP
Country: U.S.

1. Everybody Thinks I'm a Raincloud (When I'm Not Looking)
2. Sleep Over Jack
3. Girls of Wild Strawberries
4. Gonna Never Have to Die
5. Window of My World
6. The Closets of Henry
7. Tour Guide at the Winston Churchill Memorial

8. Asia Minor
9. Sons of Apollo
10. Sing for Your Meat
11. Asphyxiated Circle
12. A Second Spurt of Growth
13. (S)mothering and Coaching
14. Huffman Prairie Flying Field

Label/Catalog #: P-Vine/Blues Interactions PCD-23536
Released: 8/6/2004
Country: Japan
Format: CD

Same tracks as U.S. version but with the following bonus track:
15. The Mind Refuser

FAN CLUB ALBUMS

Tonics and Twisted Chasers
Label/Catalog #: Rockathon 002
Released: 12/1996
Format: LP

1. Satellite
2. Dayton, Ohio-19 Something and 5
3. Is She Ever?
4. My Thoughts Are a Gas [Fucked Up Version]
5. Knock 'em Flyin'
6. The Top Chick's Silver Chord
7. The Key Losers
8. Ha Ha Man
9. Wingtip Repair
10. At the Farms
11. Unbaited Vicar of Scorched Earth
12. Optional Bases Opposed
13. Look, It's Baseball
14. Maxwell Jump
15. The Stir-Crazy Pornographer
16. 158 Years of Beautiful Sex
17. Universal Nurse Finger
18. Sadness to the End
19. Reptilian Beauty Secrets

Label/Catalog #: Rockathon 002
Released: 12/1997
Format: CD

Same tracks as LP version but with the following bonus tracks:

20. Long as the Block Is Black
21. Jellyfish Reflector
22. The Kite Surfer
23. Girl from the Sun
24. The Candyland Riots

BOX SETS

Box
Label/Catalog #: Scat 40
Released: 2/28/1995
Format: 5 CD, 6 LP

Devil Between My Toes

1. Old Battery
2. Discussing Wallace Chambers
3. Cyclops
4. Crux
5. A Portrait Destroyed by Fire
6. 3 Year Old Man
7. Dog's Out
8. A Proud and Booming Industry
9. Hank's Little Fingers
10. Artboat
11. Hey Hey, Spaceman
12. The Tumblers
13. Bread Alone
14. Captain's Dead

Sandbox

1. Lips of Steel
2. A Visit to the Creep Doctor
3. Everyday
4. Barricade
5. Get to Know the Ropes
6. Can't Stop
7. The Drinking Jim Crow
8. Trap Soul Door
9. Common Rebels
10. Long Distance Man
11. I Certainly Hope Not
12. Adverse Wind

Self-Inflicted Aerial Nostalgia

1. The Future Is in Eggs
2. The Great Blake Street Canoe Race
3. Slopes of Big Ugly
4. Paper Girl
5. Navigating Flood Regions
6. An Earful o' Wax
7. White Whale
8. Trampoline
9. Short on Posters
10. Chief Barrel Belly
11. Dying to Try This
12. The Qualifying Remainder
13. Liar's Tale
14. Radio Show (Trust the Wizard)

Same Place the Fly Got Smashed

1. Airshow '88
2. Order for the New Slave Trade
3. The Hard Way
4. Drinker's Peace
5. Mammoth Cave
6. When She Turns 50
7. Club Molluska
8. Pendulum
9. Ambergris
10. Local Mix-Up/Murder Charge
11. Starboy
12. Blatant Doom Trip
13. How Loft I Am?

King Shit and the Golden Boys

1. We've Got Airplanes
2. Dust Devil
3. Squirmish Frontal Room
4. Tricyclic Looper
5. Crutch Came Slinking
6. Fantasy Creeps
7. Sopor Joe
8. Crunch Pillow
9. Indian Was An Angel
10. Don't Stop Now [Original Version]
11. Bite
12. Greenface
13. Deathtrot and Warlock Riding a Rooster
14. 2nd Moves to Twin
15. At Odds with Dr. Genesis
16. Please Freeze Me
17. Scissors
18. Postal Blowfish
19. Crocker's Favorite Song

Note: The following album was only included in the 6 LP version of Box.

Propeller

1. Over the Neptune/Mesh Gear Fox
2. Weed King
3. Particular Damaged
4. Quality of Armor
5. Metal Mothers

6. Lethargy
7. Unleashed! The Large-
Hearted Boy
8. Red Gas Circle
9. Exit Flagger
10. 14 Cheerleader Coldfront

11. Back to Saturn X Radio
Report
12. Ergo Space Pig
13. Circus World
14. Some Drilling Implied
15. On the Tundra

Suitcase: Failed Experiments and Trashed Aircraft
Label/Catalog #: Fading Captain Series 6
Released: 10/17/2000
Format: 4 CD

Fake band names were listed for each of the one hundred songs. Band names are listed first below and then the song title, separated by a dash.

Disc One

1. Styles We Paid For—The Terrible Two
2. Standard Generator—Bloodbeast
3. Huge on Pluto—The Kissing Life
4. Whitey Museum—Bottoms Up! (You Fantastic Bastard)
5. (The Amazing) Ben Zing—Tear It Out
6. Meat Kingdom Group—Cinnamon Flavored Skulls
7. Elf God—Bunco Men
8. Judas & The Piledrivers—Bad and Rare
9. Eric Pretty—Dorothy's a Planet
10. Global Witch Awakening—Pluto the Skate
11. Magic Toe—Let's Go Vike
12. Hazzard Hotrods—Sabotage [Live]
    • Recorded at MC Video
13. Tax Revlon—Pink Drink
14. Champion Hairpuller—James Riot
15. Burns Carpenter—It's Easy
16. A A Bottom—Dank Star Ground Control
17. Crushed Being Groovy—Spring Tigers
18. Rex Polaroyd—Born on Seaweed
19. Monkey Business—Flesh Ears from June
20. Ghetto Blaster—Driving in the U.S. of A.
21. Turned on Turner—My Big Day [3 Versions]
22. Maxwell Greenfield—Have It Again
23. Little Bobby Pop—Little Jimmy the Giant
24. Bozo's Octopuss—Taco, Buffalo, Birddog and Jesus
25. Mooshoo Wharf—Ding Dong Daddy (Is Back from the Bank)

Disc Two

1. Clinton Killingsworth—Supermarket the Moon
2. Stingy Queens—Hold on to Yesterday
3. Judy Plus Nine, The—Ha Ha Man [Different Version]
4. Nicotine Cranes—Our Value of Luxury
5. Arthur Psycho and the Trippy Warts—Bug House [2 Versions]
6. Groovy Lucifer—Rainbow Billy
7. Approval of Mice—Shrine to the Dynamic Years (Athens Time Change Riots)
8. Eric Pretty—On Short Wave
9. Artrock Unicorns—I Can See It in Your Eyes
10. Kuda Labranche—Tobacco's Last Stand
11. Elvis Caligula—Shifting Swift Is a Lift
12. Tabatha's Flashpot—Sing It Out
13. Ricked Wicky—Messenger
14. K.C. Turner—The Fool Ticket
15. Brown Smoothies—Mallard Smoke
16. Edison Shell—Mr. McCaslin Will Sell No More Flowers
17. Ceramic Cock Einstein—Shit Midas
18. Moonchief—Blue Gil
19. Ricked Wicky—Invest in British Steel
20. Pearly Gates Smoke Machine—Spinning Around
21. 1st Joint—Let's Go! (To War)
22. Antler—Grasshopper Rap
23. King of Cincinnati—I'm Cold
24. Ghost Fart—Damn Good Mr. Jam [Different Version]
25. Ben Zing—In Walked the Moon

Disc Three

1. Fake Organisms—Long Way to Run
2. Tom Devil—Mr. Media
3. Urinary Track Stars—Settlement Down
4. Red Hot Helicopter—Mr. Japan
5. Doctor Formula—A Kind of Love [Live]
   • Recorded at Gilly's, Dayton, OH
6. Ben Zing—Meddle
7. Hazzard Hotrods—Big Trouble [Live]
   • Recorded at MC Video
8. Eric Pretty—A Good Circuitry Soldier
9. Antler—Devil Doll
10. Indian Alarm Clock—Pantherz [Different Version]
11. Flaming Ray—Cocaine Jane
12. Grabbit—Exploding Anthills

13. 8th Dwarf—Perch Warble
14. Coward of the Hour—Medley: This View/True Sensation/On the Wall
15. Oil Can Harry—What Are We Coming Up To?
16. Too Proud to Practice—Scissors and the Clay Ox (In)
17. Zeppelin Commander—Cody's Antler
18. God's Brother—Once in a While
19. Antler—Buzzards and Dreadful Crows [Different Version]
20. Kink Zero—Carnival at the Morning Star School
21. Royal Japanese Daycare—Cruise [Different Version]
22. Stingy Queens—Gayle
23. Homosexual Flypaper—Gift
24. Fast Forward Life—The Flying Party
25. Bus of Trojan Hope—Trashed Aircraft

Disc Four

1. Pete Eastwood—Trying to Make It Work Again
2. Panzee—Turbo Boy
3. Unfriendly, The—Chain Wallet Bitch
4. King of Cincinnati—Little Head
5. Matted Pelt—Why Did You Land? [Slow Version]
6. Ben Zing—Time Machines [Different Version]
7. Hazzard Hotrods—A Farewell to Arms [Live]
   • Recorded at MC Video
8. Jumped Or Pushed?—Best Things Goin' Round
9. Good Parts Only Corporation—Sickly Sweet
10. Ben Zing—United
11. John the Croc—Unshaven Bird
12. Go Back Snowball—Black Ghost Pie
13. Brown Star Jam—Go for the Answers
14. Factory Rat—Rocking Now [Demo]
15. God's Brother—Excellent Things
16. Antler—Static Airplane Jive
17. Fake Organisms—Where I Come From
18. Fat Chance—Try to Find You
19. Antler—Deaf Ears [Different Version]
20. Academy of Crowsfeet—Good for a Few Laughs
21. Nelly & the Dirtfloor—Raphael
22. Maxwell Greenfield—My Feet's Trustworthy Existance
23. Bravery Umpire—Eggs
24. Clinton Killingsworth—Wondering Boy Poet [Piano Version]
25. Styles We Paid For—Oh, Blinky

Hardcore UFO's: Revelations, Epiphanies and Fast Food in the Western Hemisphere
Label/Catalog #: Matador OLE 550
Released: 11/4/2003
Format: 5 CD + DVD

Human Amusements at Hourly Rates:
The Best of Guided by Voices

1. Captain's Dead
2. Drinker's Peace
3. Exit Flagger
4. 14 Cheerleader Coldfront
5. Shocker in Gloomtown
6. Non-Absorbing
7. Tractor Rape Chain
8. Hot Freaks
9. Echos Myron
10. I Am a Scientist [7" Version]
11. A Salty Salute
12. Watch Me Jumpstart
13. Game of Pricks
14. Motor Away
15. Hit
16. My Valuable Hunting Knife
17. Cut-Out Witch
18. The Official Ironmen Rally Song
19. To Remake the Young Flyer
20. I Am a Tree
21. Bulldog Skin
22. Learning to Hunt
23. Teenage FBI [Original Version]
24. Things I Will Keep
25. Surgical Focus
26. Chasing Heather Crazy
27. Twilight Campfighter
28. Glad Girls
29. Back to the Lake
30. Everywhere with Helicopter
31. My Kind of Soldier
32. The Best of Jill Hives

Demons and Painkillers: Matador Out-of-Print Singles,
B-Sides & Compilation Tracks

1. Motor Away [7" Version]
2. Color of My Blade
3. My Valuable Hunting Knife [7" Version]
4. Game of Pricks [7" Version]
5. Mice Feel Nice (In My Room)
6. Not Good for the Mechanism
7. Kiss Only the Important Ones
8. Dodging Invisible Rays
9. Deaf Ears
10. Why Did You Land?
11. June Salutes You!
12. Delayed Reaction Brats
13. He's the Uncle
14. The Key Losers
15. Postal Blowfish [New Version]
16. Unleashed! The Large-Hearted Boy [Live]
17. Some Drilling Implied [Live]
18. Systems Crash
19. Catfood on the Earwig
20. The Who vs. Porky Pig
21. A Life in Finer Clothing
22. The Worryin' Song
23. Subtle Gear Shifting
24. Finks
25. The Finest Joke Is Upon Us
26. The Singing Razorblade
27. Now to War [Electric Version]
28. Mannequin's Complaint (Wax Dummy Meltdown)
29. Do They Teach You the Chase?

30. (I'll Name You) The Flame That Cries
31. The Ascended Master's Grogshop
32. My Thoughts Are a Gas
33. Running Off With the Fun City Girls
34. None of Them Any Good
35. Choking Tara [Creamy Version]

Delicious Pie & Thank You For Calling: Previously Unreleased Songs and Recordings

1. I
2. Back to Saturn X
3. H-O-M-E
4. You're the Special
5. Perhaps We Were Swinging
6. Mother & Son
7. 7 Strokes to Heaven's Edge
8. Fire 'Em Up, Abner
9. Harboring Exiles
10. Still Worth Nothing
11. Never
12. Slave Your Beetle Brain
13. It Is Divine [Different Version]
14. They
15. I Invented the Moonwalk (And the Pencil Sharpener) [Do the Collapse Demo]
16. Fly Into Ashes [Do the Collapse Demo]
17. The Various Vaults of Convenience [Do the Collapse Demo]
18. Trashed Aircraft [Do the Collapse Demo]
19. Running Off with the Fun City Girls [Mag Earwhig! Demo]
20. Bulldog Skin [Mag Earwhig! Demo]
21. Portable Men's Society [Mag Earwhig! Demo]
22. Choking Tara [Mag Earwhig! Demo]
23. Man Called Aerodynamics [Concert For Todd Version]

Live at the Wheelchair Races: Unreleased Live Recordings 1995–2002

1. Intro by Randy Campbell
   • Recorded at The Paradise, Boston, MA—06/20/1995
2. Little Lines
   • Recorded at Bogart's, Cincinnati, OH—07/25/1997
3. A Salty Salute
4. I Am Produced
   • Recorded at Bogart's, Cincinnati, OH—07/25/1997
5. Why Did You Land?
   • Recorded at Fox Theatre, Denver, CO—04/10/1995
6. Zap
   • Recorded at Cat's Cradle, Carrboro, NC, USA—04/16/2002
7. 14 Cheerleader Coldfront
   • Recorded at The Paradise, Boston, MA—06/20/1995
8. Everywhere with Helicopter
   • Recorded at Cat's Cradle, Carrboro, NC, USA—04/16/2002
9. Quicksilver
   • Recorded at Bogart's, Cincinnati, OH—07/25/1997

10. James Riot
   • Recorded at Bernie's Bagel Shop, Columbus, OH—03/28/1998
11. Pretty Bombs
   • Recorded at Cat's Cradle, Carrboro, NC—04/16/2002
12. Far-Out Crops
   • Recorded at Bimbo's, San Francisco, CA—02/27/1999
13. My Impression Now
   • Recorded at Phantasy Club, Cleveland, OH—04/26/1997
14. Look at Them
   • Recorded at The Metro, Chicago, IL—02/24/1996
15. Melted Pat
   • Recorded at The Metro, Chicago, IL—02/24/1996
16. How Loft I Am?
   • Recorded at The Metro, Chicago, IL—07/11/1998
17. King and Caroline/Motor Away
   • Recorded at First Avenue, Minneapolis, MN—02/22/1996
18. Trap Soul Door
19. Cheyenne
   • Recorded at Cat's Cradle, Carrboro, NC—04/16/2002
20. Make Use
   • Recorded at The Metro, Chicago, IL—07/11/1998
21. Burning Flag Birthday Suit
   • Recorded at The Metro, Chicago, IL—02/24/1996
22. Weed King
   • Recorded at The Metro, Chicago, IL—02/24/1996
23. Town of Mirrors
   • Recorded at Bimbo's, San Francisco, CA—02/27/1999
24. Over the Neptune/Mesh Gear Fox
   • Recorded at The Paradise, Boston, MA—06/20/1995
25. Dragons Awake!
   • Recorded at 40 Watt Club, Athens, GA—01/22/2000
26. Shrine to the Dynamic Years (Athens Time Change Riots)
   • Recorded at Bernie's Bagel Shop, Columbus, OH—03/28/1998
27. Game of Pricks
28. Tractor Rape Chain
   • Recorded at Melkweg, Amsterdam, Holland—07/10/1997
29. The Key Losers
   • Recorded at Fox Theatre, Denver, CO—04/10/1995
30. Now to War
   • Recorded at Melkweg, Amsterdam, Holland—07/10/1997
31. Johnny Appleseed
   • Recorded at Crocodile Club, Seattle, WA—04/17/1995
32. Drinker's Peace

Forever Since Breakfast: The 1986 Debut EP

1. Land of Danger
2. Let's Ride
3. Like I Do
4. Sometimes I Cry

5. She Wants To Know
6. Fountain of Youth
7. The Other Place

Watch Me Jumpstart DVD
A Guided by Voices documentary film by Banks Tarver.

EPs

Forever Since Breakfast
Label/Catalog #: I Wanna 605058X
Released: 1986
Format: 12" *(Also available on CD as part of Hardcore UFO's box set)*

Side One
1. Land of Danger
2. Let's Ride
3. Like I Do
4. Sometimes I Cry

Side Two
1. She Wants to Know
2. Fountain of Youth
3. The Other Place

The Grand Hour
Label/Catalog #: Scat 28
Released: 1/1993
Format: 7"

There were two re-pressings of the 7" with different cover art.

Label/Catalog #: Scat 28
Released: 8/18/1994
Format: CD

1. I'll Get Over It
2. Shocker in Gloomtown
3. Alien Lanes

4. Off the Floor
5. Break Even
6. Bee Thousand

Static Airplane Jive
Label/Catalog #: City Slang 04939
Released: 12/1993
Format: 7"
Country: Germany

Label/Catalog #: Recordhead LUNA 15
Released: 5/11/1999
Format: CD
Country: U.S.

1. Big School
2. Damn Good Mr. Jam
3. Rubber Man

4. Hey Aardvark
5. Glow Boy Butlers
6. Gelatin, Ice Cream, Plum ....

Fast Japanese Spin Cycle
Label/Catalog #: Engine VROOM-07
Released: 2/1994
Format: CD, 7"

1. 3rd World Birdwatching
2. My Impression Now
3. Volcano Divers
4. Snowman
5. Indian Fables

6. Marchers in Orange
   [Different Version]
7. Dusted [Different Version]
8. Kisses to the Crying Cooks

Get out of My Stations
Label/Catalog #: Siltbreeze SB 028
Released: 2/1994
Format: 7"

1. Scalding Creek
2. Mobile
3. Melted Pat
4. Queen of Second Guessing

5. Dusty Bushworms
6. Spring Tiger
7. Blue Moon Fruit

Label/Catalog #: Siltbreeze SB28
Released: 8/25/2003
Format: CD

Includes the following bonus tracks:

8. Motor Away [Live]
   • Recorded at Mys Tavern, Harrisburg, PA—02/1993
9. Hot Freaks [Live]
   • Recorded at Glenn's Hideaway, Lodi—06/1994
10. Weed King [Live]
    • Recorded at Khyber Pass, Philadelphia, PA—08/1992
11. Postal Blowfish [Live]
    • Recorded at Boot & Saddle, Philadelphia, PA—01/1993

Clown Prince of the Menthol Trailer
Label/Catalog #: Domino RUG 11
Released: 3/1994
Format: CD, 7"

1. Matter Eater Lad
2. Broadcastor House
3. Hunter Complex
4. Pink Gun

5. Scalping the Guru
6. Grandfather Westinghouse
7. Johnny Appleseed

I Am A Scientist
Label/Catalog #: Scat 38
Released: 10/15/1994
Format: CD, 7"

1. I Am a Scientist [7" Version]
2. Curse of the Black Ass Buffalo

3. Do the Earth
4. Planet's Own Brand

Tigerbomb
Label/Catalog #: Matador OLE 168
Released: 11/14/1995
Format: 7"

Side A
1. My Valuable Hunting Knife [7" Version]
2. Game of Pricks [7" Version]
3. Mice Feel Nice (In My Room)

Side B
1. Not Good for the Mechanism
2. Kiss Only the Important Ones
3. Dodging Invisible Rays

Superchunk/Guided by Voices [Split]
Label/Catalog #: Fellaheen JACK 046
Released: 1996
Format: CD
Country: Australia

1. Superchunk—A Small Definition
2. Superchunk—Her Royal Fisticuffs
3. Superchunk—The Mine Has Been Returned to the Original Owner
4. Guided by Voices—Delayed Reaction Brats
5. Guided by Voices—He's the Uncle
6. Guided by Voices—The Key Losers

Sunfish Holy Breakfast
Label/Catalog #: Matador OLE 185
Released: 11/19/1996
Format: CD, 12"

1. Jabberstroker
2. Stabbing a Star
3. Canteen Plums
4. Beekeeper Seeks Ruth
5. Cocksoldiers and Their Postwar Stubble
6. A Contest Featuring Human Beings
7. If We Wait
8. Trendspotter Acrobat
9. The Winter Cows
10. Heavy Metal Country

Plantations Of Pale Pink
Label/Catalog #: Matador OLE 208
Released: 11/19/1996
Format: 7"

Side A
1. Systems Crash
2. Catfood on the Earwig
3. The Who vs. Porky Pig

Side B
1. A Life in Finer Clothing
2. The Worryin' Song
3. Subtle Gear Shifting

Girls vs. Boys & Guided by Voices—8 Rounds: GVSB vs. GBV [Split]
Label/Catalog #: Radiopaque RR013
Released: 7/1/1997
Format: CD

1. Girls vs. Boys—Learned It
2. Girls vs. Boys—Vera Cruz
3. Girls vs. Boys—Disco 666
4. Girls vs. Boys—Kill the Sexplayer
5. Guided by Voices—Unleashed! The Large-Hearted Boy [Live]
6. Guided by Voices—Motor Away [Live]
7. Guided by Voices—My Valuable Hunting Knife [Live]
8. Guided by Voices—Shocker in Gloomtown/Some Drilling Implied [Live]

Wish in One Hand . . .
Label/Catalog #: Jass J001
Released: 3/1997
Format: 7"

Side A
1. Teenage FBI [Original Version]
2. Now I'm Crying

Side B
1. Real

Plugs for the Program
Label/Catalog #: TVT 1983
Released: 12/3/1999
Format: CD

1. Surgical Focus [Remix]
2. Sucker of Pistol City

3. Picture Me Big Time
   [Demo]

Hold on Hope
Label/Catalog #: TVT 1985
Released: 3/7/2000
Format: CD
Country: U.S.

1. Underground Initiations
2. Interest Position
3. Fly Into Ashes
4. Tropical Robots
5. A Crick Uphill

6. Idiot Princess
7. Avalanche Aminos
8. Do the Collapse
9. Hold on Hope

Label/Catalog #: TVT D12983
Released: 4/15/2000
Format: CD
Country: Australia

1. Hold on Hope
2. Perfect This Time
3. Interest Position

4. A Crick Uphill
5. Avalanche Aminos

Dayton, Ohio-19 Something and 5
Label/Catalog #: Fading Captain Series 5
Released: 4/2/2000
Format: 7"
Side A—45 RPM

1. Dayton, Ohio-19 Something and 5 [Live]
   • Recorded at The 40 Watt, Athens, GA—01/22/2000

Side B—33 1/3 RPM

1. Travels
2. No Welcome Wagons
3. Selective Service

Daredevil Stamp Collector: Do the Collapse B-sides
Label/Catalog #: Fading Captain Series 10
Released: 3/30/2001
Format: 12"

Side A
1. Underground Initiations
2. Interest Position
3. Fly Into Ashes
4. Tropical Robots
5. A Crick Uphill

Side B
1. Idiot Princess
2. Avalanche Aminos
3. Do the Collapse
4. Perfect This Time
5. Hold on Hope [Demo Version]

Guided by Voices & Airport 5 – Selective Service [Split]
Label/Catalog #: Fading Captain Series 16
Released: 12/10/2001
Format: CD

1. Guided by Voices—Dayton, Ohio-19 Something and 5 [Live]
2. Guided by Voices—Travels
3. Guided by Voices—No Welcome Wagons
4. Guided by Voices—Selective Service
5. Airport 5—Total Exposure
6. Airport 5—Cold War Water Sports
7. Airport 5—The Wheel Hits the Path (Quite Soon)
8. Airport 5—Stifled Man Casino
9. Airport 5—Peroxide
10. Airport 5—Eskimo Clockwork
11. Airport 5—In the Brain [Bonus Track]

The Pipe Dreams of Instant Prince Whippet
Label/Catalog #: Fading Captain Series 24
Released: 9/17/2002
Format: CD, 12"

1. Visit This Place
2. Swooping Energies
3. Keep It Coming
4. Action Speaks Volumes
5. Stronger Lizards
6. The Pipe Dreams of Instant Prince Whippet
7. Request Pharmaceuticals
8. For Liberty
9. Dig Through My Window
10. Beg for a Wheelbarrow

SINGLES

Guided by Voices/Jenny Mae Leffel [Split]
Label/Catalog #: Anyway 013
Released: 6/1993
Format: 7"

A pink-tinted version of the cover is also available with colored vinyl.

Side 4
1. Guided by Voices—If We Wait

Side 5
1. Jenny Mae Leffel—Red Chair

Guided by Voices/Grifters [Split]
Label/Catalog #: Now Sound NOW #2
Released: 1994
Format: 7"

Side A
1. Guided by Voices—Hey Mr. Soundman
2. Guided by Voices—Announcers and Umpires
3. Guided by Voices—Evil Speaker B
4. Guided by Voices—Uncle Dave

Side B
1. Grifters—I'm Drunk

Guided by Voices/Belreve [Split]
Label/Catalog #: Anyway 021
Released: 1994
Format: 7"

The 7" has three different covers: 2 black and white, 1 color (with colored vinyl).

Side 6
1. Belreve—The Sulk King
Side 7
1. Guided by Voices—Always Crush Me

Motor Away
Label/Catalog #: Matador OLE 148
Released: 6/6/1995
Format: 7"

Side One	Side Two
1. Motor Away [7" Version]	1. Color of My Blade

The Opposing Engineer (Sleeps Alone) [Unmixed Version]
Guided by Voices/New Radiant Storm King [Split]
Label/Catalog #: Chunk CH4520
Released: 1995
Format: 7"
Side A
   1. Guided by Voices—The Opposing Engineer (Sleeps Alone)
Side B
   1. New Radiant Storm King—I Am a Scientist

Brighton Rocks
Label/Catalog #: RCRPA 17
Released: 1996
Format: 7"
Country: United Kingdom

Recorded at The Concorde in Brighton, UK on September 6, 1995. Available with two different covers. The blue cover version has colored vinyl.

1. Hot Freaks [Live]	2. Game of Pricks [Live]

The Official Ironmen Rally Song
Label/Catalog #: Matador OLE 184
Released: 2/27/1996
Format: CD, 7"

1. The Official Ironmen Rally Song	3. Why Did You Land?
2. Deaf Ears	4. June Salutes You!

Cut-Out Witch
Label/Catalog #: Matador OLE 218
Released: 6/17/1996
Format: 7" Picture Disc
Country: United Kingdom
Side A
 1. Cut-Out Witch
 2. Rhine Jive Click

The following tracks recorded at WHFS in Washington, DC in August 1995.

Side B
 1. Unleashed! The Large-Hearted Boy [Live]
 2. Some Drilling Implied [Live]

Guided by Voices/Cobra Verde [Split]
Label/Catalog #: Wabana ORE 10
Released: 3/10/1997
Format: 7"

Two different cover versions exist.

Side A
 1. Guided by Voices—Aim Correctly
 2. Guided by Voices—Orange Jacket
Side A
 1. Cobra Verde—Terrorist

Bulldog Skin
Label/Catalog #: Matador OLE 217
Released: 5/6/1997
Format: 7"
Country: United Kingdom

Side A	Side B
1. Bulldog Skin	1. The Singing Razorblade
	2. Now to War [Electric Version]

Label/Catalog #: Matador OLE 217
Released: 5/6/1997
Format: CD
Country: United Kingdom
1. Bulldog Skin
2. The Singing Razorblade
3. Now to War [Electric Version]
4. Mannequin's Complaint (Wax Dummy Meltdown)

I Am a Tree
Label/Catalog #: Matador OLE 264
Released: 7/29/1997
Format: 7"
Side A
1. I Am a Tree
Side B
1. (I'll Name You) The Flame That Cries
2. The Ascended Master's Grogshop

Label/Catalog #: Matador OLE 264
Released: 7/29/1997
Format: CD
1. I Am a Tree
2. Do They Teach You the Chase?
3. (I'll Name You) The Flame That Cries
4. The Ascended Master's Grogshop

Hold on Hope [Promo]
Label/Catalog #: Creation CRESCD 328
Released: 11/1/1999
Format: CD
Country: United Kingdom
1. Hold on Hope [Edit]   3. Teenage FBI [Demo]
2. Perfect This Time

Surgical Focus
Label/Catalog #: TVT 1981
Released: 9/23/2003
Format: 7"
Side A   Side B
1. Surgical Focus   1. Fly Into Ashes

Teenage FBI
Label/Catalog #: Creation CRE 325
Released: 9/28/1999
Format: CD, 7"
Country: United Kingdom
  1. Teenage FBI   3. Tropical Robots
  2. Fly Into Ashes

Chasing Heather Crazy
Label/Catalog #: TVT 2162
Released: 3/13/2001
Format: 7"
Side A   Side B
  1. Chasing Heather Crazy   1. On With the Show

Glad Girls
Label/Catalog #: TVT/Festival Mushroom 020412
Released: 7/9/2001
Format: CD
Country: Australia/New Zealand
  1. Glad Girls   3. On With the Show
  2. North American Vampires   4. Isolation Drills

Back to the Lake
Label/Catalog #: Fading Captain Series 20
Released: 5/21/2002
Format: 7"
A   AA
  1. Back to the Lake   1. Dig Through My Window

Cheyenne
Label/Catalog #: Fading Captain Series 21
Released: 5/21/2002
Format: 7"
A   AA
  1. Cheyenne   1. Visit This Place

Everywhere With Helicopter
Label/Catalog #: Fading Captain Series 22
Released: 5/21/2002
Format: 7"
A   AA
  1. Everywhere With Helicopter 1. Action Speaks Volumes

Universal Truths and Cycles
Label/Catalog #: Fading Captain Series 23
Released: 5/21/2002
Format: 7"

A	AA
1. Universal Truths and Cycles	1. Beg for a Wheelbarrow

Guided by Voices/Sin Sin 77 [Split]
Label/Catalog #: Devil In The Woods 53
Released: 2002
Format: 7"
This Side
  1. Guided by Voices—Cheyenne [Live]
    • Recorded at Cat's Cradle, Carrboro, NC—04/16/2002
That Side
  1. Sin Sin 77—Radio

My Kind of Soldier
Label/Catalog #: Fading Captain Series 28
Released: 7/29/2003
Format: 7"

Side A	Side B
1. My Kind of Soldier	1. Broken Brothers

The Best of Jill Hives
Label/Catalog #: Matador OLE 598
Released: 9/23/2003
Format: CD
Country: United Kingdom

1. The Best of Jill Hives	3. Downed [Cheap Trick cover]
2. Free of This World	

COMPILATIONS

Out of Cowtown Vol. 3
Label/Catalog #: Anyway 011
Released: 1993
Format: 7"
Includes the following track:
Stabbing a Star

An Earful o' Wax
Label/Catalog #: Get Happy!!! BIG 01
Released: 1993
Format: LP

An alternate cover appears on the Earful O' Wax LP test pressings.

Side A (Over)	Side B (Here)
1. Navigating Flood Regions	1. Sometimes I Cry
2. Captain's Dead	2. A Visit to the Creep Doctor
3. The Hard Way	3. The Future Is in Eggs
4. Crux	4. The Great Blake Street Canoe Race
5. Hey Hey, Spaceman	5. Pendulum
6. An Earful o' Wax	6. Long Distance Man
7. Lips of Steel	7. Old Battery
8. How Loft I Am?	8. The Other Place
	9. Liar's Tale

Early "Best of" LP that includes material from Forever Since Breakfast *through* Same Place the Fly Got Smashed.

Vampire On Titus/Propeller
Label/Catalog #: Scat 31
Released: 1993
Format: CD

1. "Wished I Was a Giant"	18. Non-Absorbing
2. #2 in the Model Home Series	19. Over the Neptune/Mesh Gear Fox
3. Expecting Brainchild	20. Weed King
4. Superior Sector Janitor X	21. Particular Damaged
5. Donkey School	22. Quality of Armor
6. Dusted	23. Metal Mothers
7. Marchers in Orange	24. Lethargy
8. Sot	25. Unleashed! The Large-Hearted Boy
9. World of Fun	26. Red Gas Circle
10. Jar of Cardinals	27. Exit Flagger
11. Unstable Journey	28. 14 Cheerleader Coldfront
12. E-5	29. Back to Saturn X Radio Report
13. Cool Off Kid Kilowatt	30. Ergo Space Pig
14. Gleemer (The Deeds of Fertile Jim)	31. Circus World
15. Wondering Boy Poet	32. Some Drilling Implied
16. What About It?	33. On the Tundra
17. Perhaps Now the Vultures	

CD combines tracks from the Vampire On Titus *and* Propeller *albums onto one disc.*

Volume 14—Reading '95 Special
Catalog #: 14VCD14
Released: 9/26/1995
Format: 2 CD

Includes the following track, which is the same song as "Reptilian Beauty Secrets" with a different title:
Snuff Movie (She's Gone)

Brain Candy Soundtrack
Label/Catalog #: Matador OLE 183
Released: 1996
Format: CD, LP, Cassette

Includes the following track:
Postal Blowfish [New Version]

Edgefest '96 [Live]
Label/Catalog #: American Radio Systems, Inc.
MWCD103.9FM
Released: 1996
Format: CD

Includes the following tracks:
Stabbing a Star [Live]
Teenage FBI [Live]
The Official Ironmen Rally Song [Live]

Magnet Magazine
Label/Catalog #: Darla DRL-019/MAG-001
Released: 1996
Format: 7"

Includes the following track:
Tractor Rape Chain [Clean It Up]

The Lounge Ax Defense & Relocation Compact Disc
Label/Catalog #: Touch And Go TG130CD
Released: 4/30/1996
Format: CD

Includes the following track:
Beneath a Festering Moon

Threadwaxing Space Live: The Presidential Compilation '93–94
Label/Catalog #: Zero Hour ZH 1060
Released: 2/6/1996
Format: CD, LP

Includes the following track:
I Am a Scientist [Live]

God Save the Clean
Label/Catalog #: Flying Nun FNCD409
Released: 1997
Format: CD

Includes the following track:
Draw(In)g to a (W)hole [Clean cover]

KCRW: Rare on Air, Live Performances, Volume 3
Label/Catalog #: Mammoth Records MR0162
Released: 2/25/1997
Format: CD

Includes the following track:
The Official Ironmen Rally Song [Live]

Ptolemic Terrascope Magazine #24
Label/Catalog #: Ptolemic Terrascope POT 24
Released: 1997
Format: 7"

Includes the following track:
Scorpion Lounge Shutdown

Kit Kat Acoustic Break [Promo]
Label: Track Marketing
Released: 1997
Format: CD

Includes the following songs as part of a Guided by Voices radio show/interview track:

1. Quicksilver [Live, Acoustic]
2. Not Behind the Fighter Jet [Live, Acoustic]
3. Bulldog Skin [Live, Acoustic]
4. Choking Tara [Live, Acoustic]
5. My Impression Now [Live, Acoustic]
6. Now to War [Live, Acoustic]
7. Teenage FBI [Live, Acoustic]

Rebound Magazine #6
Label/Catalog #: Rebound 6
Released: 1998
Format: 7"
Country: Netherlands

Two versions exist: gray cover and pink cover with colored vinyl (back cover shown here):

Includes the following track:

Pantherz

Buffy the Vampire Slayer Soundtrack
Label/Catalog #: TVT 8300
Released: 10/19/1999
Format: CD

Includes the following track:

Teenage FBI

X Fest 99 [Live]
Label: WXEG Productions
Released: 1999
Format: CD

Includes the following tracks recorded 9/14/1999:

Teenage FBI [Live]
My Valuable Hunting Knife [Live]
I Am a Scientist [Live]

Crime & Punishment in Suburbia Soundtrack
Label/Catalog #: Milan 35909
Released: 8/22/2000
Format: CD

Includes the following track:

Learning to Hunt

Darla 100
Label/Catalog #: Darla DRL 100
Released: 2000
Format: 4 CD

Includes the following track:

Tractor Rape Chain [Clean It Up]

More Music, Less Parking: WFMU Live From Jersey City
Label: WFMU
Released: 2000
Format: 2 CD

Includes the following track:

Wrecking Now [Acoustic, Live]

 The XFM 104.9 London Live Sessions
Label: Select Magazine
Released: 2000
Format: CD

Includes the following track:

Hold on Hope [Acoustic, Live]

 Briefcase (Suitcase Abridged: Drinks and Deliveries)
Label/Catalog #: Fading Captain Series 19
Released: 10/17/2000
Format: LP

Side A
  1. The Kissing Life
  2. Bunco Men
  3. Let's Go Vike
  4. Sabotage
  5. James Riot
  6. Spring Tigers
  7. Taco, Buffalo, Birddog And Jesus
  8. Hold on to Yesterday

Side B
  1. Ha Ha Man [Different Version]
  2. Rainbow Billy
  3. Shrine to the Dynamic Years (Athens Time Change Riots)
  4. Tobacco's Last Stand
  5. Settlement Down
  6. Sensational Gravity Boy [Refraze Version]
  7. Cruise
  8. The Flying Party
  9. Turbo Boy
  10. Wondering Boy Poet [Piano Version]
  11. Oh, Blinky

 Colonel Jeffrey Pumpernickel
Label/Catalog #: Off Records 1000
Released: 3/20/2001
Format: CD, 2 LP

Includes the following tracks:

Titus and Strident Wet Nurse (Creating Jeffrey)
Reprise (Destroying Jeffrey)

Dean Quixote Soundtrack
Label/Catalog #: SpinArt SPART 99
Released: 11/20/2001
Format: CD

Includes the following track:

If We Wait

ESPN's Ultimate X Soundtrack
Label/Catalog #: Hollywood Records 162340
Released: 5/14/2002
Format: CD

Includes the following track:

Skills Like This

Scrubs Soundtrack
Label/Catalog #: Hollywood Records 162353
Released: 9/24/2002
Format: CD

Includes the following track:

Hold on Hope

**The Best Of Guided by Voices: Human Amusements
at Hourly Rates**
Label/Catalog #: Matador OLE 565
Released: 11/4/2003
Format: CD

Tracklisting is different than the Best of *CD included in the*
Hardcore UFO's *box set.*

1. A Salty Salute
2. Things I Will Keep
3. Everywhere With Helicopter
4. I Am a Tree
5. My Kind of Soldier
6. 14 Cheerleader Coldfront
7. Twilight Campfighter
8. Echos Myron
9. Learning to Hunt
10. Bulldog Skin
11. Captain's Dead
12. Tractor Rape Chain
13. Game of Pricks [7" Version]
14. To Remake the Young Flyer
15. Hit
16. Glad Girls
17. Drinker's Peace
18. Surgical Focus
19. Cut-Out Witch
20. The Best of Jill Hives
21. Hot Freaks
22. Shocker in Gloomtown
23. Chasing Heather Crazy
24. My Valuable Hunting Knife
25. The Official Ironmen Rally Song

26. Non-Absorbing
27. Motor Away [7" Version]
28. Teenage FBI [Original
    Version]

29. Watch Me Jumpstart
30. Exit Flagger
31. Back to the Lake
32. I Am a Scientist

Label/Catalog #: P-Vine/Blues Interactions PCD-4276
Released: 1/23/2004
Format: CD
Country: Japan

Includes the following bonus track:

33. I Am Produced

Who's Not Forgotten—FDR's Tribute to the Who
Label: Face Down Records
Released: 2004
Format: CD

Includes the following track:

Baba O'Riley [Live, Who cover]

OFFICIAL BOOTLEGS

Crying Your Knife Away [Live]
Label/Catalog #: Simple Solution SS-016
Reissued: 1998
Format: CD

Recorded June 18, 1994, at Stache's in Columbus, Ohio.

1. Postal Blowfish
2. Closer You Are
3. My Valuable Hunting Knife
4. Gold Star for Robot Boy
5. Lethargy
6. Striped White Jets
7. Non-Absorbing
8. The Goldheart Mountaintop
   Queen Directory
9. Shocker in Gloomtown
10. Motor Away
11. Awful Bliss
12. Tractor Rape Chain
13. Blimps Go 90

14. Exit Flagger
15. I Am a Scientist
16. Quality of Armor
17. Cruise
18. Unleashed! The Large-
    Hearted Boy
19. Some Drilling Implied
20. If We Wait
21. Weed King
22. Pimple Zoo
23. Break Even
24. Ester's Day
25. Stage Comments

Label/Catalog #: Lo-Fi Recordings LO-FI 004
Released: 1994
Format: 2 LP

Includes the following bonus track:

26. Invisible Man [Live, Breeders cover]
    • Recorded at Walnut Hills Bar, Dayton, OH—06/10/1994

For All Good Kids [Live]
No Label
Released: 1995
Format: LP

Recorded March 30, 1995 at Maxwell's in Hoboken, NJ. Two versions exist: one with colored cover and one with black-and-white cover.

Wolf Side
1. Don't Stop Now
2. King and Caroline
3. Motor Away
4. Gold Star for Robot Boy
5. Hot Freaks
6. Game of Pricks
7. Echos Myron
8. Redmen and Their Wives

Dragon Side
1. Pimple Zoo
2. Smothered In Hugs
3. Johnny Appleseed
4. Deathtrot and Warlock
   Riding a Rooster
5. Weed King
6. Postal Blowfish
7. Drinker's Peace
8. Break Even
9. The Goldheart Mountaintop
   Queen Directory

Benefit for the Winos [Live]
No Label
Released: 1996
Format: 2 LP

Recorded June 2, 1995 at Gilly's in Dayton, Ohio.

Disc 1

Side One
1. Over the Neptune
2. Mesh Gear Fox
3. The Hard Way
4. Striped White Jets
5. He's the Uncle
6. King and Caroline
7. Motor Away

Side Four
1. Weed King
2. Gold Star for Robot Boy
3. Sitting Still [R.E.M. cover]
4. Tractor Rape Chain
5. Sheetkickers
6. Non-Absorbing
7. Unleashed! The Large-
   Hearted Boy

Disc 2

Side Two
1. Kicker of Elves
2. Quality of Armor
3. Hot Freaks
4. Matter Eater Lad
5. Don't Stop Now
6. My Son Cool
7. Game of Pricks
8. Postal Blowfish
9. Buzzards and Dreadful
   Crows

Side Three
1. My Valuable Hunting Knife
2. Some Drilling Implied
3. Color of My Blade
4. The Goldheart Mountaintop
   Queen Directory
5. Shocker in Gloomtown
6. I Am a Scientist
7. Yours to Keep
8. Echos Myron
9. Exit Flagger
10. A Salty Salute

Jellyfish Reflector [Live]
Label: Jellyfish
Released: 8/9/1999
Format: CD

Recorded February 17, 1996 at Patio Club in Indianapolis, Indiana.

1. Man Called Aerodynamics
2. Rhine Jive Click
3. Cut-Out Witch
4. Burning Flag Birthday Suit
5. The Official Ironmen Rally
   Song
6. Bright Paper Werewolves
7. Lord of Overstock
8. Your Name Is Wild
9. Look at Them
10. Underwater Explosions
11. Don't Stop Now
12. Office of Hearts
13. Lethargy
14. Game of Pricks
15. Striped White Jets
16. Melted Pat
17. Hot Freaks
18. Postal Blowfish
19. My Son Cool
20. King and Caroline
21. Motor Away
22. Pimple Zoo
23. Some Drilling Implied
24. Shocker in Gloomtown
25. A Salty Salute
26. Gold Star for Robot Boy
27. Tractor Rape Chain
28. Yours to Keep
29. Echos Myron
30. Weed King

LP available in two versions: one U.S. version with white image shown above and a UK version with pink cover paper marked "UK Edition."

Label: Jellyfish
Released: 2/17/1996
Format: 2 LP
Country: U.S. & United Kingdom

Includes the following studio bonus tracks:

Bug House
Pantherz
I'll Buy You a Bird

King's Ransom—Happy Motherfuckers and Sad Clowns [Live]

No Label
Released: 2001
Format: 2 LP + 7"

Recorded April 28, 2000 at Be Here Now Club in Asheville, North Carolina. Bonus 7" recorded July 11, 1998 at Metro in Chicago, Illinois.

Disc 1

Side A
1. I Am the Walrus [Beatles cover]
2. Whiskey Ships
3. Lethargy
4. Submarine Teams
5. Surgical Focus
6. Alone, Stinking and Unafraid
7. Waved Out
8. In Stitches
9. Tight Globes

Side B
1. Choking Tara
2. Mushroom Art
3. Frequent Weaver Who Burns
4. Zoo Pie
5. Things I Will Keep
6. Teenage FBI
7. Baba O'Riley [Who cover]
8. Happy Jack [Who cover]
9. Shocker in Gloomtown

Disc 2

Side A
1. Soul Train College Policeman
2. Ziggy Stardust [David Bowie cover]
3. The Goldheart Mountaintop Queen Directory
4. Watch Me Jumpstart
5. I Am a Scientist
6. Peep-Hole
7. Release the Sunbird
8. Get Under It

Side B
1. Psychic Pilot Clocks Out
2. Hot Freaks
3. Wild Horses [Rolling Stones cover]
4. Your Name Is Wild
5. Highway to Hell [AC/DC cover]
6. I Am a Tree
7. The Old Grunt
8. Bulldog Skin
9. Motor Away

Disc 3 (7")
Side A
  1. Just Say the Word

Side B
  1. Catfood on the Earwig
  2. The Who vs. Porky Pig

King's Ransom is a pseudonym for Guided by Voices.

**The Cum Engines (Featuring The Cannot Changes)—
Live at the Athens Time Change Riots [Live]**
No Label
Released: 11/30/2001
Format: LP

Recorded January 22, 2000 at 40 Watt in Athens, Georgia.

Side A
  1. Tight Globes
  2. Cut-Out Witch
  3. The Goldheart Mountaintop
    Queen Directory
  4. Mushroom Art
  5. Submarine Teams
  6. Shocker in Gloomtown
  7. Big School
  8. Maggie Turns to Flies
  9. Don't Stop Now
  10. Circling Motorhead
    Mountain

Side B
  1. Subspace Biographies
  2. Whiskey Ships
  3. Tropical Robots
  4. Liar's Tale
  5. Echos Myron
  6. Get Under It
  7. Peep-Hole
  8. Postal Blowfish
  9. Smothered in Hugs
  10. The Official Ironmen Rally
    Song

*The Cum Engines (Featuring The Cannot Changes) is a pseudonym
for Guided by Voices.*

VIDEO

Live at the Whisky A Go Go [Live]
Recorded May 10, 1996 at Whisky A Go Go in Los Angeles,
California.
Label: Rockathon
Released: 1996
Format: VHS

  1. Postal Blowfish
  2. Gold Star for Robot Boy
  3. Over The Neptune/Mesh
    Gear Fox
  4. Man Called Aerodynamics
  5. Rhine Jive Click

  6. Cut-Out Witch
  7. Smothered in Hugs
  8. Exit Flagger
  9. My Valuable Hunting Knife
  10. Bright Paper Werewolves
  11. Lord of Overstock

12. Underwater Explosions
13. Game of Pricks
14. Break Even
15. Shocker in Gloomtown
16. Your Name Is Wild
17. Marchers in Orange
18. Jar of Cardinals
19. "Wished I Was a Giant"
20. Non-Absorbing
21. King and Caroline
22. Motor Away
23. I Am a Scientist
24. Don't Stop Now
25. My Son Cool
26. Tractor Rape Chain
27. The Goldheart Mountaintop Queen Directory
28. Echos Myron
29. 14 Cheerleader Coldfront
30. The Official Ironmen Rally Song
31. Unleashed! The Large-Hearted Boy
32. Matter Eater Lad
33. Weed King
34. Lethargy
35. Office of Hearts
36. Awful Bliss
37. Striped White Jets
38. Quality of Armor
39. A Salty Salute
40. Melted Pat
41. Johnny Appleseed [Partial]

Watch Me Jumpstart

Label/Catalog #: Matador OLE 284
Released: 7/21/1998
Format: VHS

This is a documentary film by Banks Tarver. The film documents the history of the band leading up to the release of their album Under the Bushes Under the Stars.

The following versions include an additional short film by Tarver called Beautiful Plastic *and thirty more minutes of live performances and videos.*

Label/Catalog #: Matador OLE 595
Released: 11/4/2003
Format: DVD
Packaging: Amaray

Label/Catalog #: Matador OLE 596
Released: 11/4/2003
Format: DVD
Packaging: Jewel Case

The Who Went Home and Cried

This is a documentary film of Greg Demos last show that includes live footage from a porch practice session (where Bob plays guitar!) and the live show.
Released: 2000
Format: VHS

1. Submarine Teams
2. The Big Make-Over
3. Big School
4. Cut-Out Witch
5. Tractor Rape Chain

6. Strumpet Eye
7. Psychic Pilot Clocks Out
8. Far-Out Crops
9. Strictly Comedy

Released: 11/20/2001 Format: DVD

Includes the following bonus footage:

10. A Salty Salute
11. Hot Freaks
12. Tractor Rape Chain
13. Shocker in Gloomtown
14. I Am a Scientist

15. Echos Myron
16. Liar's Tale
17. Motor Away
18. Peep-Hole
19. Smothered in Hugs

Some Drinking Implied

This is a collection of early GbV footage: unreleased videos, early studio clips, backstage footage, Bob's high school home movie Wild People, *and early live performances from 1992.*

Label: Rockathon
Released: 2001
Format: VHS

Label: Rockathon
Released: 10/12/2002
Format: DVD

INTERNET

Care for Kosovo
Internet Site: Emusic.com
Released: 1999
Format: MP3

Includes the following track:

Surgical Focus [Demo]

TVT Bootleg Web site
Internet Site: TVT Records Web site (accessible when using enhanced *Isolation Drills* CD).
Released: 2001
Format: MP3

1. Guided by Voices—Invisible Train to Earth
2. Guided by Voices—On With the Show

The following tracks were recorded live at CBGB:

3. Guided by Voices—Alone, Stinking and Unafraid
4. Guided by Voices—Big School
5. Guided by Voices—Cut-Out Witch
6. Guided by Voices—Game of Pricks
7. Guided by Voices—Hot Freaks
8. Guided by Voices—I Am a Scientist
9. Guided by Voices—Mushroom Art
10. Guided by Voices—Shocker in Gloomtown
11. Guided by Voices—Submarine Teams
12. Guided by Voices—Teenage FBI
13. Guided by Voices—Tight Globes
14. Guided by Voices—Waved Out

Napster
Internet Site: Napster.com
Released: 8/19/2003
Format: MP3

1. My Kind of Soldier [Live]
2. The Best of Jill Hives [Live]
3. Secret Star [Live]
4. Of Mites and Men [Live]

Window of My World
Internet Site: Apple.com iTunes Music Store
Label/Catalog #: Matador OLE 9005 6 IS
Released: 8/16/2004
Format: Apple AAC

1. Window of My World

SOLO AND SIDE PROJECTS OF GUIDED BY VOICES SELECTED DISCOGRAPHY 1983–2004

This discography includes selected recordings from solo and side projects related to Guided by Voices. Most promo items, non-U.S. releases or compilations without exclusive tracks are not included.

ROBERT POLLARD
Lineup: Robert Pollard

ALBUMS

Not in My Airforce
Label/Catalog #: Matador OLE 215
Released: 9/10/1996
Format: CD, LP

1. Maggie Turns to Flies
2. Quicksilver
3. Girl Named Captain
4. Get Under It
5. Release the Sunbird
6. John Strange School
7. Parakeet Troopers
8. One Clear Minute
9. Chance to Buy An Island
10. I've Owned You for Centuries
11. The Ash Gray Proclamation
12. Flat Beauty
13. King of Arthur Avenue
14. Roofer's Union Fight Song
15. Psychic Pilot Clocks Out
16. Prom Is Coming
17. Party
18. Did It Play?
19. Double Standards Inc.
20. Punk Rock Gods
21. Meet My Team
22. Good Luck Sailor

Waved Out
Label/Catalog #: Matador OLE 316
Released: 6/23/1998
Format: CD, LP

1. Make Use	9. Artificial Light
2. Vibrations in the Woods	10. People Are Leaving
3. Just Say the Word	11. Steeple of Knives
4. Subspace Biographies	12. Rumbling Joker
5. Caught Waves Again	13. Showbiz Opera Walrus
6. Waved Out	14. Pick Seeds from My Skull
7. Whiskey Ships	15. Second Step Next Language
8. Wrinkled Ghost	

Label/Catalog #: Bandai/Matador APCY-8435
Released: 6/23/1998
Format: CD
Country: Japan

Includes the following bonus track:

> 16. Aim Correctly [Different Version]

Kid Marine
Label/Catalog #: Fading Captain Series 1
Released: 2/2/1999
Format: CD, LP

1. Submarine Teams	8. Living Upside Down
2. Flings of the Waistcoat Crowd	9. Snatch Candy
	10. White Gloves Come Off
3. The Big Make-Over	11. Enjoy Jerusalem!
4. Men Who Create Fright	12. You Can't Hold Your Women
5. Television Prison	13. Town of Mirrors
6. Strictly Comedy	14. Powerblessings
7. Far-Out Crops	15. Island Crimes

Motel of Fools
Label/Catalog #: Fading Captain Series 26
Released: 1/14/2003
Format: CD, LP

1. In the House of Queen Charles Augustus	6. The Spanish Hammer
	A. She Drives Camaro
2. Captain Black	B. Lift
3. Red Ink Superman	C. Love Set
4. The Vault of Moons	D. Wildlife Energy
5. Saga of the Elk	7. Harrison Adams

Fiction Man
Label/Catalog #: Fading Captain Series 30
Released: 5/10/2004
Format: CD, LP

1. Run Son Run
2. I Expect a Kill
3. Sea of Dead
4. Children Come On
5. The Louis Armstrong of
   Rock and Roll
6. Losing Usage
7. Built to Improve
8. Paradise Style
9. Conspiracy of Owls
10. It's Only Natural
11. Trial of Affliction and Light
    Sleeping
12. Every Word in the World
13. Night of the Golden
    Underground
14. Their Biggest Win

COMPILATIONS

**I Stayed Up All Night Listening to Records:
A Collection of Field Recordings**
Label/Catalog #: Anyway AW50
Released: 1999
Format: CD

Includes the following track:

As Long as the Block Is Black

Matter Dominates Spirit – Jim Shepard Tribute
Label: Meta Records
Released: 2001
Format: 2 LP

Includes the following track:

Bristol Girl [Jim Shepard cover]

Single Wish
Label/Catalog #: Luna LUNA65
Released: 2002
Format: CD

Includes the following track:

In the States (That I Go Through)

OFFICIAL BOOTLEGS & DEMOS

Edison's Demos
No Label
Released: 1/6/2004
Format: LP
Side A
  1. Mix Up the Satellite [Demo]
  2. I'll Replace You With Machines [Demo]
  3. Beat Your Wings [Demo]
  4. Useless Inventions [Demo]
  5. Dirty Water [Demo]
  6. She Goes Off at Night [Demo]
  7. She Goes Off at Night [Vocals Only Mix—Demo]
  8. Dead Cloud [Demo]
Side B
  1. My Son, My Secretary, My Country [Demo]
  2. A Trophy Mule in Particular [Demo]
  3. Main Street Wizards [Demo]
  4. Main Street Wizards [Homemade Click Track Mix—Demo]
  5. Blasted But It's Easy [Demo]
  6. Apology in Advance [Demo]
  7. Secret Star [Demo]

INTERNET VIDEO

TVT Bootleg Web site
Internet Site: TVT Records Web site (accessible when using
enhanced *Isolation Drills* CD).
Released: 2001
Format: Quicktime Movie

Includes the following video for an unreleased track:

Headache Revolution

OTHER APPEARANCES

S/T
Label/Catalog #: AF4 Records 02002
Released: 1987
Format: LP

Label/Catalog #: Recordhead LUNA6
Released: 1998
Format: CD

Bob sings backing vocals on the following tracks:
A Hard Place
At Bay
Fishin'
Naola
Train Brain

New Creatures—Rafter Tag
Label/Catalog #: Scumfish SF002
Released: 1987
Format: LP

Bob sings backing vocals on the following tracks:
Collapse
Life's Masquerade
Nature's Way

Tobin Sprout—Carnival Boy
Label/Catalog #: Matador OLE 216
Released: 9/10/1996
Format: CD, LP

Bob plays guitar on the following tracks:
E's Navy Blue

Cobra Verde—Egomania (Love Songs)
Label/Catalog #: Scat 67
Released: 1997
Format: CD

Bob sings backing vocals on the following track:
Still Breaking Down

The Minus 5—The Lonesome Death of Buck McCoy
Label/Catalog #: Hollywood 162115
Released: 5/5/1997
Format: CD

Bob cowrote and sang backing vocals on the following track:
Boeing Spacearium

J. Mascis & The Fog—More Light
Label/Catalog #: Ultimatum Music/Artemis Records 76665
Released: 10/24/2000
Format: CD

Bob sings backing vocals on the following tracks:
All the Girls
I'm Not Fine
Same Day

3 Dream Bag—The Fertile Octogenarian
Label: Naked Fat Baby Records
Released: 10/2/2001
Format: LP

Bob did the cover art and sings backing vocals on the following track:
Perfect Friday

The song also appears on an earlier 3 Dream Bag *EP called*
A Frenzy in Frownland.

Superdrag—Last Call for Vitriol
Label/Catalog #: Arena Rock Recording Company 23
Released: 7/9/2002
Format: CD

Bob sings backing vocals on the following track:
Baby Goes to 11

TOBIN SPROUT
Lineup: Tobin Sprout

ALBUMS

Carnival Boy
Label/Catalog #: Matador OLE 216
Released: 9/10/1996
Format: CD, LP

1. The Natural Alarm
2. Cooler Jocks
3. E's Navy Blue
4. The Bone Yard
5. Carnival Boy

6. Martin's Mounted Head
7. Gas Daddy Gas
8. To My Beloved Martha
9. White Flyer
10. I Didn't Know

11. Gallant Men
12. It's Like Soul Man [Different Version]

13. Hermit Stew
14. The Last Man Well Known to Kingpin

Moonflower Plastic (Welcome to My Wigwam)
Label/Catalog #: Matador OLE 244
Released: 8/26/1997
Format: CD, LP

1. Get Out of My Throat
2. Moonflower Plastic (You're Here)
3. Paper Cut
4. Beast of Souls
5. A Little Odd
6. Angels Hang Their Socks on the Moon
7. All Used Up
8. Since I. . . .
9. Back Chorus
10. Curious Things
11. Exit Planes
12. A Little Bit of Dread
13. Hit Junky Dives
14. Water on the Boater's Back

Let's Welcome the Circus People
Label/Catalog #: Recordhead/Wigwam LUNA13
Released: 2/23/1999
Format: CD

1. Smokey Joe's Perfect Hair
2. Digging Up Wooden Teeth
3. Mayhem Stone
4. And So On
5. Making a Garden
6. Vertical Insect (The Lights Are On)
7. Maid to Order
8. Liquor Bag
9. Who's Adolescence
10. Lucifer's Flaming Hour
11. 100% Delay
12. And the Crowd Showed Up

Label/Catalog #: Recordhead/Wigwam LUNA13
Released: 2/23/1999
Format: LP + 7"

Includes the following bonus tracks on the 7" record:

Side A
1. Once I Had a Day

Side B
1. When Were You In?
2. The Sniffing Hounds of Plaster Paris

Lost Planets & Phantom Voices
Label/Catalog #: Luna LUNA64
Released: 2003
Format: CD, LP

LP cover is different than the CD cover.

Label/Catalog #: Luna LUNA64
Released: 2003
Format: LP

1. Indian Ink
2. Doctor #8
3. Catch the Sun
4. All Those Things We've Done
5. Martini
6. Rub Your Buddha Tummy
7. Courage the Tack
8. Earth Links
9. As Lovely As You
10. Shirley the Rainbow
11. Fortunes Theme No. 1
12. Cleansing From the Storm
13. Let Go of My Beautiful Balloon

Live at the Horseshoe Tavern 2004 [Live]
Label/Catalog #: Recordhead/Wigwam LUNA76
Released: 9/7/2004
Format: 2 CD

Disc 1

1. Indian Ink
2. Get Out of My Throat
3. Gleemer (The Deeds of Fertile Jim)
4. Pure Flesh
5. The Crawling Backward Man
6. Dodging Invisible Rays
7. Beast of Souls
8. Ester's Day
9. The Last Man Well Known to Kingpin
10. War & Wedding
11. To My Beloved Martha
12. To Remake the Young Flyer
13. Awful Bliss
14. All Used Up
15. Inside the Blockhouse
16. Sadder Than You
17. Gas Daddy Gas
18. Hit Junky Dives
19. Scissors

Disc 2

1. A Good Flying Bird
2. Atom Eyes
3. 14 Cheerleader Coldfront
4. Exit Planes
5. Water on the Boater's Back
6. It's Like Soul Man
7. Seed
8. Martin's Mounted Head
9. Marriage Incorporated
10. Little Whirl
11. Over Then, and Back Again
12. Inside Your Serious
13. And I Wonder

Note: The last three tracks are studio demos recorded on 9/14/2004.

EPS

Popstram
Label/Catalog #: Recordhead LUNA4
Released: 11/19/1996
Format: 7"

Available in two different cover versions: black and white and colored (with colored vinyl).

Side A	Side B
1. Toaster	1. Bottle of the Ghost of Time
2. Sadder Than You	

Wax Nails
Label/Catalog #: Recordhead/Wigwam LUNA12
Released: 1998
Format: CD

1. Get Your Calcium	4. The Crawling Backward Man
2. Cereal Killer	5. In Good Hands
3. Seed	6. How's Your House? [Demo]

Sentimental Stations
Label/Catalog #: Recordhead LUNA59
Released: 9/17/2002
Format: CD

1. Secret Service	5. Are You Happening?
2. Branding Dennis	6. Doctor #8 [Piano Version]
3. I Think You Would	7. Sentimental Stations
4. Inside the Blockhouse	

SINGLES

Let Go of My Beautiful Balloon
Label/Catalog #: Recordhead/Wigwam LUNA45
Released: 8/21/2001
Format: 7"

Side A	Side B
1. Let Go of My Beautiful Balloon	1. Shirley the Rainbow

Tobin Sprout/The Minders [Split]
Label/Catalog #: Sprite Recordings/Caffeinated Robots 3
Released: 2002
Format: 7"

Side A
1. Tobin Sprout—Can I Have This?
2. Tobin Sprout—Lust

Side B
1. The Minders—Empty Bubble

COMPILATIONS

What's Up Matador?
Label/Catalog #: Matador OLE 163
Released: 8/26/1997
Format: 2 CD, 2 LP

Includes the following track:

Small Parade

Regain the Lost Conversation
Label: Sarang Bang
Released: 1999
Format: CD
Country: New Zealand

Includes the following track:

Once I Had a Day [Different Version]

I Stayed Up All Night Listening to Records: A Collection of Field Recordings
Label/Catalog #: Anyway AW50
Released: 1999
Format: CD

Includes the following track:

Cryptic Shapes

Hydroponic Mascara Volume II
Label/Catalog #: Mr. Whiggs MWR006
Released: 2000
Format: CD

Includes the following track:

How's Your House?

Single Wish
Label/Catalog #: Luna LUNA65
Released: 2002
Format: CD

Includes the following track:

Atom Eyes [Sprite Version]

OFFICIAL BOOTLEGS & DEMOS

Demos & Outtakes
Label/Catalog #: Recordhead/Wigwam LUNA35
Released: 8/21/2001
Format: CD

1. Seven and Nine [Demo]
2. The Lords of Pretty Things
3. To Remake the Young Flyer [Demo]
4. Jealous Mantles [Demo]
5. To My Beloved Martha [Demo]
6. Quarter Turn Here
7. Dusting Coattails [Demo]
8. E's Navy Blue [Demo]
9. Little Bit of Dread [Demo]
10. Hit Junky Dives [Demo]
11. Sot #1 [Demo]
12. Ketiling Park [Demo]
13. Slow Flanges [Demo]
14. Silicone Slugs
15. Paper Cut [Demo]
16. Smokey Joe's Perfect Hair [Demo]
17. Exit Planes [Demo]
18. Water on the Boater's Back [Demo]
19. Hint #9 [Demo]
20. Piano

Label/Catalog #: Recordhead/Wigwam LUNA21
Released: 1999
Format: 2 LP

Includes the following additional tracks:

I Didn't Know [Demo]
Making a Garden [Demo]
Highrise
Cereal Killer [Demo]
Blankets of Hair
I Wonder If It's Cold Outside
Something Today
Digging Up Wooden Teeth [Demo]
Curved Warlords
There She Goes Again [Demo]
MP

OTHER APPEARANCES

Various Artists—Love & a .45 Soundtrack
Label/Catalog #: Immortal/Epic Soundtrax EK 66632
Released: 1994
Format: CD

Tobin plays guitar on the following track:
Kim Deal & Bob Pollard—Love Hurts

Robert Pollard—Not in My Airforce
Label/Catalog #: Matador OLE 215
Released: 9/10/1996
Format: CD, LP

Tobin sings backing vocals on the following track:
Roofer's Union Fight Song

Robert Pollard—Waved Out
Label/Catalog #: Matador OLE 316
Released: 6/23/1998
Format: CD, LP

Tobin adds piano and high hat to the following track:
Wrinkled Ghost

Robert Pollard—Kid Marine
Label/Catalog #: Fading Captain Series 1
Released: 2/2/1999
Format: CD, LP

Tobin plays piano on the following track:
Powerblessings

Robert Pollard—Motel of Fools
Label/Catalog #: Fading Captain Series 26
Released: 1/14/2003
Format: CD, LP

Tobin plays backward lead guitar on the following track:
Red Ink Superman

DOUG GILLARD
Lineup: Doug Gillard

ALBUMS

Salamander
Label/Catalog #: Pink Frost/Big Takeover PFCD-001
Released: 10/19/2004
Format: CD

1. Valpolicella
2. Wait for You
3. Going Back (To You)
4. Present
5. Momma
6. Me & the Wind
7. Give Me Something
8. Blockout
9. Symbols, Signs
10. Landmarks (In My Mind)
11. Fate, Say It Again
12. Drip-Nose Boy
13. Cape and Bay
14. (But) I See Something

EPs

Malamute Jute
Label: Cushion Records CR002
Released: 2000
Format: CD

1. Malamute Jute
2. Flying Backwards
3. Livery
4. Going Round
5. Western World

COMPILATIONS

Scat Semi-Annual Report May 5, 1997
Label/Catalog #: Scat 97
Released: 1997
Format: CD

Includes the following track:

J.H.-S.

U.S. Poplife Volume 2
Label: Contact Records
Released: 2000
Format: LP
Country: Japan

Includes the following track:

Flying Backwards

Hydroponic Mascara Volume II
Label/Catalog #: Mr. Whiggs MWR006
Released: 2000
Format: CD

Includes the following track:

Gloaming Blue [Mix II]

The Tigers Remixes
Label/Catalog #: 78 Records SRP005D
Released: 2001
Format: 2 CD
Country: Australia

Includes the following track, which is a remix of a Tigers song:

Cramer's Jungle

Creative Process 473 Soundtrack
Label: Acme Pictures
Released: 2002
Format: CD

1. Theme From the Writer's Garret
2. Subway Chase I
3. White Room Music
4. Let's Light Matches
5. Give Me Something
6. Coney Island
7. Shakespearean Theme
8. Shakespearean Theme (Porno)
9. Subway Chase II
10. Give Me Something (Industrial)
11. The Fight
12. Music to Pitch By
13. Give Me Something (Instrumental)
14. Drip-Nosed Boy
15. Goin' Back (Demo)
16. Gloaming Blue

OTHER APPEARANCES

Dipsomaniacs—Whatever Misery for Miles
Label/Catalog #: Apartment Records/Stickman/Progress
APAREC012
Released: 1999
Format: 7"
Country: Norway

Doug plays guitar, bass, drums, and contributes backing vocals on this track:
Second Honeymoon

The Revelers—Day In, Day Out
Label/Catalog #: SpinArt SPART71
Released: 1999
Format: CD

Doug adds the guitar solo on these tracks:
The Last Mistake
Five Will Get You Ten

Robert Pollard—Waved Out
Label/Catalog #: Matador OLE 316
Released: 6/23/1998
Format: CD, LP

Doug plays guitar on this track:
Caught Waves Again

Yuji Oniki—Orange
Label/Catalog #: Future Farmer 8
Released: 8/1/2000
Format: CD

Doug plays guitar on this record.

Yuji Oniki—Tvi
Label/Catalog #: Future Farmer 26915
Released: 11/13/2001
Format: CD

Doug plays guitar on this record.

3 DREAM BAG
Lineup: Greg Demos, Don Thrasher

ALBUMS

3 Dream Bag—The Fertile Octogenarian
Label: Naked Fat Baby Records
Released: 10/2/2001
Format: LP

1. Farmer Says
2. Daisy
3. Chaos Killed the Dinosaur
4. Pot Luck and the Insanity Mile
5. War Orphan
6. Saline Man
7. Moon Beam
8. Electric Billboards Trampoline
9. Freak Pony
10. Perfect Friday
11. Invitation to the Beheading
12. Unborn Widow
13. Honeymoon Babies
14. Bad Rice Stew/Chase and Sandborn
15. Mr. O'Malley

EPs

A Frenzy in Frownland
Label/Catalog #: Gas, Daddy, Go! GDG001
Released: 1993
Format: 7"

1. Perfect Friday
2. Chaos Killed the Dinosaur
3. Mr. O'Malley
4. Honeymoon Babies

Bevil Web/3 Dream Bag [Split]
Label/Catalog #: Simple Solution SS-009
Released: 1994
Format: 7"

3 Dream Bag Side
1. 3 Dream Bag—Saline Man
2. 3 Dream Bag—Demons Become Doves
3. 3 Dream Bag—Bad Rice Stew/Chase & Sanborn
Bevil Web Side
1. Bevil Web—Dig the Catacombs
2. Bevil Web—Apple Cores & Plums
3. Bevil Web—Gleemer (The Deeds of Fertile Jim) [Different Version]

ACID RANCH
Lineup: Robert Pollard, Jim Pollard, Mitch Mitchell

ALBUMS

Some of the Magic Syrup Was Preserved
Label/Catalog #: Fading Captain Series 19
Released: 2002
Format: 2 LP

Disc 1

Side A
1. The Theory of Broken Circles
2. Underdogs
3. Doctor Moon
4. Pictures From the Brainbox
5. Song of Love
6. Redboots and the Helmet
7. Hey, Baby
8. Love Beat

Side B
1. Morning Has Broken
2. Daily Planet
3. Look to the Left
4. You Will Be There
5. Mongoose Orgasm
6. Exploratory Rat Fink Committee
7. Dungeon of Drunks
8. The Megaphonic Thrift (An Odd Assembly)
9. Lonely Street

Disc 2

Side C
1. Mr. Gene-O
2. 10–5–55–30
3. I Hate Your Perfume
4. Steak and Eggs
5. Dying
6. Edison's Memos
7. What Kind of Love Affair?
8. Fly
9. Electric Indians
10. Newton's Hopeless Marriage
11. That Girl Moore

Side D
1. Some of the Magic Syrup Was Preserved
2. You the Doctor
3. Let's Go to China (Where The East Is Good to Me)
4. Cherry-Ann Doesn't Love Me No More
5. Scary Out There
6. Cath
7. Frogmen
8. Beatles and Stones
9. Salvation Army Bacon and Eggs

AIRPORT 5
Lineup: Robert Pollard, Tobin Sprout

ALBUMS

Tower in the Fountain of Sparks
Label/Catalog #: Fading Captain Series 13
Released: 8/21/2001
Format: CD, LP

1. Burns Carpenter, Man of Science
2. Total Exposure
3. Subatomic Rain
4. One More
5. Mission Experiences
6. The Cost of Shipping Cattle
7. Circle of Trim
8. War & Wedding
9. Stifled Man Casino
10. Up the Nails
11. Tomorrow You May Rise
12. Feathering Clueless (The Exotic Freebird)
13. Mansfield on the Sky
14. White Car Creek
15. Remain Lodging (At Airport 5)

Life Starts Here
Label/Catalog #: Fading Captain Series 18
Released: 2/5/2002
Format: CD, LP

1. Intro
2. We're in the Business
3. Yellow Wife No. 5
4. Wrong Drama Addiction (. . . And Life Starts Here . . .)
5. However Young They Are
6. The Dawntrust Guarantee
7. Forever Since
8. Impressions of a Leg
9. How Brown?
10. Natives Approach Our Plane
11. I Can't Freeze Anymore
12. Out in the World

EPs

Guided by Voices & Airport 5—Selective Service [Split]
Label/Catalog #: Fading Captain Series 16
Released: 12/10/2001
Format: CD

1. Guided by Voices—Dayton, Ohio-19 Something And 5 [Live]
2. Guided by Voices—Travels
3. Guided by Voices—No Welcome Wagons
4. Guided by Voices—Selective Service
5. Airport 5—Total Exposure
6. Airport 5—Cold War Water Sports

7. Airport 5—The Wheel Hits the Path (Quite Soon)
8. Airport 5—Stifled Man Casino
9. Airport 5—Peroxide
10. Airport 5—Eskimo Clockwork
11. Airport 5—In the Brain [Bonus Track]

SINGLES

Total Exposure
Label/Catalog #: Fading Captain Series 11
Released: 2001
Format: 7"

Side A	Side B
1. Total Exposure	1. Cold War Water Sports
	2. The Wheel Hits the Path (Quite Soon)

Stifled Man Casino
Label/Catalog #: Fading Captain Series 12
Released: 2001
Format: 7"

Side A	Side B
1. Stifled Man Casino	1. Peroxide
	2. Eskimo Clockwork

BEVIL WEB
Lineup: Tobin Sprout

EPs

Bevil Web/3 Dream Bag [Split]
Label/Catalog #: Simple Solution SS-009
Released: 1994
Format: 7"
Bevil Web Side
1. Bevil Web—Dig the Catacombs
2. Bevil Web—Apple Cores & Plums
3. Bevil Web—Gleemer (The Deeds of Fertile Jim) [Different Version]
3 Dream Bag Side
1. 3 Dream Bag—Saline Man
2. 3 Dream Bag—Demons Become Doves
3. 3 Dream Bag—Bad Rice Stew/Chase & Sanborn

SINGLES

Minutemen
Label/Catalog #: Wabana/Spirit Of Orr ORE 5
Released: 1996
Format: 7"

Side A	Side B
1. Minutemen	1. Lariat Man

CIRCUS DEVILS
Lineup: Robert Pollard, Tim Tobias, Todd Tobias

ALBUMS

Ringworm Interiors
Label/Catalog #: Fading Captain Series 15
Released: 10/31/2001
Format: CD, LP

1. Devilspeak	16. Playhouse Hostage
2. Feel Try Fury	17. Straps Hold Up the Jaw
3. Buffalo Spiders	18. Correcto
4. World 3	19. Star Peppered Wheatgerm
5. Blanks	20. Silver Eyeballs
6. North Morning Silver Trip	21. Decathalon
7. Ringworm Interiors	22. Peace Needle
8. Spectacle	23. Drill Sgt. Soul
9. You First	24. Protect Thy Interests
10. Knife Song	25. Let's Go Back to Bed
11. Kingdom of Teeth	26. Sterility Megaplant
12. Oil Birds	27. New You (You Can See and
13. Lizard Food	Believe)
14. Not So Fast	28. Circus Devils Theme
15. Apparent the Red Angus	

The Harold Pig Memorial
Label/Catalog #: Fading Captain Series 25
Released: 10/31/2002
Format: CD, LP

1. Alaska to Burning Men	3. Soldiers of June
2. Saved Herself, Shaved	4. I Guess I Needed That
Herself	5. Festival of Death

6. Dirty World News
7. May We See the Hostage?
8. Do You Feel Legal?
9. A Birdcage Until Further Notice
10. Injured?
11. Foxhead Delivery
12. Last Punk Standing
13. Bull Spears
14. Discussions in the Cave
15. Recirculating Hearse
16. Pigs Can't Hide (On Their Night Off)
17. Exoskeleton Motorcade
18. Real Trip No. 3
19. Vegas
20. The Pilot's Crucifixion/ Indian Oil
21. Tulip Review
22. The Harold Pig Memorial

Pinball Mars
Label/Catalog #: Fading Captain Series 29
Released: 10/31/2003
Format: LP

Label/Catalog #: Fading Captain Series 29
Released: 3/29/2004
Format: CD

1. Are You Out With Me?
2. Gargoyle City
3. Pinball Mars
4. Sick Color
5. Don't Be Late
6. Inkster and the King
7. A Puritan for Storage
8. Alien
9. Plasma
10. Dragging the Medicine
11. Bow Before Your Champion
12. Glass Boots
13. (No) Hell for Humor
14. Raw Reaction
   A. Nutrition Is Vital
   B. Strange Journey (See You Inside)
   C. Inside
   D. Come Out Swinging

EYESINWEASEL
Lineup: Tobin Sprout, Dan Toohey, Nick Kizirnis, John Peterson

ALBUMS

Wrinkled Thoughts
Label/Catalog #: Recordhead/Wigwam LUNA23
Released: 9/15/2000
Format: LP

Label/Catalog #: Recordhead/Wigwam LUNA23
Released: 10/17/2000
Format: CD

1. Seven and Nine
2. Dusting Coattails
3. Slow Flanges
4. Marriage Incorporated
5. Pure Flesh
6. Preferred Company
7. Daughters of the Moon

8. There She Goes Again
9. Little Bored
10. Jealous Mantles
11. Hint #9
12. Hands and Covers
13. Slow Flanges [Reprise]
14. Ketiling Park

Live in The Middle East
Label/Catalog #: Recordhead/Wigwam LUNA33
Released: 2001
Format: CD

All tracks recorded live at Middle East, Cambridge, MA on 10/28/2000

1. Get Out of My Throat
2. Seven and Nine
3. Marriage Incorporated
4. E's Navy Blue
5. The Crawling Backward Man
6. Preferred Company
7. Gleemer (The Deeds of
   Fertile Jim)
8. Pure Flesh
9. Awful Bliss
10. Slow Flanges
11. To My Beloved Martha
12. You're Not an Airplane
13. All Used Up
14. Dodging Invisible Rays

15. A Good Flying Bird
16. Scissors
17. To Remake the Young Flyer
18. The Last Man Well Known
    to Kingpin
19. Atom Eyes
20. White Flyer
21. Bottle of the Ghost of Time
22. Mincer Ray
23. Ester's Day
24. Toaster
25. Hermit Stew
26. The Natural Alarm
27. Little Whirl

SINGLES

Seven and Nine
Label: Recordhead/Wigwam
Released: 3/6/2000
Format: 7"

Side A
1. Seven and Nine

Side B
1. Daughters of the Moon

2000 Tour 7"
Label: Recordhead/Wigwam
Released: 2001
Format: 7"

Side One
1. Gas Daddy Gas [Live]

Side Two
1. Strawdogs [Live]

Maviola/Eyesinweasel [Split]
Label/Catalog #: Recordhead/Wigwam/Spirit Of Orr
QWS1
Released: 2001
Format: 7"
Side A
 1. Maviola—Spark
Side B
 1. eyesinweasel—Sadder Than You [Live]
  • Recorded at Middle East, Cambridge, MA—10/28/2000

COMPILATIONS

Hangin' From the Devil's Tree
Label: Your Flesh
Released: 2000
Format: CD

Includes the following track:

Hint #9

FIG. 4
Lineup: Tobin Sprout, Dan Toohey, John Peterson

ALBUMS

S/T
Label/Catalog #: AF4 Records 02002
Released: 1987
Format: LP

1. Way Way Gone	6. Fishin'
2. Train Brain	7. She Loves Her Gown
3. A Hard Place	8. Score
4. Strangler	9. Naola
5. At Bay	10. Contra Koo

Label/Catalog #: Recordhead LUNA6
Released: 1998
Format: CD

Includes the following bonus tracks:

11. Jump Now	15. Bottle of the Ghost of Time
12. Dig the Catacombs	16. I'll Buy You Everything You
13. Sadder Than You	Own
14. Busy Bodies	

EPs

Fig. 4
Label/Catalog #: QCA
Released: 1984
Format: 7"

Side A
  1. Behind Her Eyes
  2. Dirt and Dog

Side B
  1. Thief
  2. I Saw It There

FREEDOM CRUISE
Lineup: Robert Pollard, Tobin Sprout

SINGLES

Freedom Cruise/Nightwalker [Split]
Label/Catalog #: Simple Solution SS-002
Released: 1994
Format: 7"

A jukebox edition exists that has a larger hole in the record and a jukebox label.

Side A
  1. Freedom Cruise—Cruise

Side B
  1. Nightwalker—Lucifer's
    Aching Revolver

COMPILATIONS

Red Hot & Bothered: The Indie-Rock Guide to Dating
Label/Catalog #: The Red Hot Organization/Kinetic 9
45983
Released: 9/22/1995
Format: 2 10"

Label/Catalog #: The Red Hot Organization/Kinetic 9
45983
Released: 10/3/1995
Format: CD

Includes the following track:

Sensational Gravity Boy

GO BACK SNOWBALL
Lineup: Robert Pollard, Mac McCaughan

ALBUMS

Calling Zero
Label/Catalog #: Fading Captain Series 17
Released: 2/26/2002
Format: CD, LP

1. Radical Girl	7. Go Gold
2. Calling Zero	8. Lifetime for the Mavericks
3. Never Forget Where You Get Them	9. Throat of Throats
4. Red Hot Halos	10. Ironrose Worm
5. Again the Waterloo	11. It Is Divine
6. Climb	12. Dumbluck Systems Stormfront

HAZZARD HOTRODS
Lineup: Robert Pollard, Tobin Sprout, Mitch Mitchell,
Larry Keller

ALBUMS

Big Trouble
Label/Catalog #: Fading Captain Series 8
Released: 2000
Format: LP

Side A	Side B
1. A Farewell to Arms	1. Big Trouble
2. The Lawless 90's	2. Runaway
3. 39 Steps	3. Get Dirty
4. Tit for Tat	4. Clue
5. Sabotage	5. Solid Gold

HOWLING WOLF ORCHESTRA
Lineup: Robert Pollard, Nate Farley, Jim Pollard

ALBUMS

Speedtraps for the Bee Kingdom
Label/Catalog #: Fading Captain Series 9
Released: 12/5/2000
Format: CD, LP

1. You Learn Something Old Every Day
2. I.B.C.
3. I'm Dirty
4. It's a Bad Ticket
5. Satyr at Styx & Rubicon
6. Is It Mostly? (It Is Mostly)
7. Where Is Out There?
8. Fruit Weapon

KIM DEAL & BOB POLLARD
Lineup: Robert Pollard, Kim Deal

COMPILATIONS

Love & a .45 Soundtrack
Label/Catalog #: Immortal/Epic Soundtrax EK 66632
Released: 1994
Format: CD

Includes the following track:

Love Hurts

KUDA LABRANCHE
Lineup: Robert Pollard

COMPILATIONS

Tractor Tunes, Volume 1
Label/Catalog #: Fresh Cow Pie TTV1
Released: 2000
Format: CD

Includes the following track:

My Big Day

LEXO AND THE LEAPERS
Lineup: Robert Pollard, Gale Bonham, Tere Lerma, Jay Madewell

EPs

Ask Them
Label/Catalog #: Fading Captain Series 2
Released: 5/25/1999
Format: CD, 12"
1. Time Machines
2. Alone, Stinking and Unafraid
3. Plainskin
4. Will You Show Me Your Gold?
5. Fair Touching [Original Version]
6. Circling Motorhead Mountain

LIFEGUARDS
Lineup: Robert Pollard, Doug Gillard

ALBUMS

Mist King Urth
Label/Catalog #: Fading Captain Series 27
Released: 3/25/2003
Format: CD, LP
1. Gift of the Mountain
2. Starts at the River
3. First of an Early Go-Getter
4. Society Dome
5. Shorter Virgins
6. No Chain Breaking
7. Sea of Dead
8. Surgeon Is Complete
9. Then We Agree
10. Fether Herd
11. Red Whips and Miracles

NIGHTWALKER
Lineup: Robert Pollard and various members

ALBUMS

In Shop We Build Electric Chairs:
Professional Music by Nightwalker 1984–1993
Label/Catalog #: Fading Captain Series 3
Released: 5/25/1999
Format: CD, LP

1. Drum Solo
2. The Fink Swan (Swims Away)
3. Kenneth Ray
4. Dogwood Grains
5. Amazed
6. Signifying UFO
7. Ceramic Cock Einstein
8. U235
9. Weird Rivers & Sapphire Sun
10. Trashed Canned Goods
11. Those Little Bastards Will Bite

SINGLES

Firehouse Mountain
No Label
Released: 1997
Format: 7"

1. Firehouse Mountain

Freedom Cruise/Nightwalker [Split]
Label/Catalog #: Simple Solution SS-002
Released: 1994
Format: 7"

Side A
1. Freedom Cruise—Cruise

Side B
1. Nightwalker—Lucifer's Aching Revolver

COMPILATIONS

Sponic Magazine #3
Label: Sponic
Released: 9/1998
Format: 7"

Includes the following track:

One Track Record

PHANTOM TOLLBOOTH
Lineup: Robert Pollard, Dave Rick, Gerard Smith, Jon Coats

ALBUMS

Beard of Lightning
Label/Catalog #: Off Records 995
Released: 5/20/2003
Format: CD, LP

1. Mascara Snakes	7. Capricorn's Paycheck
2. Atom Bomb Professor	8. Gratification to Concrete
3. Asleep Under Control	9. Crocodile to the Crown
4. Iceland Continuations	10. Janus Pan
5. A Good Looking Death	11. Work Like Bullies
6. The Cafe Interior	

RICHARD MELTZER, ROBERT POLLARD, SMEGMA, & ANTLER
Lineup: Robert Pollard, Richard Meltzer

EPs

The Tropic of Nipples EP
Label/Catalog #: Off Records 999
Released: 2/4/2002
Format: 7"

Side A
1. Smegma—The Valium Restaurant
2. Antler—Ovarian Angel Architect
3. Smegma—Kerouac Never Drove, So He Never Drove Alone
4. Antler—Industry Standard
5. Smegma—Corduroy
6. Antler—Mosquitoes Dropped Their Javelins

Side B
1. Antler—Pressurized
2. Smegma—Chowder, Anyone?
3. Antler—All for Sex and Better Whiskey
4. Smegma—The Sonny Liston Fan Club
5. Antler—Tykie Love (Text Book Memorial Hemmingway)
6. Smegma—Tropic of Nipples

RICHARD MELTZER, ROBERT POLLARD, SMEGMA, ANTLER, AND VOM
Lineup: Robert Pollard, Richard Meltzer

ALBUMS

The Completed Soundtrack for the Tropic of Nipples
Label/Catalog #: Off Records 998
Released: 6/4/2002
Format: CD

1. Smegma—The Valium Restaurant
2. Antler—Ovarian Angel Architect
3. Smegma—Kerouac Never Drove, So He Never Drove Alone
4. Antler—Industry Standard
5. Smegma—Corduroy
6. Antler—Mosquitoes Dropped Their Javelins
7. Antler—Pressurized
8. Smegma—Chowder, Anyone?
9. Antler—All for Sex and Better Whiskey
10. Smegma—The Sonny Liston Fan Club
11. Antler—Tykie Love (Text Book Memorial Hemmingway)
12. Smegma—Tropic of Nipples
13. Vom—Electrocute Your Cock
14. Smegma—Tropic of Labia
15. Antler—World's Coolest Rock Star
16. Vom—Too Animalistic
17. Antler—Revolver Tricks
18. Smegma—Gotta
19. Vom—Punkmobile
20. Vom—God Save the Whales (Live at Rhino 12–77)
21. Vom—I Live With the Roaches
22. Vom—I'm in Love With Your Mom

ROBERT POLLARD AND HIS SOFT ROCK RENEGADES
Lineup: Robert Pollard, Jim Macpherson, Greg Demos

ALBUMS

Choreographed Man of War
Label/Catalog #: Fading Captain Series 14
Released: 7/24/2001
Format: CD, LP

1. I Drove a Tank
2. She Saw the Shadow
3. Edison's Memos
4. 7th Level Shutdown
5. 40 Yards to the Burning Bush
6. Aeriel
7. Citizen Fighter
8. Kickboxer Lightning
9. Bally Hoo
10. Instrument Beetle

ROBERT POLLARD WITH DOUG GILLARD
Lineup: Robert Pollard, Doug Gillard

ALBUMS

Speak Kindly of Your Volunteer Fire Department
Label/Catalog #: Fading Captain Series 4
Released: 11/5/1999
Format: CD, LP

1. Frequent Weaver Who Burns
2. Soul Train College Policeman
3. Pop Zeus
4. Slick As Snails
5. Do Something Real
6. Port Authority
7. Soft Smoke
8. Same Things
9. And I Don't (So Now I Do)
10. Tight Globes
11. I Get Rid of You
12. Life Is Beautiful
13. Messiahs
14. Larger Massachusetts
15. And My Unit Moves

TERRIFYING EXPERIENCE (ALSO CALLED MITCH MITCHELL'S TERRIFYING EXPERIENCE)
Lineup: Mitch Mitchell and various members

ALBUMS

Supreme Radial
Label/Catalog #: Albert Ayler's Jukebox Records AAJ112
Released: 1998
Format: CD

1. Two Day Mini-War
2. Snakes Are Arrows of the Moon
3. Cocktail Party Effect
4. Dynasty of the Last Star Children Have Come to an End
5. Attacking the Padded Assailant
6. Genesis Flood
7. Get Out of My World
8. Everytime I Turn Around
9. Exhilarating Ether Jags
10. Cash Money Runaway
11. You Don't Recognize "Sweet Leaf"
12. Critics Assert Influence Once In Office

Magnetic Breakthrough
Label/Catalog #: Mental Telemetry TELE002
Released: 2000
Format: CD

1. Woodshed Fist Fight
2. A Hard Line to Tread
3. The Road to Hell
4. Anvil Jumper
5. Juvenile Martyrs Behavior Under Fire
6. "Absolute Bloody Shocker"
7. Universal Sheep Coma
8. From Chariots to Garbage Cans
9. The Tearful Champion
10. If You Lived a Minute of My Life
11. Static Arrival
12. Leprechaun
13. Elizabeth and Mercury
14. Underground Pressure

EPs

Search for Omega Minus
Label/Catalog #: Albert Ayler's Jukebox Records AAJ109
Released: 1997
Format: CD

1. Reaching for a Whisper
2. Noble's Last Will & Testament
3. Seeing Betty's Headache Again
4. Correspondence Course by Tape
5. Stress Is the Best Reliever

SINGLES

Terrifying Experience/Illyah Kuryahkin [Split]
Label/Catalog #: Arena Rock Recording Company AR004
Released: 1996
Format: 7"

Side A
1. Terrifying Experience—Friday Night Fights
2. Terrifying Experience—Big City
Side B
1. Illyah Kuryahkin—Takin' a Train

I'm Invisible
Label/Catalog #: Albert Ayler's Jukebox Records AAJ016
Released: 1997
Format: 7"

Side A
1. I'm Invisible

Side B
1. Legacy of Conquest

One After the End
Label: Southern Records
Released: 1998
Format: 7"

Side A
1. One After the End

Side B
1. Hollis Put His Hands
Around My Neck

Anvil Jumper
Label/Catalog #: Mental Telemetry TELE001
Released: 2000
Format: 7"

Side A
1. Anvil Jumper

Side B
1. The Tearful Champion

COMPILATIONS

Fuel Soundtrack
Label: Arena Rock Recording Company
Released: 1997
Format: CD

Includes the following track:

Get Out of My World

The Nervous System
Label: Albert Ayler's Jukebox Records
Released: 1999
Format: CD

Includes the following track:

Look Into the Magic Book for the Answers

Tractor Tunes, Volume 1
Label/Catalog #: Fresh Cow Pie TTV1
Released: 2000
Format: CD

Includes the following track:

We're the Sissy Shockers

OTHER
Other miscellaneous items

TRIBUTE ALBUMS

Blatant Doom Trip (Guided by Voices Tribute)
Label/Catalog #: Simple Solution SS-015
Released: 1998
Format: CD

1. Cobra Verde—Striped White Jets
2. Male Slut (Thurston Moore)—Stabbing a Star
3. Chapter 18—Matter Eater Lad
4. Gem—My Impression Now
5. Rally for Japan—Rubber Man
6. New Radiant Storm King—I Am a Scientist
7. Shove—Melted Pat
8. Local H—Smothered in Hugs
9. Earnest—Back to Saturn X
10. Resolve—The Future Is in Eggs
11. Real Lulu—Postal Blowfish
12. O-Matic—Motor Away
13. Swearing At Motorists—Volcano Divers
14. This Busy Monster—Gleemer (The Deeds of Fertile Jim)
15. 84 Nash—Hot Freaks
16. Gem—Kisses to the Crying Cooks
17. Portastatic—Echos Myron
18. Lotion—Quality of Armor

GUIDED BY VOICES
FAMILY TREE

Family Tree layout and execution by Jason Pierce for mperfectdesignco. (www.mperfectdesign.com)

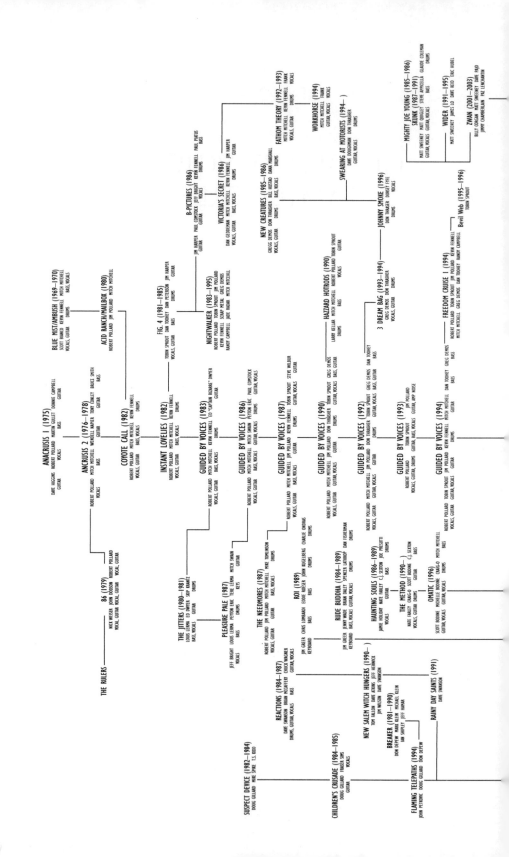

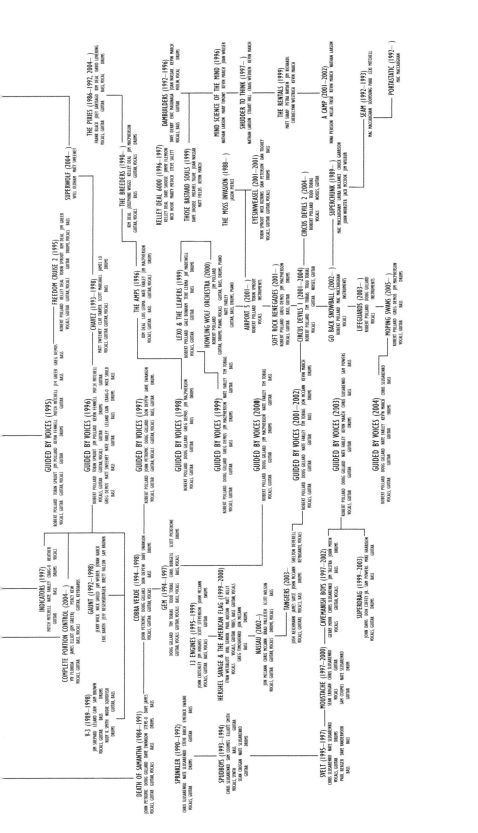

GIGOGRAPHY & SELECTED SET LISTS 1984–2004

All known shows played are listed. There were definitely more shows played than what is included here—especially during the earlier years—but those dates were never recorded. For some gigs that didn't have specific dates identified just a month or year is given. Gigs that are underlined also have the full set list for the show listed. These set lists were selected because they are typical of the material played live at that time.

1984

| Jun | 7 | Canal Street Tavern - Dayton, OH |

1985

| May | 16 | Gilly's - Dayton, OH |
| Jul | | Brookwood Hall - Dayton, OH |

1986

Mar	23	Canal Street Tavern - Dayton, OH
May	26	Island Park - Dayton, OH
May	29	Canal Street Tavern - Dayton, OH
Dec	13	Building Lounge - Dayton, OH

1992

| Aug | | Khyber Pass – Philadelphia, PA |

1993

| Jan | | Boot & Saddle – Philadelphia, PA |
| Feb | | Mys Tavern – Harrisburg, PA |

Jul   20   CBGB - New York, NY [New Music Seminar]

1. My Impression Now	10. Smothered in Hugs
2. Unleashed! The Large-	11. Stabbing a Star
Hearted Boy	12. Sot
3. Jar of Cardinals	13. Tractor Rape Chain
4. Expecting Brainchild	14. Old Battery
5. Shocker in Gloomtown	15. Marchers in Orange
6. Postal Blowfish	16. Weed King
7. Break Even	17. Non-Absorbing
8. Queen of Cans and Jars	18. Some Drilling Implied
9. Lethargy	19. Exit Flagger

Oct   2   CBGB - New York, NY
Nov   6   Under Acme - New York, NY [CMJ Convention]
Nov   24   Canal Street Tavern - Dayton, OH
Dec   Canal Street Tavern - Dayton, OH
Dec   Euclid Tavern - Cleveland, OH

1994

		Urban Art Bar - Houston, TX
Jan	22	Thurston's - Chicago, IL
Feb	19	Euclid Tavern - Cleveland, OH
May	7	Canal Street Tavern - Dayton, OH
May	8	Southgate House - Newport, KY
Jun		*Unknown Venue* - Toledo, OH
Jun		Glenn's Hideaway – Lodi, OH
Jun	18	Stache's - Columbus, OH
Jun	25	Threadwaxing Space - New York, NY
Jun	26	Maxwell's - Hoboken, NJ
Jun	30	Crocodile Cafe - Seattle, WA
Jul	1	University of Oregon - Eugene, OR
Jul	2	I-Beam - San Francisco, CA
Jul	3	Jabberjaw - Los Angeles, CA
Jul	6	Cicero's - St. Louis, MO
Jul	7	University of Wisconsin - Madison, WI
Jul	8	Euclid Tavern - Cleveland, OH
Jul	9	Lounge Ax - Chicago, IL
Jul	20	Riverbend Music Center - Cincinnati, OH [Lollapalooza]
Jul	23	Pine Knob Ampitheater - Clarkston, MI [Lollapalooza]
Aug	6	Khyber - Philadelphia, PA
Sep	29	Union Bar - Athens, OH
Sep	30	Special Occasions - Dayton, OH

Oct   1   <u>Lounge Ax - Chicago, IL</u>

1. A Salty Salute	14. Smothered in Hugs
2. Gold Star for Robot Boy	15. Awful Bliss
3. Buzzards and Dreadful Crows	16. Non-Absorbing
	17. Always Crush Me
4. Pantherz	18. Echos Myron
5. My Son Cool	19. Motor Away
6. Evil Speakers	20. Cruise
7. Watch Me Jumpstart	21. Unleashed! The Large-
8. The Goldheart Mountaintop Queen Directory	Hearted Boy
	22. Tractor Rape Chain
9. Shocker in Gloomtown	23. I Am a Scientist
10. Striped White Jets	24. 14 Cheerleader Coldfront
11. Pimple Zoo	25. Lethargy
12. Closer You Are	26. Weed King
13. Postal Blowfish	

Oct   7   Euclid Tavern - Cleveland, OH
Oct   14   Trocadero - Philadelphia, PA
Oct   15   Roseland - New York, NY
Oct   31   *Unknown Venue* - State College, PA
Nov   2   CBGB - New York, NY
Nov   4   Tramps - New York, NY
Nov   5   Black Cat - Washington, DC
Nov   9   40 Watt Club - Athens, GA
Nov   11   Nite Lights (Stetson University) - Deland, FL
Nov   16   Howlin' Wolf - New Orleans, LA
Nov   20   Antenna Club - Memphis, TN

1995

Mar   18   Terrace - Austin, TX [SXSW]
Mar   30   Maxwell's - Hoboken, NJ
Mar   31   Jon Stewart Show - New York, NY
Apr   3   Canal Street Tavern - Dayton, OH
Apr   5   Lounge Ax - Chicago, IL
Apr   6   Lounge Ax - Chicago, IL
Apr   8   Uptown Bar - Minneapolis, MN
Apr   10   Fox Theatre - Boulder, CO
Apr   14   Crocodile Cafe - Seattle, WA
Apr   15   Reed College - Portland, OR
Apr   17   Great American Music Hall - San Francisco, CA
Apr   18   Bottom of the Hill - San Francisco, CA
Apr   20   Troubador - Los Angeles, CA
Apr   21   Spaceland - Los Angeles, CA

Apr   22   Casbah - San Diego, CA
Apr   22   Price Center (UCSD) - San Diego, CA [Spring Music Festival 95]
May   17   Crocodile Cafe - Seattle, WA
Jun   2   <u>Gilly's - Dayton, OH</u>

1. Over the Neptune / Mesh Gear Fox
2. The Hard Way
3. Striped White Jets
4. He's the Uncle
5. King and Caroline
6. Motor Away
7. Weed King
8. Gold Star for Robot Boy
9. Sitting Still   *(R.E.M.)*
10. Tractor Rape Chain
11. Sheetkickers
12. Non-Absorbing
13. Unleashed! The Large-Hearted Boy
14. Kicker of Elves
15. Quality of Armor
16. Hot Freaks
17. Matter Eater Lad
18. Don't Stop Now
19. My Son Cool
20. Game of Pricks
21. Postal Blowfish
22. Buzzards and Dreadful Crows
23. My Valuable Hunting Knife
24. Some Drilling Implied
25. Color of My Blade
26. The Goldheart Mountaintop Queen Directory
27. Shocker in Gloomtown
28. I Am a Scientist
29. Yours to Keep
30. Echos Myron
31. Exit Flagger
32. A Salty Salute

Jun   16   Southgate House - Newport, KY
Jun   17   Stache's - Columbus, OH
Jun   20   Paradise - Boston, MA
Jun   21   Irving Plaza - New York, NY
Jul   15   St. Andrew's Hall - Detroit, MI
Jul   21   Cat's Cradle - Carrboro, NC
Jul   22   Masquerade - Atlanta, GA
Jul   23   *Unknown Venue* - Knoxville, TN
Jul   24   Exit-In - Nashville, TN
Jul   25   Barristers - Memphis, TN
Jul   26   Sheldon Ballroom - St. Louis, MO
Aug   WHFS - Washington, DC [Inside Dave's Garage]
Aug   16   Gleis 22 - Munster, Germany
Aug   17   Luxor - Koln, Germany [Popkomm]
Aug   19   Die Insel - Berlin, Germany
Aug   20   Muffathalle - Munich, Germany
Aug   21   Cooky's - Frankfurt, Germany
Aug   23   Logo - Hamburg, Germany
Aug   25   Reading Festival - Reading, UK [Reading Festival]
Aug   26   Pukkelpop Festival - Hasselt, Belgium [Pukkelpop Festival]
Aug   27   Walibi Flevo - Dronten, Netherlands [Lowlands Festival]

Aug 29   Bataclan - Paris, France
Aug 30   Vera - Gronigen, Netherlands
Aug 31   Doornroosje - Nijmegen, Netherlands
Sep   2   Leadmill - Sheffield, UK
Sep   3   Cathouse - Glasgow, UK
Sep   5   Clinton Rooms - Nottingham, UK
Sep   6   The Concorde - Brighton, UK
Sep   7   Kings College - London, UK
Sep 13   NPR Morning Edition
Sep 15   *Unknown Venue* - St. Louis, MO
Sep 16   Patio - Indianapolis, IN
Oct 12   Pub (University Of Dayton) - Dayton, OH
Oct 13   Post Office - Tipp City, OH
Oct 23   Amherst College - Amherst, MA
Oct 25   Phoenix - Toronto, ON, Canada
Oct 26   Embassy - London, ON, Canada
Oct 27   Harrow East Theatre - Rochester, NY
Oct 27   MuchMusic - Toronto, ON, Canada [The Wedge]
Oct 28   Metropolis - Montreal, QB, Canada
Oct 30   Toad's Place - New Haven, CT
Oct 31   Paradise - Boston, MA
Nov   2   Academy - New York, NY
Nov   3   Capital Ballroom - Washington, DC
Nov   4   Electric Factory - Philadelphia, PA

1996

Jan   20   Khyber - Philadelphia, PA
Feb 17   Patio - Indianapolis, IN
Feb 22   First Avenue - Minneapolis, MN
Feb 23   Council Fire Ballroom (University of Wisconsin) - Eau Claire, WI
Feb 24   Metro - Chicago, IL
Mar   2   Southgate House - Newport, KY

1. Man Called Aerodynamics	11. Lethargy
2. Game of Pricks	12. Look at Them
3. Rhine Jive Click	13. My Valuable Hunting Knife
4. Cut-Out Witch	14. Postal Blowfish
5. King and Caroline	15. Bright Paper Werewolves
6. Motor Away	16. Lord of Overstock
7. Burning Flag Birthday Suit	17. Smothered in Hugs
8. Pimple Zoo	18. Hot Freaks
9. The Official Ironmen Rally Song	19. Shocker in Gloomtown
10. Gold Star for Robot Boy	20. Striped White Jets
	21. Underwater Explosions

22. Your Name Is Wild	28. Echos Myron
23. I Am a Scientist	29. A Salty Salute
24. Some Drilling Implied	30. Matter Eater Lad
25. Don't Stop Now	31. Tractor Rape Chain
26. My Son Cool	32. Melted Pat
27. Yours to Keep	33. Break Even

Mar	16	Liberty Lunch - Austin, TX [SXSW]
Apr	6	Canal Street Tavern - Dayton, OH
Apr	19	Alrosa Villa - Columbus, OH
Apr	20	North Lawn (Grand Valley State University) - Allendale, MI [Rights Of Spring]
Apr	25	Phoenix Hill Tavern - Louisville, KY
Apr	26	Blue Note - Columbia, MO
Apr	27	Bottleneck - Lawrence, KS
Apr	29	Mercury Cafe - Denver, CO
May	2	Commodore Ballroom - Vancouver, BC, Canada
May	3	Moe's Cafe - Seattle, WA
May	4	Berbati's Pan - Portland, OR
May	6	Great American Music Hall - San Francisco, CA
May	7	Great American Music Hall - San Francisco, CA
May	9	Whiskey a Go Go - Los Angeles, CA
May	10	Whiskey a Go Go - Los Angeles, CA
May	11	Gibson's - Tempe, AZ
May	13	Dingo Bar - Albuquerque, NM
May	13	KCRW - Los Angeles, CA [Morning Becomes Eclectic]
May	14	Bricktown Live - Oklahoma City, OK
Jun	1	RFK Stadium Parking Lot - Washington, DC [WHFStival]
Jun	6	Graffiti - Pittsburgh, PA
Jun	7	Trocadero - Philadelphia, PA
Jun	8	9:30 Club - Washington, DC
Jun	10	Opera House - Toronto, Canada
Jun	13	Axis - Boston, MA
Jun	14	Irving Plaza - New York, NY
Jun	15	Irving Plaza - New York, NY
Jun	18	BBC Maida Vale Studios (Radio 1) - London, UK [John Peel Session]
Jun	21	Garage - London, UK
Jun	25	Vooruit - Gent, Belgium
Jun	30	Cooky's - Frankfurt, Germany
Sep	8	University Of Dayton Arena Backyard - Dayton, OH [Edgefest]

1997

Feb	21	Westbeth Theater - New York, NY [Gerard Cosloy Wedding Party]
Apr	26	Phantasy Nite Club - Cleveland, OH
May	2	Westbeth Theater - New York, NY

May   3   Haverford College - Haverford, PA
May   3   Nick's - Philadelphia, PA
May   4   Princeton University - Princeton, NJ
May   7   Dionysus Club - Oberlin, OH
May 13   Haverford College - Haverford, PA
May 17   University of Chicago - Chicago, IL
Jun   6   Asylum - Dayton, OH
Jun   7   Little Brother's - Columbus, OH
Jun 12   Metro - Chicago, IL
Jun 13   Union Terrace (University of Wisconsin) - Madison, WI
Jun 14   First Avenue - Minneapolis, MN
Jun 17   Showbox - Seattle, WA
Jun 18   La Luna - Portland, OR
Jun 20   Bimbo's 365 - San Francisco, CA
Jun 21   El Rey Theatre - Los Angeles, CA
Jun 23   Brick By Brick - San Diego, CA
Jun 23   KCRW - Los Angeles, CA [Morning Becomes Eclectic]
Jun 25   Dingo Bar - Albuquerque, NM
Jun 27   Liberty Lunch - Austin, TX

1. Can't Hear the Revolution	20. Lord of Overstock
2. Little Lines	21. Shocker in Gloomtown
3. Jane of The Waking Universe	22. Knock 'Em Flyin'
	23. Mute Superstar
4. I've Owned You for Centuries	24. Sad if I Lost It
	25. Maggie Turns to Flies
5. Tractor Rape Chain	26. Game of Pricks
6. I Am a Tree	27. Motor Away
7. The Old Grunt	Encore #1
8. Bulldog Skin	28. Metal Mothers
9. Hot Freaks	29. Get Under It
10. Quicksilver	30. Striped White Jets
11. Not Behind the Fighter Jet	31. Postal Blowfish
12. Choking Tara	32. My Valuable Hunting Knife
13. Psychic Pilot Clocks Out	33. Smothered in Hugs
14. I Am a Scientist	Encore #2
15. Flat Beauty	34. A Salty Salute
16. My Impression Now	35. Stabbing a Star
17. Teenage FBI	36. Weed King
18. I Am Produced	37. Now to War
19. John Strange School	38. Shakin' All Over *(Guess Who)*

Jun 28   Bricktown Live - Oklahoma City, OK
Jun 29   Bottleneck - Lawrence, KS
Jul 10   Graffiti - Pittsburgh, PA

Jul   11   Trocadero - Philadelphia, PA
Jul   12   Central Park - New York, NY [Summerstage]
Jul   14   Met Cafe - Providence, RI
Jul   15   Paradise - Boston, MA
Jul   17   9:30 Club - Washington, DC
Jul   18   Cat's Cradle - Carrboro, NC
Jul   19   Cotton Club - Atlanta, GA
Jul   21   Howlin' Wolf - New Orleans, LA
Jul   22   Barristers - Memphis, TN
Jul   24   Galaxy - St. Louis, MO
Jul   25   Bogarts - Cincinnati, OH
Jul   26   Phoenix Hill Tavern - Louisville, KY
Aug   Phantasy Nite Club - Cleveland, OH
Aug   21   WXPN - Philadelphia, PA [World Cafe - National Public Radio]
Sep   18   MTV - New York, NY [Oddville]
Sep   27   Irving Plaza - New York, NY
Sep   27   Quad Recording - New York, NY [Kit Kat Acoustic Break]
Oct   4   Outdoor Venue - Pradajon, La Rioja, Spain [Serie B Independent Music Festival]
Oct   6   Unknown Venue - Paris, France
Oct   7   Melkweg - Amsterdam, Netherlands
Oct   8   Garage - London, UK
Oct   8   Greater London Radio (GLR) - London, UK
Oct   11   Vogue - Indianapolis, IN
Oct   17   CBC Studios - Vancouver, BC, Canada [Radio Sonic Session]
Oct   17   Starfish Room - Vancouver, BC, Canada
Oct   18   Crocodile Cafe - Seattle, WA
Oct   20   Bimbo's 365 - San Francisco, CA
Oct   21   Billboard Live - Los Angeles, CA
Oct   24   Newport Music Hall - Columbus, OH

1998

Mar   28   Bernie's - Columbus, OH
Apr   18   Lake Cheston Amphitheatre (Univ. of The South) - Sewanee, TN
May   9   Main Street - Cincinnati, OH [Jammin' On Main]
Jun   20   Tramps - New York, NY
Jul   11   Metro - Chicago, IL
Aug   8   Theater of the Living Arts - Philadelphia, PA
Oct   16   Phantasy Nite Club - Cleveland, OH
Oct   17   Magic Stick - Detroit, MI
Nov   7   Little Brother's - Columbus, OH

            1. Cut-Out Witch   4. In Stitches
            2. An Unmarketed Product   5. Make Use
            3. Mushroom Art   6. Peep-Hole

7. Surgical Focus
8. Teenage FBI
9. Just Say the Word
10. Much Better Mr. Buckles
11. Maggie Turns to Flies
12. Zoo Pie
13. Things I Will Keep
14. Waved Out
15. Liquid Indian
16. Subspace Biographies
17. Drinker's Peace
18. Psychic Pilot Clocks Out
19. Burning Flag Birthday Suit
20. Tractor Rape Chain
21. The Old Grunt
22. Bulldog Skin
23. Strumpet Eye
24. Whiskey Ships

25. I Am a Tree
26. Hold on Hope
27. Shocker in Gloomtown
28. Hot Freaks
29. Picture Me Big Time
30. Some Drilling Implied
31. Acorns & Orioles
32. Echos Myron
33. I Am a Scientist
Encore #1
34. Dog's Out
35. Postal Blowfish
36. Liar's Tale
37. Motor Away
Encore #2
38. Tropical Robots
39. Smothered in Hugs
40. Your Name Is Wild

Nov 17   Whiskey a Go Go - Los Angeles, CA
Nov 21   Southgate House - Newport, KY
Dec 31   Maxwell's - Hoboken, NJ

1999

Jan 23   Gilly's - Dayton, OH
Feb 13   Irving Plaza - New York, NY
Feb 27   Bimbo's 365 - San Francisco, CA [Noise Pop Festival]

1. Submarine Teams
2. The Big Make-Over
3. Cut-Out Witch
4. Subspace Biographies
5. Men Who Create Fright
6. Teenage FBI
7. Zoo Pie
8. Far-Out Crops
9. Waved Out
10. Tractor Rape Chain
11. Strumpet Eye
12. Quicksilver
13. Surgical Focus
14. I Am a Tree
15. Shocker in Gloomtown
16. Strictly Comedy
17. Make Use

18. Liquid Indian
19. Wrinkled Ghost
20. Flat Beauty
21. Hot Freaks
22. Drinker's Peace
23. In Stitches
24. Maggie Turns to Flies
25. Peep-Hole
26. Living Upside Down
27. The Old Grunt
28. Bulldog Skin
29. Some Drilling Implied
30. Town of Mirrors
31. Your Name Is Wild
32. Hold On Hope
33. Psychic Pilot Clocks Out
34. A Salty Salute

35. Motor Away	38. Postal Blowfish
36. I Am a Scientist	39. Acorns & Orioles
37. Echos Myron	40. Smothered in Hugs

Mar	20	Waterloo Park - Austin, TX [SXSW]
Apr	18	University of Missouri Field House - Columbia, MO
Apr	24	Pollock Fields (Penn State University) - University Park, PA
May	1	Hill of Three Oaks (Carleton College) - Northfield, MN
May	21	South Oval Lawn (Ohio State University) - Columbus, OH [Spring Festival]
Jun	25	WOXY (97X) - Oxford, OH
Jun	26	Bogarts - Cincinnati, OH
Jul	2	Greek Theatre - Berkeley, CA [This Is Not A Festival]
Jul	4	Oak Creek Ranch - Irvine, CA [This Ain't No Picnic Festival]
Jul	23	Bowery Ballroom - New York, NY
Jul	27	Crocodile Cafe - Seattle, WA
Jul	30	Berbati's Pan - Portland, OR
Jul	31	WFMU - Jersey City, NJ
Aug	1	Liquid Joe's - Salt Lake City, UT
Aug	2	Fox Theatre - Boulder, CO
Aug	4	First Avenue - Minneapolis, MN
Aug	5	Shank Hall - Milwaukee, WI
Aug	6	Metro - Chicago, IL
Aug	24	BBC Maida Vale Studios (Radio 1) - London, UK [Evening Session]
Aug	25	Garage - London, UK
Aug	27	Reading Festival - Reading, UK [Reading Festival]
Sep	8	Cotton Club - Atlanta, GA
Sep	9	Cat's Cradle - Carrboro, NC
Sep	10	9:30 Club - Washington, DC
Sep	12	Edgefest - Dayton, OH
Sep	13	123 Pleasant Street - Morgantown, WV
Sep	15	Roseland - New York, NY
Sep	16	Avalon - Boston, MA
Sep	18	Electric Factory - Philadelphia, PA
Sep	19	Lupo's - Providence, RI
Sep	21	Higher Ground - Winooski, VT
Sep	22	Cabaret - Montreal, QB, Canada
Sep	24	Opera House - Toronto, ON, Canada
Sep	25	Showplace Theatre - Buffalo, NY
Oct	16	Cockpit - Leeds, UK
Oct	17	Fleece And Firkin - Bristol, UK
Oct	20	London Astoria 2 - London, UK
Oct	21	Hop & Grape (Manchester University) - Manchester, UK
Oct	23	Leadmill - Sheffield, UK
Oct	24	King Tuts - Glasgow, UK
Oct	27	Royal Court - Liverpool, UK

Nov 4   Mississippi Nights - St. Louis, MO
Nov 5   Blue Note - Columbia, MO
Nov 6   Bottleneck - Lawrence, KS
Nov 8   Bluebird Theatre - Denver, CO
Nov 11   Maritime Hall - San Francisco, CA
Nov 12   Roxy - Los Angeles, CA
Nov 13   Bellyup Tavern - Solana Beach, CA
Nov 15   Green Room - Tempe, AZ
Nov 16   Club Congress - Tucson, AZ
Nov 18   Trees - Dallas, TX
Nov 19   Fitzgerald's - Houston, TX
Nov 20   La Zona Rosa - Austin, TX
Nov 22   Last Place on Earth - Memphis, TN
Nov 23   328 Performance Hall - Nashville, TN
Nov 24   Headliner's Music Hall - Louisville, KY
Dec 3   Agora Ballroom - Cleveland, OH
Dec 4   Majestic Theater - Detroit, MI
Dec 10   Metro - Chicago, IL
Dec 11   High Dive - Champaign, IL
Dec 14   BBC Maida Vale Studios (Radio 1) - London, UK [John Peel Session]
Dec 16   Vogue - Indianapolis, IN

2000

Jan 13   Theater of the Living Arts - Philadelphia, PA
Jan 14   9:30 Club - Washington, DC
Jan 15   Irving Plaza - New York, NY
Jan 17   Middle East - Cambridge, MA
Jan 18   Middle East - Cambridge, MA
Jan 20   Traxx - Charlottesville, VA
Jan 21   Elbow Room - Columbia, SC
Jan 22   40 Watt Club - Athens, GA
Jan 24   Sapphire Supper Club - Orlando, FL
Jan 25   Covered Dish - Gainesville, FL
Jan 26   Cow Haus - Tallahassee, FL
Jan 28   Nick - Birmingham, AL
Jan 29   Be Here Now Club - Asheville, NC
Feb   ABC Rippon Lea Studios (Studio 31) - Melbourne, Australia [The 10:30 Slot]
Feb   Fox Studios (Channel [V] HQ) - Sydney, Australia [The Joint With Jabba]
Feb 16   Powerstation - Auckland, New Zealand
Feb 18   Adelaide Uni Bar - Adelaide, Australia
Feb 19   Watershed - Perth, Australia [Festival Of Perth]
Feb 20   Zoo - Brisbane, Australia
Feb 22   Corner Hotel - Melbourne, Australia

Feb 23   Corner Hotel - Melbourne, Australia
Feb 25   Goldman's - Sydney, Australia
Feb 26   Goldman's - Sydney, Australia
Mar   1   Club Quattro - Osaka, Japan
Mar   3   Club Quattro - Tokyo, Japan
Mar 18   SE Corner of 4th & Lavaca (in Empty Building) - Austin, TX
          [*Revolver* Magazine Party]
Mar 24   Alrosa Villa - Columbus, OH
Mar 25   Southgate House - Newport, KY
Mar 28   Bluebird - Bloomington, IN
Apr   1   Sapphire Supper Club - Orlando, FL
Apr   6   Regent Street Retreat Annex - Madison, WI
Apr   7   Gabe's Oasis - Iowa City, IA
Apr   8   Sokol Underground - Omaha, NE
Apr 11   Liquid Joe's - Salt Lake City, UT
Apr 12   Neurolux - Boise, ID
Apr 14   Crystal Ballroom - Portland, OR
Apr 15   Showbox - Seattle, WA
Apr 17   Bimbo's 365 - San Francisco, CA
Apr 18   Bimbo's 365 - San Francisco, CA
Apr 20   El Rey Theatre - Los Angeles, CA
Apr 21   El Rey Theatre - Los Angeles, CA
Apr 22   Casbah - San Diego, CA
Apr 27   328 Performance Hall - Nashville, TN
Apr 28   <u>Be Here Now Club - Asheville, NC</u>

1. I Am the Walrus *(The Beatles)*
2. A Salty Salute
3. Whiskey Ships
4. Lethargy
5. Flat Beauty
6. Submarine Teams
7. Surgical Focus
8. Far-Out Crops
9. Time Machines
10. Alone, Stinking and Unafraid
11. Game of Pricks
12. Waved Out
13. In Stitches
14. Tight Globes
15. Choking Tara
16. Mushroom Art
17. Frequent Weaver Who Burns
18. Zoo Pie
19. Things I Will Keep
20. Teenage FBI
21. Baba O'Riley   *(The Who)*
22. Happy Jack   *(The Who)*
23. Shocker in Gloomtown
24. Tropical Robots
25. Subspace Biographies
26. Soul Train College Police-man
27. Ziggy Stardust *(David Bowie)*
28. Pop Zeus
29. The Goldheart Mountaintop Queen Directory
30. Big School
31. Don't Stop Now
32. Dayton, Ohio-19 Something And 5
33. Watch Me Jumpstart
34. I Am a Scientist

35. Circling Motorhead Mountain
36. Peep-Hole
37. Release the Sunbird
38. Get Under It
39. Psychic Pilot Clocks Out
40. Hot Freaks
41. Wild Horses *(The Rolling Stones)*
42. Your Name Is Wild
43. Echos Myron
44. Highway to Hell *(AC/DC)*
45. Postal Blowfish
46. I Am a Tree
47. The Old Grunt
48. Bulldog Skin
49. Motor Away
50. My Valuable Hunting Knife
51. Smothered in Hugs

May	9	CBGB - New York, NY
May	9	NBC Studios - New York, NY [*Late Night with Conan O'Brien*]
May	13	Dionysus Club - Oberlin, OH
Jul	26	Bowery Ballroom - New York, NY [Concrete Media.com Party]
Aug	24	Asylum - Dayton, OH
Aug	25	Beachland Ballroom - Cleveland, OH
Sep	2	Rocket Bar - St. Louis, MO
Sep	3	Liberty Memorial Park - Kansas City, MO [KC Spirit Festival]
Sep	15	Beehive - Pittsburgh, PA
Sep	21	Metro - Chicago, IL
Sep	22	State Theatre - Kalamazoo, MI
Sep	28	Lee's Palace - Toronto, ON, Canada
Sep	29	Barrymore's - Ottawa, ON, Canada
Sep	30	Lee's Palace - Toronto, ON, Canada
Dec	30	40 Watt Club - Athens, GA
Dec	31	Cat's Cradle - Carrboro, NC

2001

Feb	11	Empty Bottle - Chicago, IL
Feb	12	Empty Bottle - Chicago, IL
Feb	14	Bowery Ballroom - New York, NY
Feb	16	Theater of the Living Arts - Philadelphia, PA
Feb	17	Black Cat - Washington, DC
Mar	1	Moose's Music Hall - Knoxville, TN
Mar	2	Elbow Room - Columbia, SC
Mar	3	40 Watt Club - Athens, GA
Mar	5	Sapphire Supper Club - Orlando, FL
Mar	6	Jackrabbit's - Jacksonville, FL
Mar	8	Echo Lounge - Atlanta, GA
Mar	9	Asheville Music Zone - Asheville, NC
Mar	10	Headliner's Music Hall - Louisville, KY
Mar	22	Rave - Milwaukee, WI
Mar	23	400 Bar - Minneapolis, MN
Mar	24	400 Bar - Minneapolis, MN

Mar	26	Hurricane - Kansas City, MO
Mar	27	Bluebird Theatre - Denver, CO
Mar	30	Showbox - Seattle, WA
Mar	31	Crystal Ballroom - Portland, OR
Apr	2	Fillmore - San Francisco, CA
Apr	3	Amoeba Records - San Francisco, CA
Apr	4	Catalyst - Santa Cruz, CA
Apr	6	House Of Blues - Hollywood, CA
Apr	7	Brick By Brick - San Diego, CA
Apr	8	Nita's - Tempe, AZ
Apr	10	Launchpad - Albuquerque, NM
Apr	12	Waterloo Records - Austin, TX
Apr	13	Gypsy Tea Room - Dallas, TX
Apr	14	Stubb's - Austin, TX
Apr	25	Opera House - Toronto, ON, Canada
Apr	27	Armory High - Syracuse, NY
Apr	28	Valentine's - Albany, NY
Apr	30	Higher Ground - Winooski, VT
May	1	Paradise - Boston, MA
May	1	WXRV River Music Hall - Haverhill, MA
May	3	Irving Plaza - New York, NY
May	4	Irving Plaza - New York, NY
May	5	9:30 Club - Washington, DC
May	7	Beehive - Pittsburgh, PA
May	8	Little Brother's - Columbus, OH
May	9	Birdy's - Indianapolis, IN
May	11	Majestic Theater - Detroit, MI
May	12	Vic Theatre - Chicago, IL
May	14	Mississippi Nights - St. Louis, MO
May	15	Last Place on Earth - Memphis, TN
May	16	Variety Playhouse - Atlanta, GA
May	18	Cat's Cradle - Carrboro, NC
May	19	Fletcher's - Baltimore, MD
May	20	Trocadero - Philadelphia, PA
Jun	13	Southgate House - Newport, KY
Jun	15	Shim Sham Club - New Orleans, LA
Jun	16	Engine Room - Houston, TX
Jun	17	Mercury - Austin, TX
Jun	19	Nita's - Tempe, AZ
Jun	20	House Of Blues - Hollywood, CA
Jun	21	4th & B - San Diego, CA
Jun	23	Cactus Club - San Jose, CA
Jun	24	Fillmore - San Francisco, CA
Jun	27	Ogden - Denver, CO

Jun 29   Other Side - Tulsa, OK
Jun 30   Bottleneck - Lawrence, KS
Jul 12   Asylum - Dayton, OH
Jul 14   Beachland Ballroom - Cleveland, OH
Jul 15   Embassy - London, ON, Canada
Jul 21   Coney Island - New York, NY [Siren Fest]
Jul 24   Irving Plaza - New York, NY
Jul 25   Camden Tweeter Center - Philadelphia, PA [Y100 Fez-Tival]
Aug 10   Marquee - Halifax, NS, Canada
Aug 11   Marquee - Halifax, NS, Canada
Aug 23   <u>Garage - London, UK</u>

1. I'm Dirty	17. Get Under It
2. Titus and Strident Wet Nurse	18. Shocker in Gloomtown
	19. Tight Globes
3. Settlement Down	20. Game of Pricks
4. Skills Like This	21. Mushroom Art
5. Stifled Man Casino	22. In Stitches
6. Waved Out	23. Soul Train College Policeman
7. Submarine Teams	24. Pop Zeus
8. The Brides Have Hit Glass	25. Twilight Campfighter
9. I Drove a Tank	26. Don't Stop Now
10. Edison's Memos	27. Teenage FBI
11. Tractor Rape Chain	28. I Am a Scientist
12. Alone, Stinking and Unafraid	29. Cut-Out Witch
13. Glad Girls	30. Instrument Beetle
14. Pivotal Film	31. A Salty Salute
15. Things I Will Keep	32. Psychic Pilot Clocks Out
16. The Enemy	33. Baba O'Riley *(The Who)*

Aug 24   Pukkelpop Festival - Hasselt, Belgium [Pukkelpop Festival]
Aug 25   Reading Festival - Reading, UK [Reading Festival]
Aug 26   Leeds Festival - Leeds, UK [Leeds Festival]
Sep 1   Roseland Theater - Portland, OR
Sep 3   Key Arena - Seattle, WA [Bumbershoot]
Oct 18   Irving Plaza - New York, NY
Oct 19   Maxwell's - Hoboken, NJ
Oct 20   Middle East - Cambridge, MA
Oct 21   Toad's Place - New Haven, CT
Dec 7   Southgate House - Newport, KY
Dec 8   Birdy's - Indianapolis, IN
Dec 29   Trocadero - Philadelphia, PA
Dec 30   Apollo Theater - New York, NY
Dec 31   Apollo Theater - New York, NY

2002

Feb	21	*Unknown Venue* - Columbus, OH
Feb	22	Bluebird - Bloomington, IN
Feb	23	Mojo's - Columbia, MO
Feb	24	Hurricane - Kansas City, MO
Feb	26	Fox Theatre - Boulder, CO
Mar	1	House of Blues - Anaheim, CA
Mar	2	Colonial Theatre - Sacramento, CA
Mar	3	Bimbo's 365 - San Francisco, CA [Noise Pop Festival]
Mar	5	Crocodile Cafe - Seattle, WA
Mar	6	Richard's on Richards - Vancouver, BC, Canada
Mar	9	First Avenue - Minneapolis, MN
Mar	10	High Dive - Champaign, IL
Mar	16	Dublin Pub - Dayton, OH
Apr	2	Intersection - Grand Rapids, MI
Apr	3	Magic Stick - Detroit, MI
Apr	5	Beachland Ballroom - Cleveland, OH
Apr	6	Continental - Buffalo, NY
Apr	9	Warsaw - Brooklyn, NY
Apr	10	Warsaw - Brooklyn, NY
Apr	11	Chameleon Club - Lancaster, PA
Apr	13	Recher Theatre - Towson, MD
Apr	14	Alley Katz - Richmond, VA
Apr	16	Cat's Cradle - Carrboro, NC
Apr	17	Music Farm - Charleston, SC
Apr	19	40 Watt Club - Athens, GA
Apr	20	Exit-In - Nashville, TN

1. Hit
2. Everywhere with Helicopter
3. Hardcore UFO's
4. I Drove a Tank
5. Eureka Signs
6. Back to the Lake
7. Buzzards and Dreadful Crows
8. Instrument Beetle
9. Chasing Heather Crazy
10. Zap
11. Christian Animation Torch Carriers
12. Edison's Memos
13. Cheyenne
14. Tight Globes
15. The Official Ironmen Rally Song
16. Wire Greyhounds
17. Skin Parade
18. Things I Will Keep
19. My Valuable Hunting Knife
20. From a Voice Plantation
21. Skills Like This
22. Game of Pricks
23. The Weeping Bogeyman
24. Car Language
25. Drinker's Peace
26. Twilight Campfighter
27. Wings of Thorn
28. Submarine Teams
29. The Brides Have Hit Glass

30. Love 1
31. Storm Vibrations
32. Alone, Stinking and Unafraid
33. Glad Girls
34. Waved Out
35. The Enemy
36. Factory of Raw Essentials
37. Watch Me Jumpstart
38. Pretty Bombs
39. Cut-out Witch
40. The Ids Are Alright
41. Universal Truths and Cycles
42. Fair Touching
43. Don't Stop Now
44. Teenage FBI

45. Father Sgt. Christmas Card
46. Tractor Rape Chain
Encore #1
47. Shocker in Gloomtown
48. The Goldheart Mountaintop
   Queen Directory
49. Peep-Hole
50. I Am a Scientist
51. Echos Myron
Encore #2
52. Hot Freaks
53. Pop Zeus
54. Psychic Pilot Clocks Out
55. Baba O'Riley *(The Who)*

May	8	Metro - Chicago, IL
May	9	Gabe's Oasis - Iowa City, IA
May	10	Gabe's Oasis - Iowa City, IA
Jun	7	Young Avenue Deli - Memphis, TN
Jun	8	Shim Sham Club - New Orleans, LA
Jun	10	Engine Room - Houston, TX
Jun	11	Trees - Dallas, TX
Jun	12	La Zona Rosa - Austin, TX
Jun	14	Club Congress - Tucson, AZ
Jun	15	Canes - San Diego, CA
Jun	17	CBS Studios - Los Angeles, CA [*Craig Kilborn Show*]
Jun	18	Amoeba Records - Los Angeles, CA
Jun	19	AOL Sessions - Los Angeles, CA
Jun	19	House of Blues - Hollywood, CA
Jun	20	Warfield - San Francisco, CA
Jun	22	Crystal Ballroom - Portland, OR
Jun	23	Showbox - Seattle, WA
Jun	27	First Avenue - Minneapolis, MN
Jun	28	Regent Street Retreat Annex - Madison, WI
Jun	29	Metro - Chicago, IL
Jun	30	Summerfest - Milwaukee, WI [Summerfest]
Jul	6	Bogarts - Cincinnati, OH
Jul	7	Summerstages - Indianapolis, IN [Summerstages]
Jul	9	Echo Lounge - Atlanta, GA
Jul	10	Echo Lounge - Atlanta, GA
Jul	17	Paradise - Boston, MA
Jul	19	Horseshoe Tavern - Toronto, ON, Canada
Jul	20	Horseshoe Tavern - Toronto, ON, Canada
Jul	21	Rosebud - Pittsburgh, PA

Aug 3 Mather Memorial Ct. (Case Western Reserve Univ.) - Cleveland, OH [WRUW Studio-A-Rama]
Aug 9 Irving Plaza - New York, NY
Aug 10 Theater Of The Living Arts - Philadelphia, PA
Aug 23 Reading Festival - Reading, UK [Reading Festival]
Aug 24 Leeds Festival - Leeds, UK [Leeds Festival]
Aug 25 Glasgow Festival - Glasgow, UK [Glasgow Festival]
Aug 27 Limelight - Belfast, Ireland
Aug 28 Half Moon - Cork, Ireland
Aug 29 Ambassador - Dublin, Ireland
Aug 31 Paradiso - Amsterdam, Netherlands
Sep 2 Rockefeller - Oslo, Norway
Sep 3 Gota Kallare - Stockholm, Sweden
Sep 4 KB - Malmo, Sweden
Sep 6 Gebaude - Koln, Germany
Sep 7 Ancienne Belgique - Brussels, Belgium
Sep 8 Garage - London, UK
Sep 21 Hideout - Chicago, IL [Hideout Block Party]
Sep 22 Grog Shop - Cleveland, OH
Sep 23 Grog Shop - Cleveland, OH
Oct 5 Oak Creek Ranch - Irvine, CA [This Ain't No Picnic Festival]
Oct 11 9:30 Club - Washington, DC
Oct 12 Stone Pony - Asbury Park, NJ
Oct 17 Alrosa Villa - Columbus, OH
Oct 18 Headliner's Music Hall - Louisville, KY
Oct 19 Chukker - Tuscaloosa, AL
Oct 21 State Theatre - St. Petersburg, FL
Oct 22 Factory - Ft. Lauderdale, FL
Oct 23 Social - Orlando, FL
Oct 25 40 Watt Club - Athens, GA
Oct 26 Cat's Cradle - Carrboro, NC
Oct 27 Blue Cats - Knoxville, TN
Dec 31 American Cabaret Theatre - Indianapolis, IN

2003

Jan 24 Metro - Chicago, IL
Jan 25 Nevin's Pub - Evanston, IL
Feb 21 Music Factory - Columbus, OH
Feb 22 Bluebird - Bloomington, IN
Apr 8 Historic State Theatre - Minneapolis, MN
Apr 9 Modjeska Theatre - Milwaukee, WI
Apr 11 Coronado Theatre - Rockford, IL
Apr 12 Vic Theatre - Chicago, IL

Apr 13   State Theatre - Detroit, MI
Apr 18   Dame - Lexington, KY
Apr 19   Sawyer Point Amphitheatre - Cincinnati, OH [WOXY Earth Day Celebration]
Apr 25   Mississippi Nights - St. Louis, MO
Apr 26   Jesse Hall (University Of Missouri) - Columbia, MO [Springfest 2003]
Jun 21   Westword's Music Showcase - Denver, CO [Westword's Music Showcase]
Jun 26   Intersection - Grand Rapids, MI
Jun 26   Nate Farley Session
Jun 27   Lime Spider - Akron, OH
Jun 28   Continental - Buffalo, NY
Jul 12   Pennsylvania Avenue - Washington, DC [Live On Penn]
Aug 14   Southgate House - Newport, KY
Aug 15   Finkl Steel - Chicago, IL [Goose Island Festival]
Aug 16   Birdy's - Indianapolis, IN
Aug 19   Napster - Los Angeles, CA
Aug 20   Bimbo's 365 - San Francisco, CA
Aug 21   Amoeba Records - San Francisco, CA
Aug 22   Spaceland - Los Angeles, CA
Aug 23   Sunset Boulevard - Los Angeles, CA [Sunset Junction Festival]
Sep   3   Paradise - Boston, MA
Sep   4   Irving Plaza - New York, NY
Sep   5   Trocadero - Philadelphia, PA
Sep 10   Muffathalle - Munich, Germany
Sep 11   Flex - Vienna, Austria
Sep 12   Hiroshima - Turin, Italy
Sep 13   Piazza Dei Cinquencento - Rome, Italy [Enzimi Festiva]
Sep 16   Space Place - Frankfurt, Germany
Sep 17   Knaack Club - Berlin, Germany
Sep 18   Logo - Hamburg, Germany

1. I Drove a Tank
2. Mascara Snakes
3. I'll Replace You with Machines
4. My Kind of Soldier
5. Christian Animation Torch Carriers
6. Back to the Lake
7. Smothered in Hugs
8. Red Ink Superman
9. Bull Spears
10. Useless Inventions
11. Dirty Water
12. The Best of Jill Hives
13. Game of Pricks
14. Storm Vibrations
15. The Official Ironmen Rally Song
16. Mix Up the Satellite
17. A Trophy Mule in Particular
18. Apology in Advance
19. Secret Star
20. The Goldheart Mountaintop Queen Directory
21. Get Under It
22. Shocker in Gloomtown
23. Starts at the River
24. From a Voice Plantation

25. Skills Like This
26. Beg for a Wheelbarrow
27. Things I Will Keep
28. Motor Away
29. Buzzards and Dreadful Crows
30. Alone, Stinking and Unafraid
31. Glad Girls
32. Tractor Rape Chain
33. Cut-Out Witch
34. Liar's Tale
35. Watch Me Jumpstart
36. Of Mites and Men
Encore #1
37. A Salty Salute
38. Everywhere with Helicopter
39. Teenage FBI
40. Don't Stop Now
41. Echos Myron
42. I Am a Scientist
43. Baba O'Riley *(The Who)*

Sep	20	Les Nuits Botanique - Brussels, Belgium
Sep	21	Paradiso - Amsterdam, Netherlands
Sep	23	Cockpit - Leeds, UK
Sep	24	Rescue Rooms - Nottingham, UK
Sep	25	Clwb Ifor Bach - Cardiff, UK
Sep	27	Barfly - Glasgow, UK
Sep	28	Princess Charlotte - Leicester, UK
Sep	29	Roadhouse - Manchester, UK
Sep	30	University of London Union (ULU) - London, UK
Oct	16	House of Blues - Hollywood, CA
Oct	17	Slim's - San Francisco, CA
Oct	18	Slim's - San Francisco, CA
Oct	20	Berbati's Pan - Portland, OR
Oct	21	Graceland - Seattle, WA
Oct	22	Drink - Vancouver, BC, Canada
Oct	24	Harlow's - Sacramento, CA
Oct	25	Canes - San Diego, CA
Oct	26	House of Blues - Anaheim, CA
Nov	6	Variety Playhouse - Atlanta, GA
Nov	7	Orange Peel - Asheville, NC
Nov	8	Cat's Cradle - Carrboro, NC
Nov	10	Recher Theatre - Towson, MD
Nov	11	Theater of the Living Arts - Philadelphia, PA
Nov	12	Warsaw - Brooklyn, NY
Nov	14	Opera House - Toronto, ON, Canada
Nov	15	Magic Stick - Detroit, MI
Nov	16	Grog Shop - Cleveland, OH
Nov	18	First Avenue - Minneapolis, MN
Nov	19	Regent Street Retreat Annex - Madison, WI
Nov	21	Otto's - Dekalb, IL
Nov	22	Abbey Pub - Chicago, IL
Nov	23	Abbey Pub - Chicago, IL
Dec	31	4th & B - San Diego, CA

2004

Jan	8	Exit-In - Nashville, TN
Jan	9	40 Watt Club - Athens, GA
Jan	10	Market Street Pub - Gainesville, FL
Jan	12	Social - Orlando, FL
Jan	13	Jackrabbit's - Jacksonville, FL
Jan	14	Beta Bar - Tallahassee, FL
Jan	16	Engine Room - Houston, TX
Mar	5	Trees - Dallas, TX
Mar	6	La Zona Rosa - Austin, TX
Mar	8	Blue Note - Columbia, MO
Mar	9	Mississippi Nights - St. Louis, MO
Mar	11	Little Brother's - Columbus, OH
Mar	12	Headliner's Music Hall - Louisville, KY
Mar	13	Bluebird - Bloomington, IN
Apr	22	Conduit - Trenton, NJ
Apr	23	Pearl Street - Northampton, MA
Apr	24	Bowery Ballroom - New York, NY
Jun	4	Foundry - Dayton, OH
Jun	6	Dixie's on Grand - St. Paul, MN [Grand Old Day]
Jun	17	High Dive - Champaign, IL
Jun	18	Gabe's Oasis - Iowa City, IA
Jun	19	Clinton Lake - Lawrence, KS [Wakarusa Festival]
Aug	19	Pier 54, Hudson River Park - New York, NY [Hudson River Rocks]
Aug	25	Uptown Mix - Nashville, TN
Sep	9	Paradise - Boston, MA
Sep	10	Theater of the Living Arts - Philadelphia, PA
Sep	11	9:30 Club - Washington, DC
Sep	22	Pageant - St. Louis, MO
Sep	28	Cat's Cradle - Carrboro, NC
Oct	21	Alrosa Villa - Columbus, OH
Oct	22	Southgate House - Newport, KY
Oct	23	Beachland Ballroom - Cleveland, OH
Oct	25	Bluebird - Bloomington, IN
Oct	26	Majestic Theater - Detroit, MI
Nov	3	40 Watt Club - Athens, GA
Nov	5	Stubb's - Austin, TX
Nov	6	Gypsy Ballroom - Dallas, TX
Nov	7	Engine Room - Houston, TX
Nov	9	KLRU Studio 6A - Austin, TX [Austin City Limits]
Nov	11	Canes - San Diego, CA
Nov	12	Henry Fonda Theatre - Los Angeles, CA
Nov	13	Fillmore - San Francisco, CA

Nov 15 Berbati's Pan - Portland, OR
Nov 16 Berbati's Pan - Portland, OR
Nov 17 Neumos - Seattle, WA
Dec   2 NBC Studios - New York, NY [Late Night With Conan O'Brien]
Dec   3 Irving Plaza - New York, NY
Dec   4 Irving Plaza - New York, NY
Dec   5 Irving Plaza - New York, NY
Dec 13 Tabu Night Club - Orlando, FL
Dec 30 Metro - Chicago, IL
Dec 31 <u>Metro - Chicago, IL</u>

1. Over the Neptune / Mesh Gear Fox
2. Watch Me Jumpstart
3. Pimple Zoo
4. Everybody Thinks I'm a Raincloud (When I'm Not Looking)
5. Fair Touching
6. Things I Will Keep
7. Glow Boy Butlers
8. Lethargy
9. The Best of Jill Hives
10. Red Ink Superman
11. 14 Cheerleader Coldfront
12. Girls of Wild Strawberries
13. Back to the Lake
14. Demons Are Real
15. Do the Earth
16. Tropical Robots
17. Beg for a Wheelbarrow
18. My Kind of Soldier
19. "Wished I Was a Giant"
20. Bright Paper Werewolves
21. Lord of Overstock
22. Window of My World
23. Navigating Flood Regions
24. The Goldheart Mountaintop Queen Directory
25. Tractor Rape Chain
26. I Am a Tree
27. Drinker's Peace
28. Chief Barrel Belly
29. Game of Pricks
30. Pink Gun
31. Matter Eater Lad
32. Redmen and Their Wives
33. Gonna Never Have to Die
34. I Drove a Tank
35. Shocker in Gloomtown
36. Secret Star
37. If We Wait
38. Huffman Prairie Flying Field
39. Sad If I Lost It
40. Cut-Out Witch
41. Buzzards and Dreadful Crows
42. Alone, Stinking and Unafraid
43. Unleashed! The Large-Hearted Boy
44. Glad Girls
45. Johnny Appleseed
46. Heavy Metal Country
47. Murder Charge
Encore #1
48. My Impression Now
49. My Valuable Hunting Knife
50. Queen of Cans and Jars
51. Hot Freaks
52. Motor Away
53. I Am a Scientist
54. Teenage FBI
55. Echos Myron
56. Smothered in Hugs
Encore #2
57. A Salty Salute
58. Postal Blowfish

59. Pendulum
60. Dayton, Ohio-19 Something and 5
61. He's the Uncle
62. Exit Flagger
63. Don't Stop Now

The selected discographies and set lists/gigography were compiled by Jeff Warren. Jeff runs a Guided by Voices database Web site (GBVDB.com), which features discography and gigography information for GbV and related solo/side projects. Jeff would like especially to thank Rich Turiel (GBV.com and RobertPollard.net), Rhys Davies, Robert Gray, Jack Stenner, and Andy Gower for their assistance in compiling the discography.